CAPTAIN AMERICA: HAIL HYDRA. Contains material originally published in magazine form as CAPTAIN AMERICA: HAIL HYDRA #1-5. First printing 2011. ISBN# 978-0-7851-5127-2. Published by MARVEL WORLDWIDE, INC., a subsidiary of MARVEL ENTERTAINMENT, LLC. OFFICE OF PUBLICATION: 135 West 50th Street, New York, NY 10020. Copyright © 2011 Marvel Characters, Inc. All rights reserved. $14.99 per copy in the U.S. and $16.50 in Canada (GST #R127032852); Canadian Agreement #40668537. All characters featured in this issue and the distinctive names and likenesses thereof, and all related indicia are trademarks of Marvel Characters, Inc. No similarity between any of the names, characters, persons, and/or institutions in this magazine with those of any living or dead person or institution is intended, and any such similarity which may exist is purely coincidental. **Printed in the U.S.A.** ALAN FINE, EVP - Office of the President, Marvel Worldwide, Inc. and EVP & CMO Marvel Characters B.V.; DAN BUCKLEY, Publisher & President - Print, Animation & Digital Divisions; JOE QUESADA, Chief Creative Officer; JIM SOKOLOWSKI, Chief Operating Officer; DAVID BOGART, SVP of Business Affairs & Talent Management; TOM BREVOORT, SVP of Publishing; C.B. CEBULSKI, SVP of Creator & Content Development; DAVID GABRIEL, SVP of Publishing Sales & Circulation; MICHAEL PASCIULLO, SVP of Brand Planning & Communications; JIM O'KEEFE, VP of Operations & Logistics; DAN CARR, Executive Director of Publishing Technology; JUSTIN F. GABRIE, Director of Publishing & Editorial Operations; SUSAN CRESPI, Editorial Operations Manager; ALEX MORALES, Publishing Operations Manager; STAN LEE, Chairman Emeritus. For information regarding advertising in Marvel Comics or on Marvel.com, please contact John Dokes, SVP Integrated Sales and Marketing, at jdokes@marvel.com. For Marvel subscription inquiries, please call 800-217-9158. **Manufactured between 6/2/11 and 6/21/2011 by QUAD/GRAPHICS, DUBUQUE, IA, USA.**

10 9 8 7 6 5 4 3 2 1

CAPTAIN AMERICA
HAIL HYDRA!

Writer: **Jonathan Maberry**

Artists: **Sergio Cariello, Tom Scioli, Phil Winslade, Kyle Hotz & Graham Nolan**

Colorists: **Chris Sotomayor, Bill Crabtree, Chris Chuckry, Dan Brown & Ian Hannin**

Letterers: **VC's Joe Caramagna, Clayton Cowles & Joe Sabino**

Cover Artist: **Adi Granov**

Assistant Editor: **Rachel Pinnelas**
Editors: **Bill Rosemann & Tom Brennan**

Captain America created by **Joe Simon** and **Jack Kirby**

Collection Editor: **Nicole Boose**
Editorial Assistants: **James Emmett & Joe Hochstein**
Assistant Editors: **Alex Starbuck & Nelson Ribeiro**
Editors, Special Projects: **Jennifer Grünwald & Mark D. Beazley**
Senior Editor, Special Projects: **Jeff Youngquist**
Senior Vice President of Sales: **David Gabriel**
SVP of Brand Planning & Communications: **Michael Pasciullo**
Book Designer: **Spring Hoteling**
Production: **Jerry Kalinowski**

Editor in Chief: **Axel Alonso**
Chief Creative Officer: **Joe Quesada**
Publisher: **Dan Buckley**
Executive Producer: **Alan Fine**

During the dark days of the early 1940s, a covert military experiment turned
Steve Rogers into America's first Super-Soldier, CAPTAIN AMERICA.

Throughout the war, Cap and his partner Bucky fought alongside our infantry and with a group
of heroes known as the Invaders. In the closing months of WWII, Captain America and Bucky
were both presumed dead in an explosion over the English Channel.

Decades later, a figure was found trapped in ice, and Captain America was revived. Having
slept through more than half of the 20th century, Steve Rogers awakened to a world he never
imagined, a world where war had moved from the battlefield to the city streets...

CAPTAIN AMERICA

Whenever a major evil has threatened the world, they
have been there. Whatever their name—the Cathari,
Sons of Anubis, Ariosophists, Wotanists, the Seven
Kings, the Black Order, the Green and Red Societies,
the Thule Society—their malevolence knows no end.

Every aspect of history, politics, science, magic and
faith has been influenced by their many tentacles;
when one of their vile heads is cut off, two more take
its place. Their evil is exponential. They are eternal
and infinite—no matter who stands against them they
will not stop. They are HYDRA.

HAIL HYDRA!

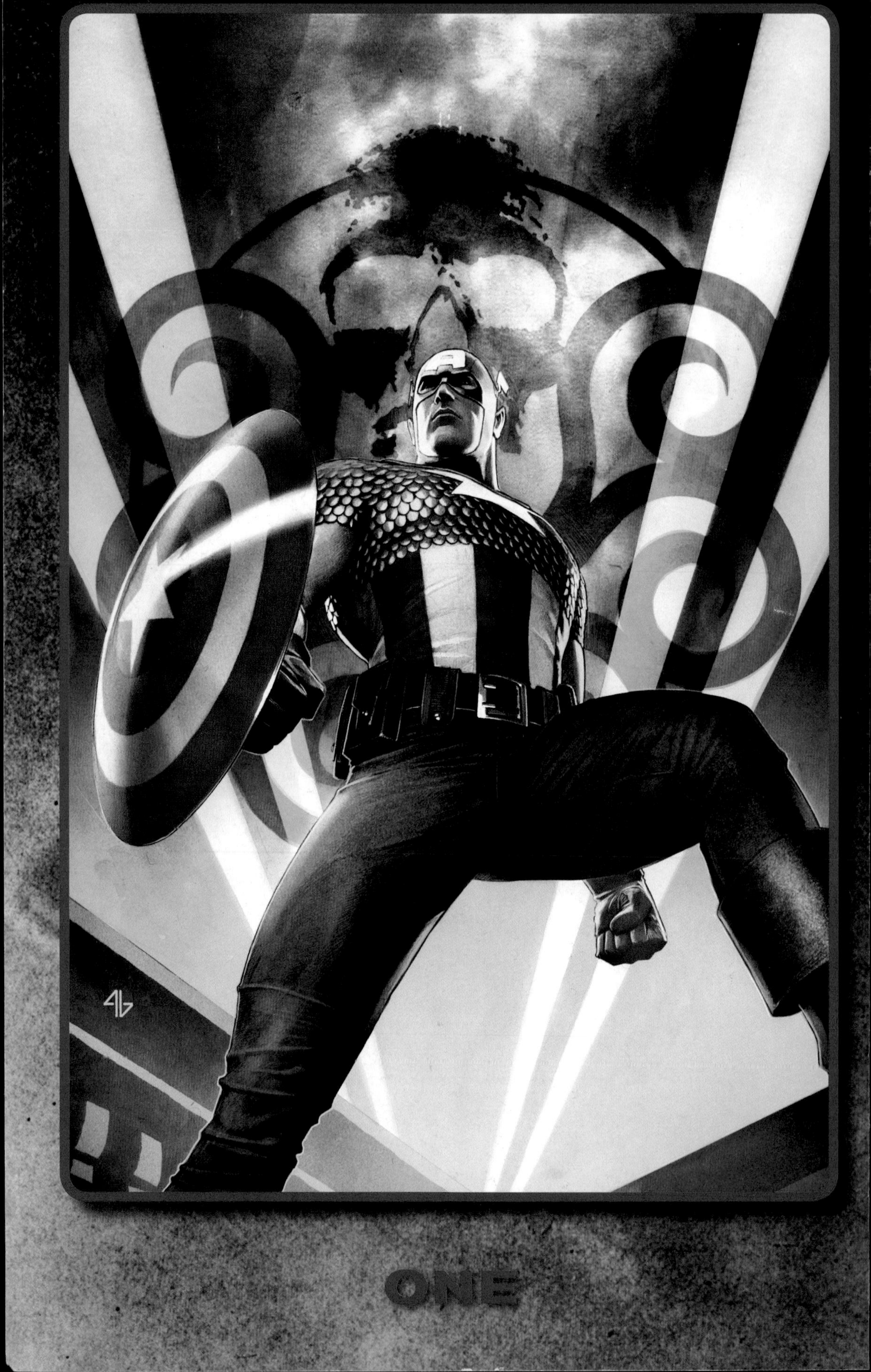

ONE

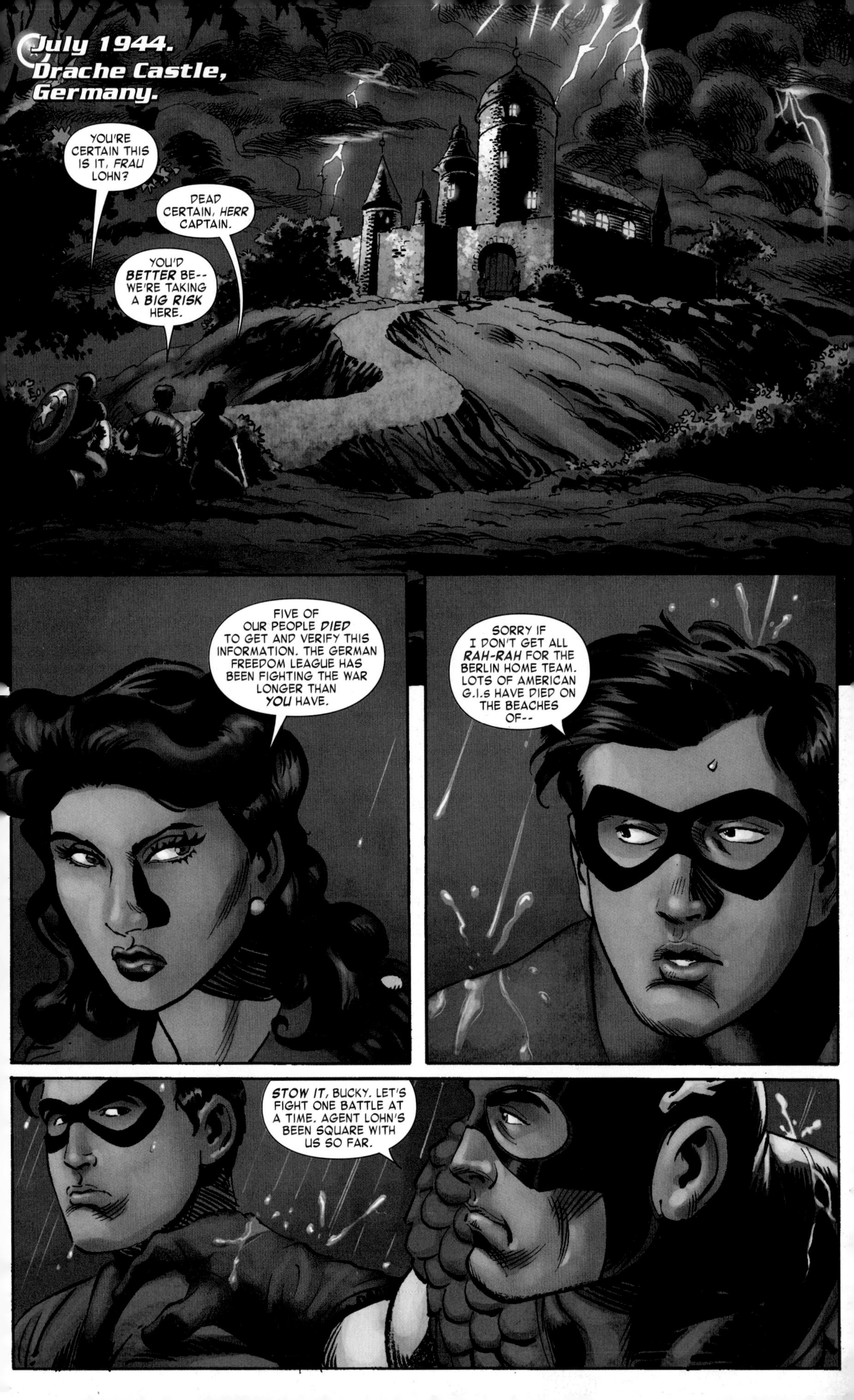

July 1944. Drache Castle, Germany.
YOU'RE CERTAIN THIS IS IT, FRAU LOHN?
DEAD CERTAIN, HERR CAPTAIN.
YOU'D BETTER BE-- WE'RE TAKING A BIG RISK HERE.
FIVE OF OUR PEOPLE DIED TO GET AND VERIFY THIS INFORMATION. THE GERMAN FREEDOM LEAGUE HAS BEEN FIGHTING THE WAR LONGER THAN YOU HAVE.
SORRY IF I DON'T GET ALL RAH-RAH FOR THE BERLIN HOME TEAM. LOTS OF AMERICAN G.I.s HAVE DIED ON THE BEACHES OF--
STOW IT, BUCKY. LET'S FIGHT ONE BATTLE AT A TIME. AGENT LOHN'S BEEN SQUARE WITH US SO FAR.

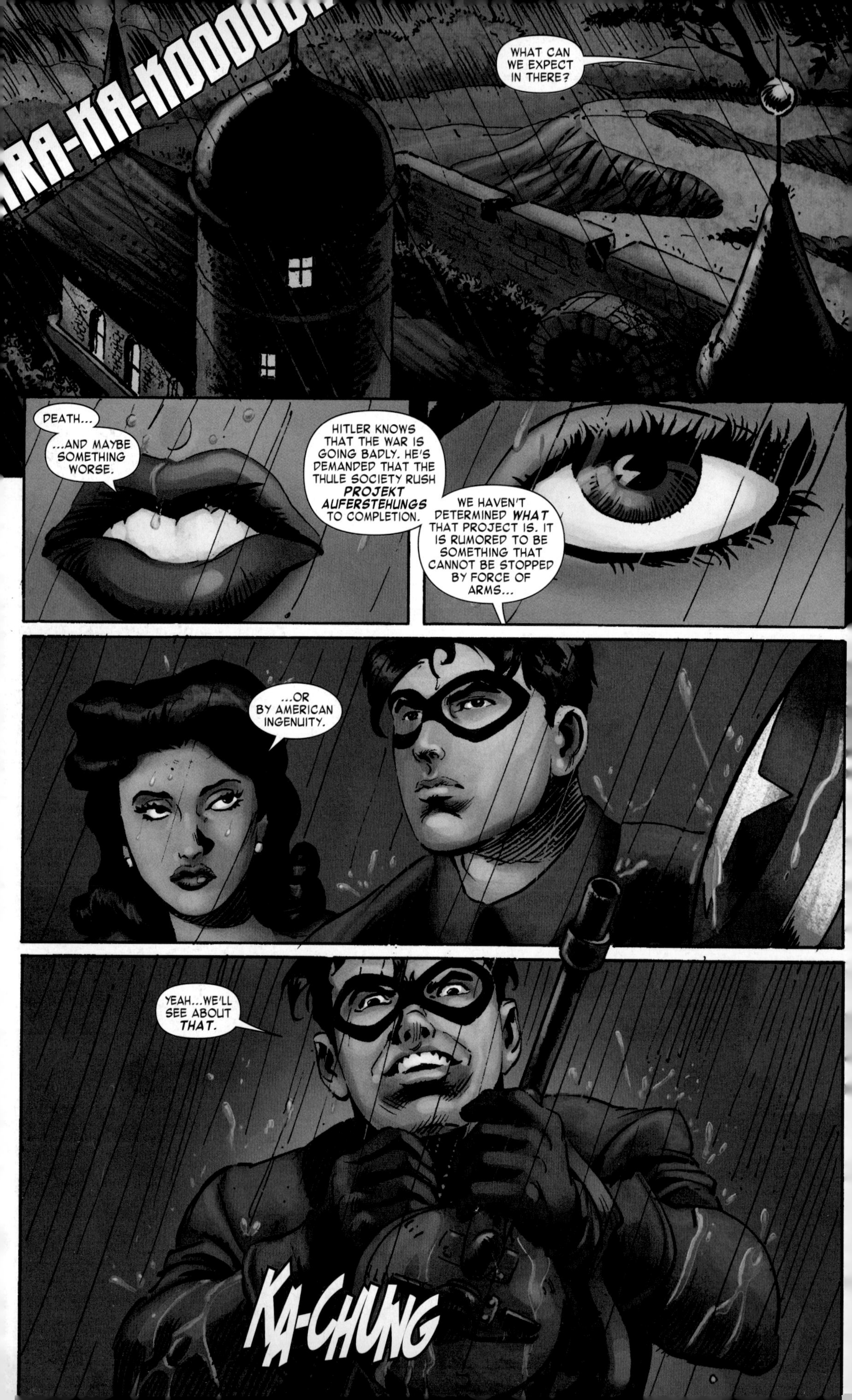

RA-KA-KOOOOO
WHAT CAN WE EXPECT IN THERE?
DEATH...
...AND MAYBE SOMETHING WORSE.
HITLER KNOWS THAT THE WAR IS GOING BADLY. HE'S DEMANDED THAT THE THULE SOCIETY RUSH *PROJEKT AUFERSTEHUNGS* TO COMPLETION.
WE HAVEN'T DETERMINED *WHAT* THAT PROJECT IS. IT IS RUMORED TO BE SOMETHING THAT CANNOT BE STOPPED BY FORCE OF ARMS...
...OR BY AMERICAN INGENUITY.
YEAH...WE'LL SEE ABOUT *THAT.*
KA-CHUNG

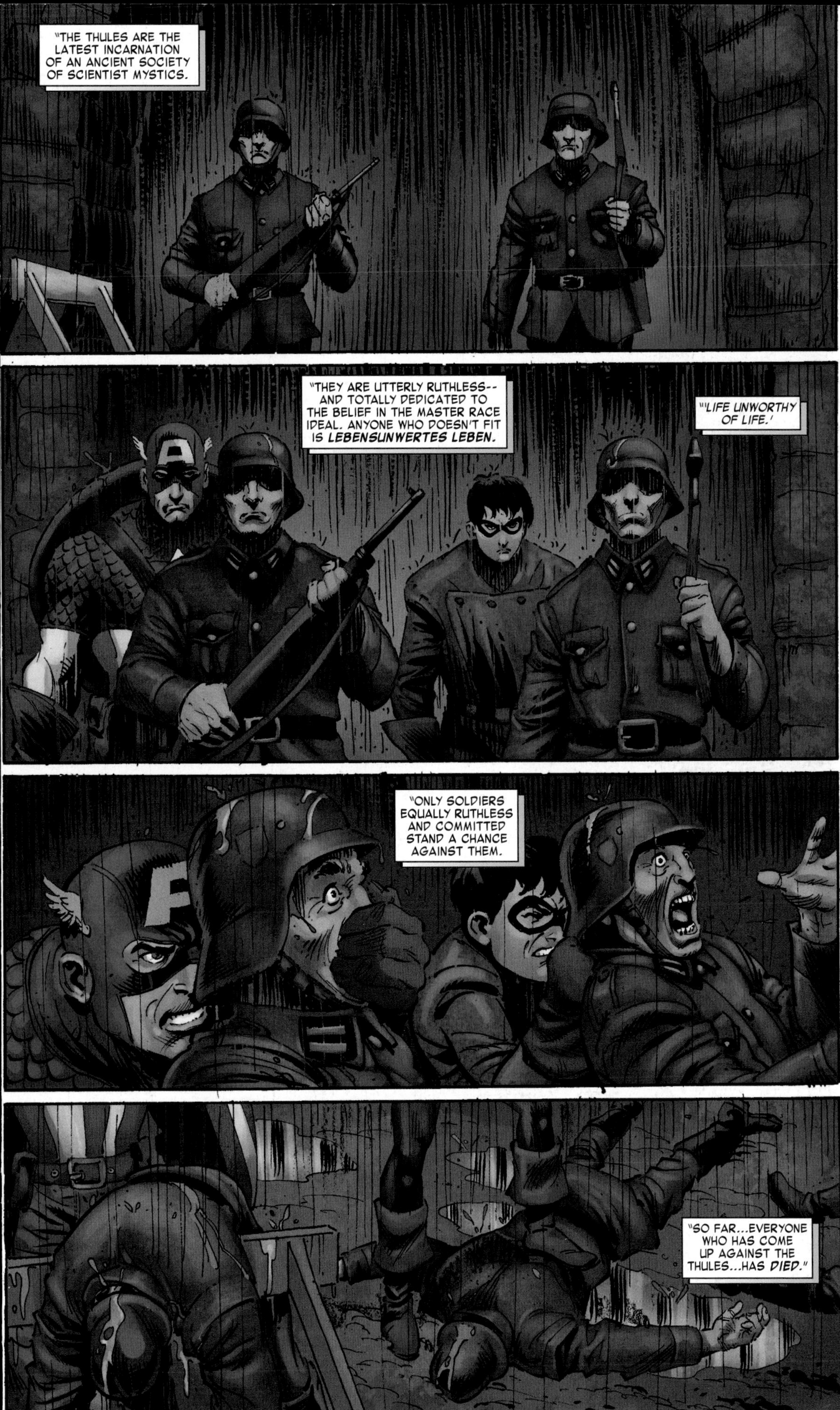
"THE THULES ARE THE LATEST INCARNATION OF AN ANCIENT SOCIETY OF SCIENTIST MYSTICS.
"THEY ARE UTTERLY RUTHLESS-- AND TOTALLY DEDICATED TO THE BELIEF IN THE MASTER RACE IDEAL. ANYONE WHO DOESN'T FIT IS *LEBENSUNWERTES LEBEN.*
"*LIFE UNWORTHY OF LIFE.*'
"ONLY SOLDIERS EQUALLY RUTHLESS AND COMMITTED STAND A CHANCE AGAINST THEM.
"SO FAR...EVERYONE WHO HAS COME UP AGAINST THE THULES...HAS *DIED.*"

CAPTAIN AMERICA: HAIL HYDRA Part 1

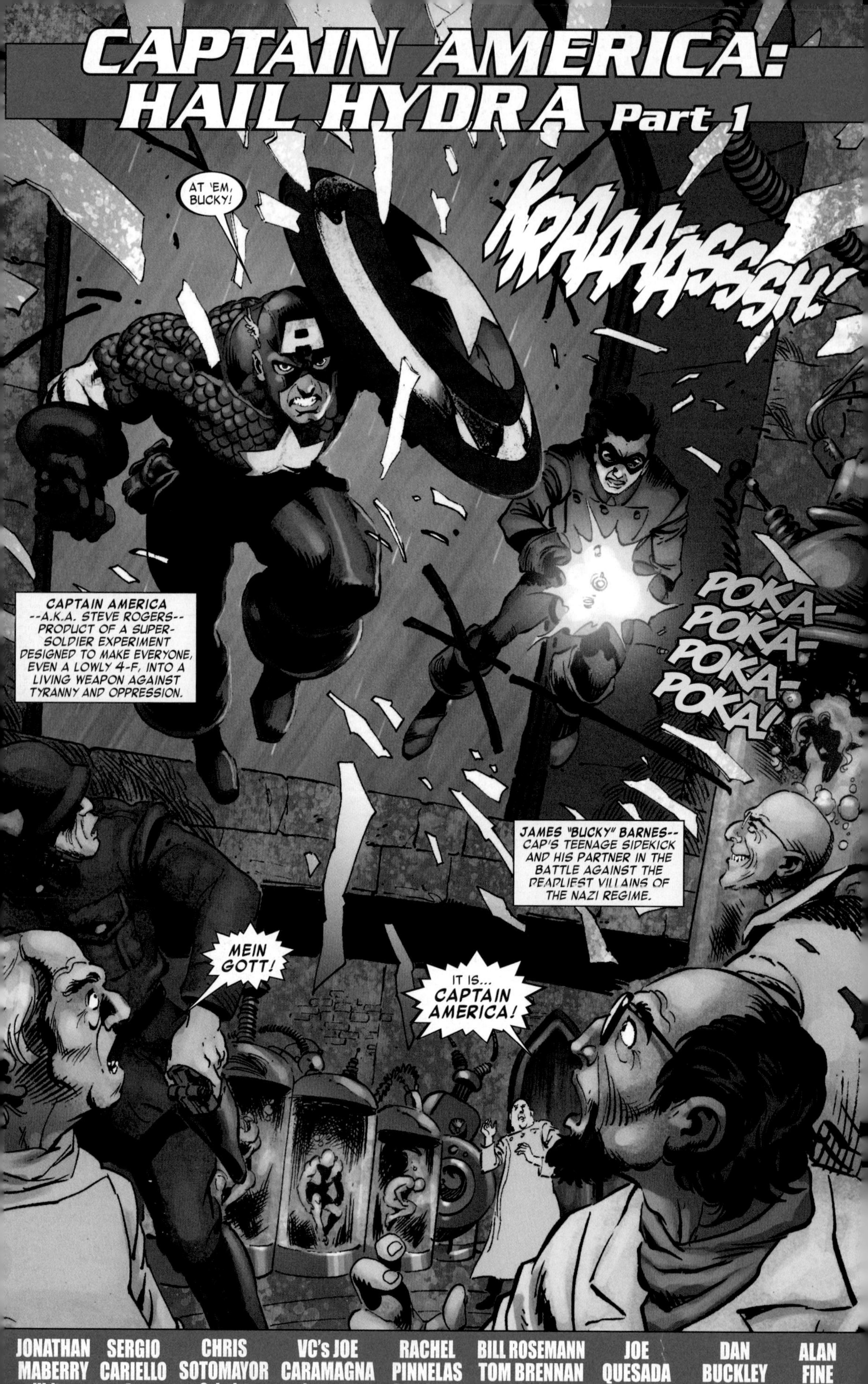
AT 'EM, BUCKY!
KRAAAASSSH!
CAPTAIN AMERICA --A.K.A. STEVE ROGERS-- PRODUCT OF A SUPER-SOLDIER EXPERIMENT DESIGNED TO MAKE EVERYONE, EVEN A LOWLY 4-F, INTO A LIVING WEAPON AGAINST TYRANNY AND OPPRESSION.
POKA-POKA-POKA-POKA!
JAMES "BUCKY" BARNES-- CAP'S TEENAGE SIDEKICK AND HIS PARTNER IN THE BATTLE AGAINST THE DEADLIEST VILLAINS OF THE NAZI REGIME.
MEIN GOTT!
IT IS... CAPTAIN AMERICA!

JONATHAN MABERRY Writer | SERGIO CARIELLO Art | CHRIS SOTOMAYOR Colorist | VC's JOE CARAMAGNA Letterer | RACHEL PINNELAS Asst. Editor | BILL ROSEMANN TOM BRENNAN Editors | JOE QUESADA Editor in Chief | DAN BUCKLEY Publisher | ALAN FINE Exec. Producer

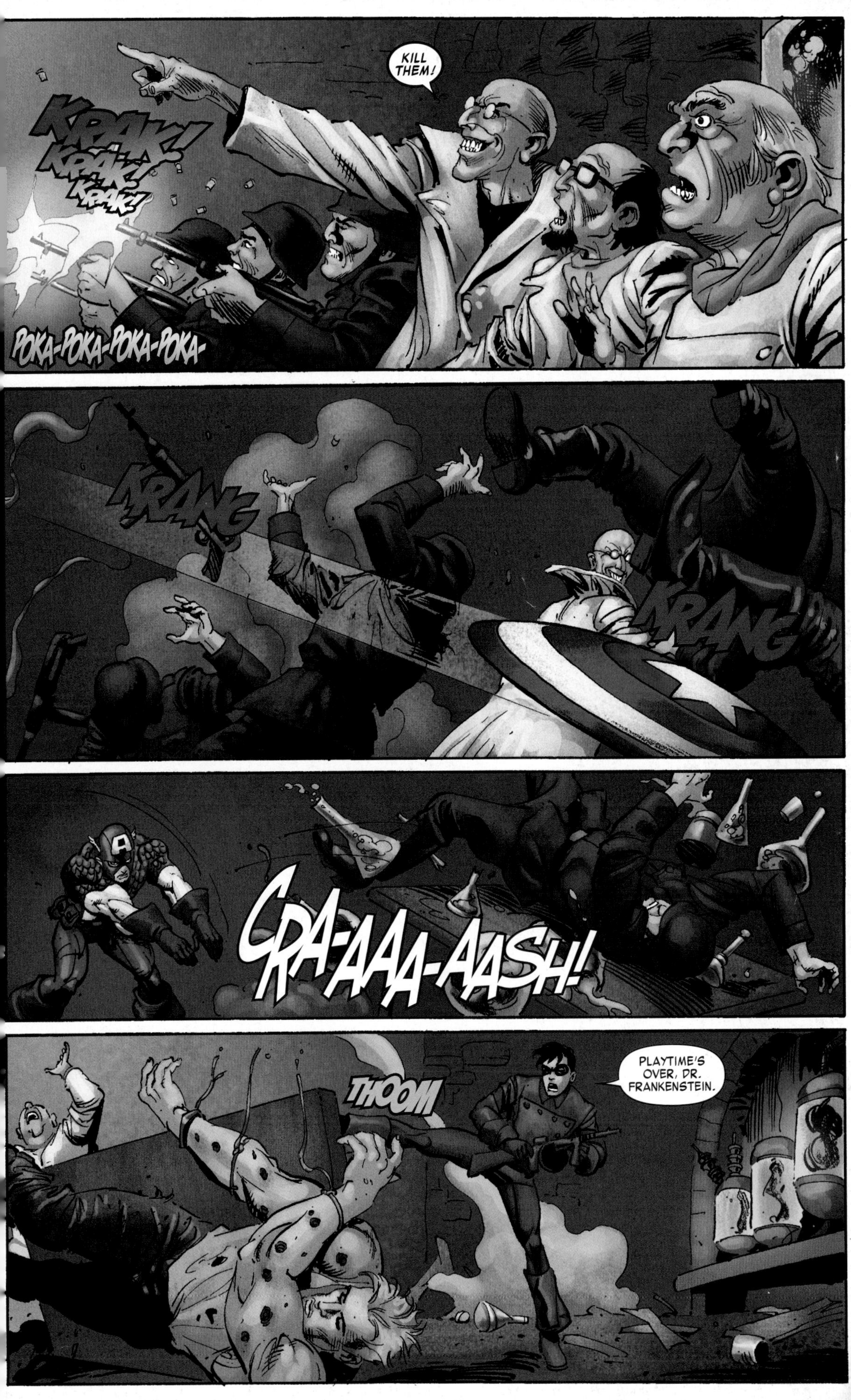
KILL THEM!
KRAK! KRAK! KRAK!
POKA-POKA-POKA-POKA-
KRANG
KRANG
CRA-AAA-AASH!
THOOM
PLAYTIME'S OVER, DR. FRANKENSTEIN.

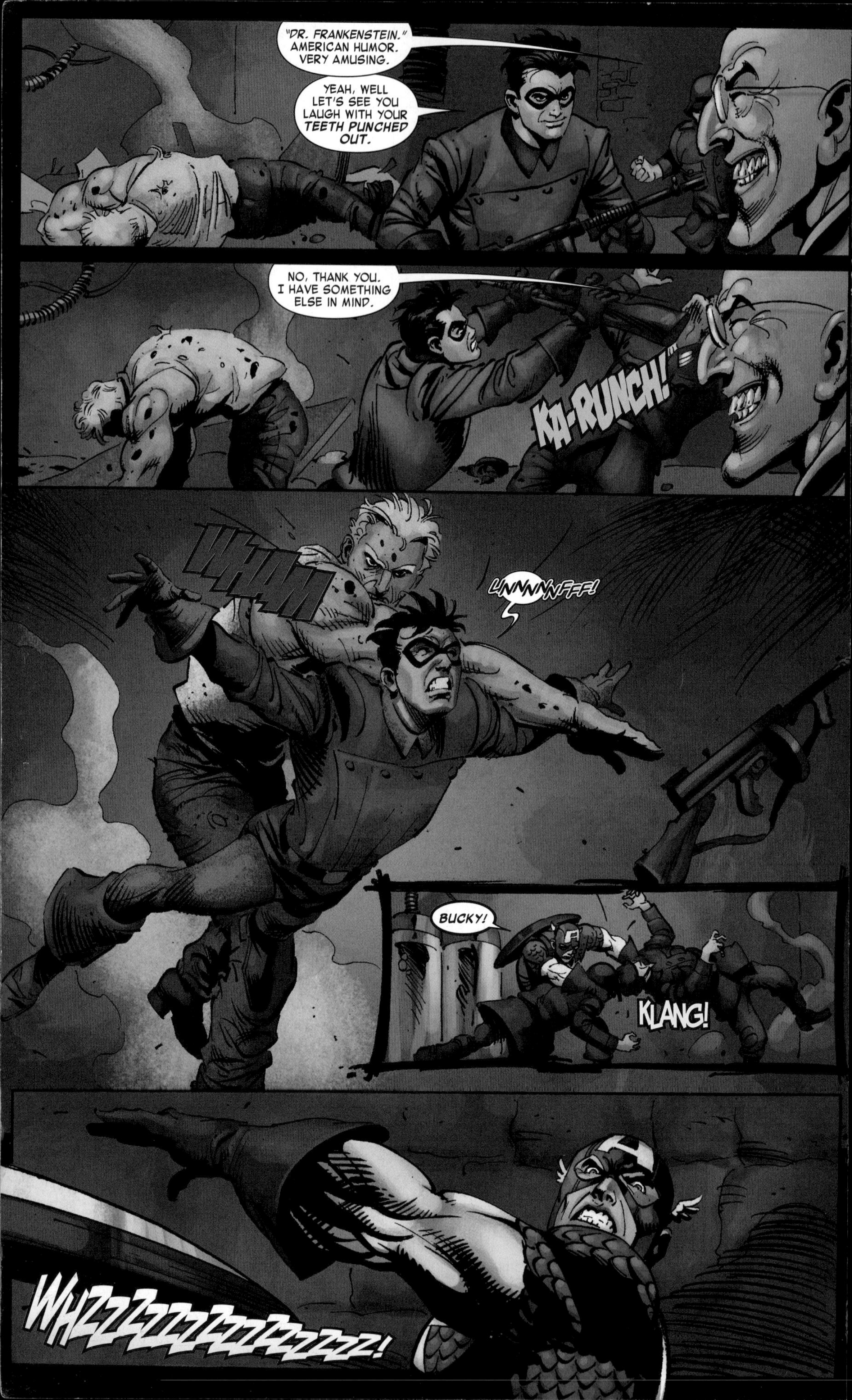
"DR. FRANKENSTEIN." AMERICAN HUMOR. VERY AMUSING.
YEAH, WELL LET'S SEE YOU LAUGH WITH YOUR TEETH PUNCHED OUT.
NO, THANK YOU. I HAVE SOMETHING ELSE IN MIND.
KA-RUNCH!
WHAM
UNNNNNFFF!
BUCKY!
KLANG!
WHZZZZZZZZZZZZZZZ!

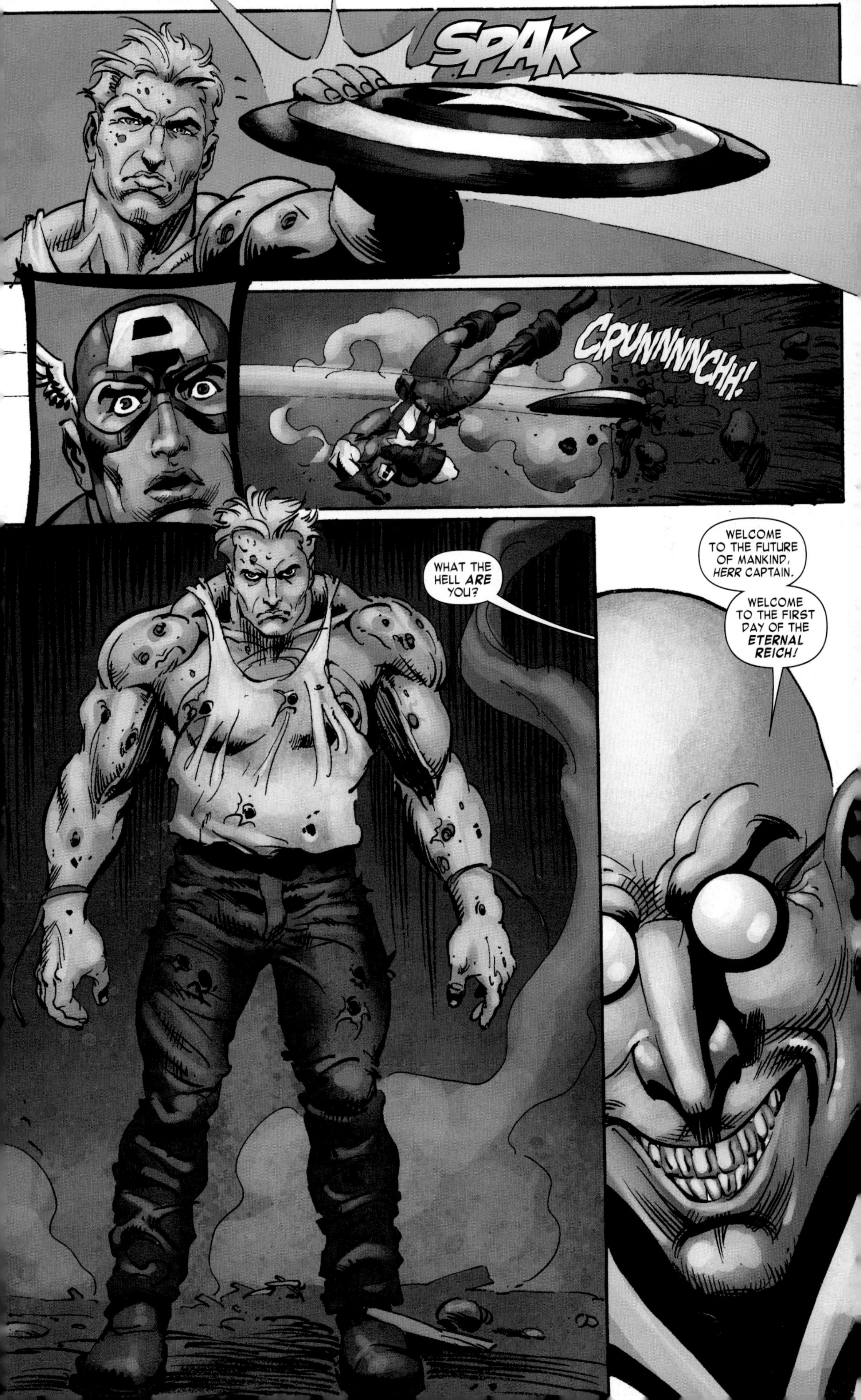
SPAK
CRUNNNNCHH!
WHAT THE HELL ARE YOU?
WELCOME TO THE FUTURE OF MANKIND, HERR CAPTAIN.
WELCOME TO THE FIRST DAY OF THE ETERNAL REICH!

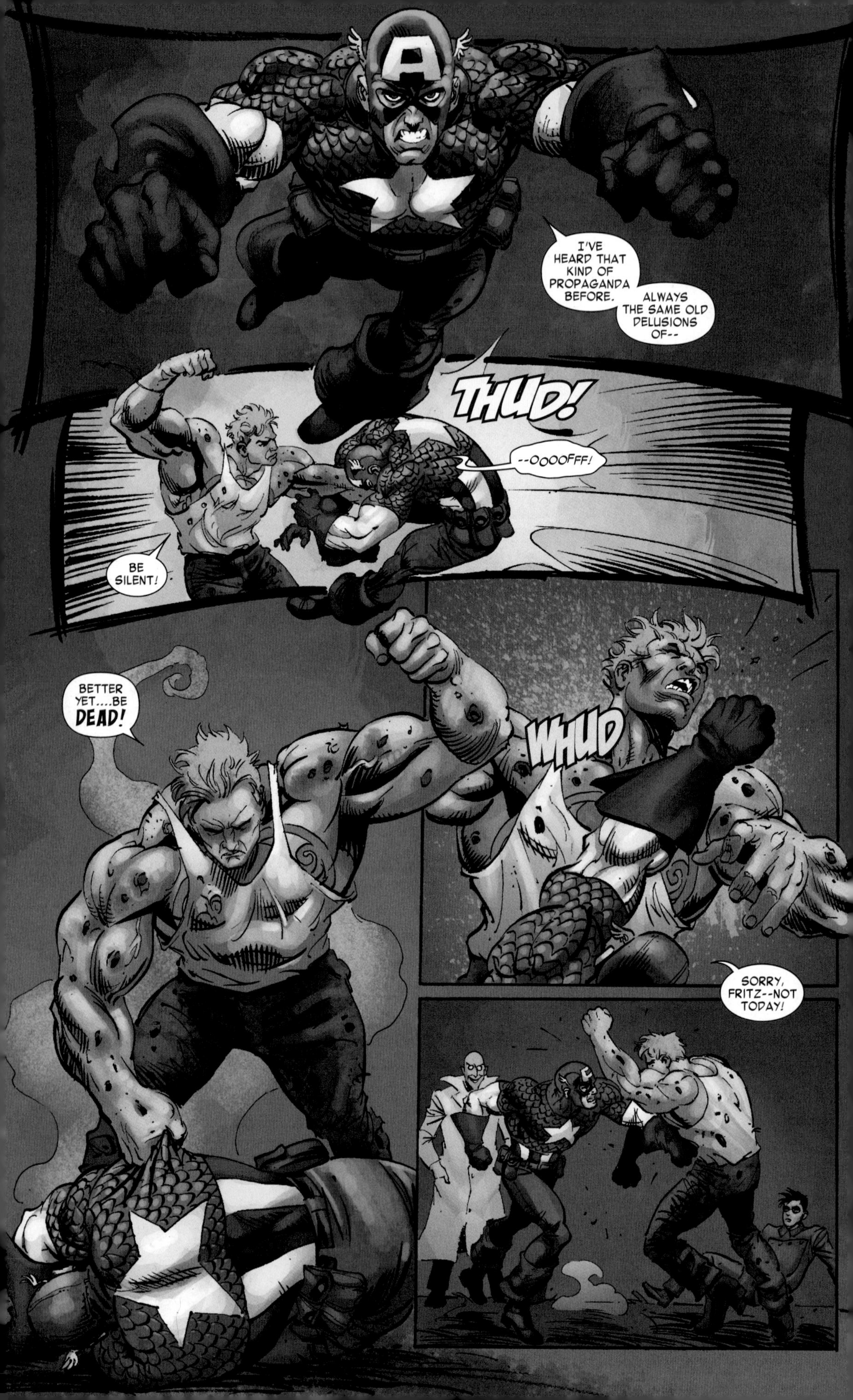

I'VE HEARD THAT KIND OF PROPAGANDA BEFORE.
ALWAYS THE SAME OLD DELUSIONS OF--
THUD!
--OOOOFFF!
BE SILENT!
BETTER YET....BE DEAD!
WHUD
SORRY, FRITZ--NOT TODAY!

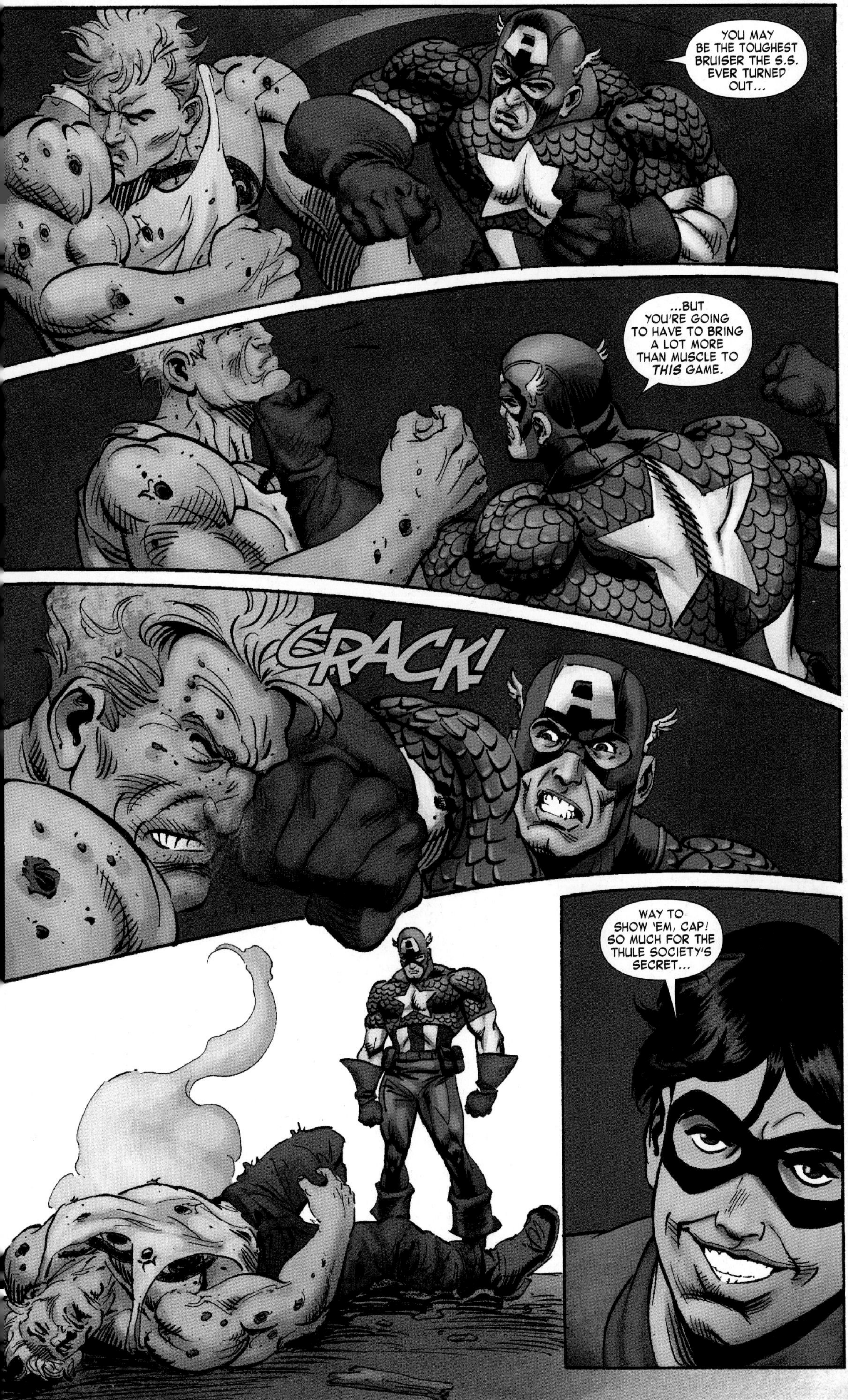
YOU MAY BE THE TOUGHEST BRUISER THE S.S. EVER TURNED OUT...
...BUT YOU'RE GOING TO HAVE TO BRING A LOT MORE THAN MUSCLE TO THIS GAME.
CRACK!
WAY TO SHOW 'EM, CAP! SO MUCH FOR THE THULE SOCIETY'S SECRET...

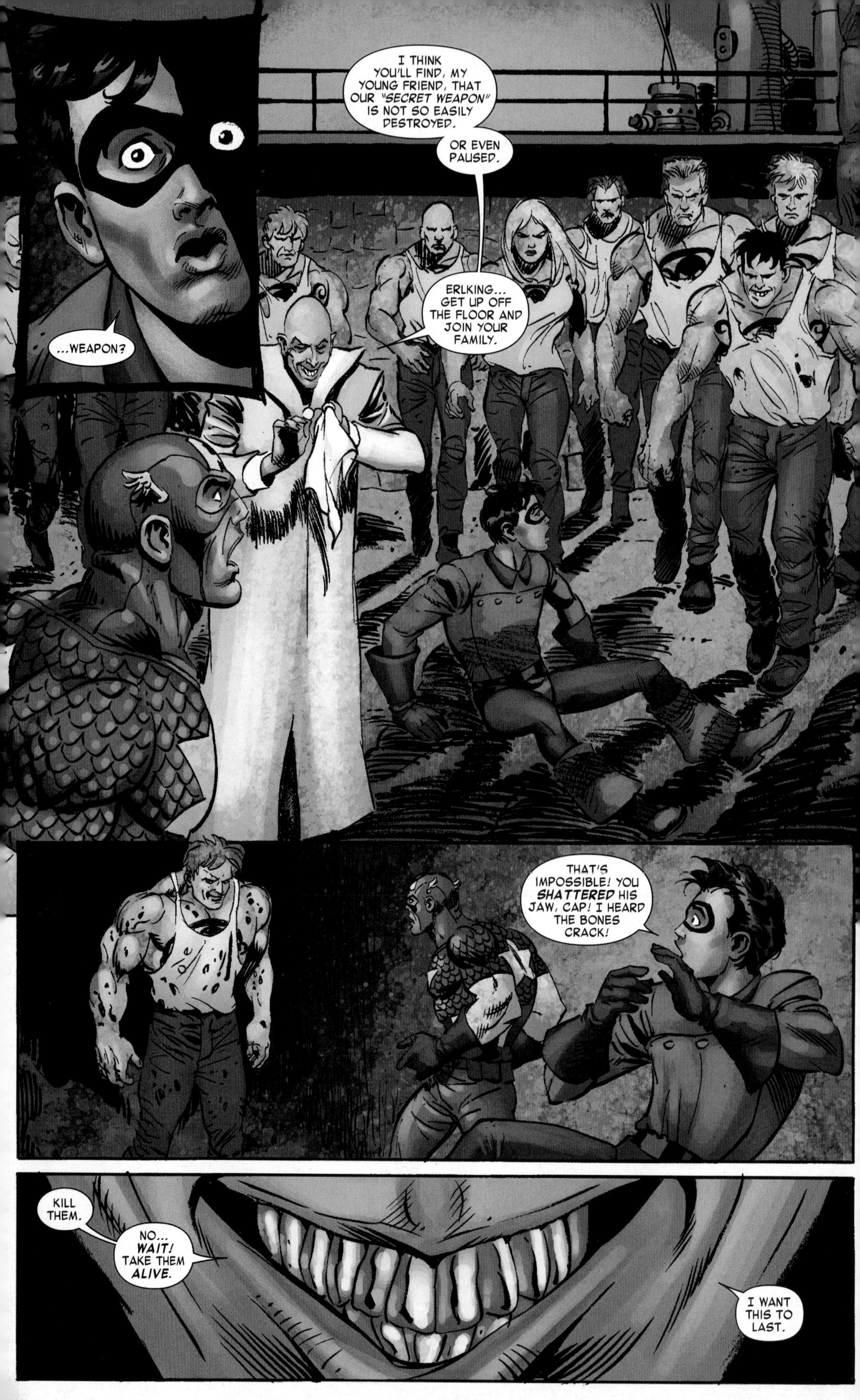
...WEAPON?
I THINK YOU'LL FIND, MY YOUNG FRIEND, THAT OUR "SECRET WEAPON" IS NOT SO EASILY DESTROYED.
OR EVEN PAUSED.
ERLKING... GET UP OFF THE FLOOR AND JOIN YOUR FAMILY.
THAT'S IMPOSSIBLE! YOU SHATTERED HIS JAW, CAP! I HEARD THE BONES CRACK!
KILL THEM.
NO... WAIT! TAKE THEM ALIVE.
I WANT THIS TO LAST.

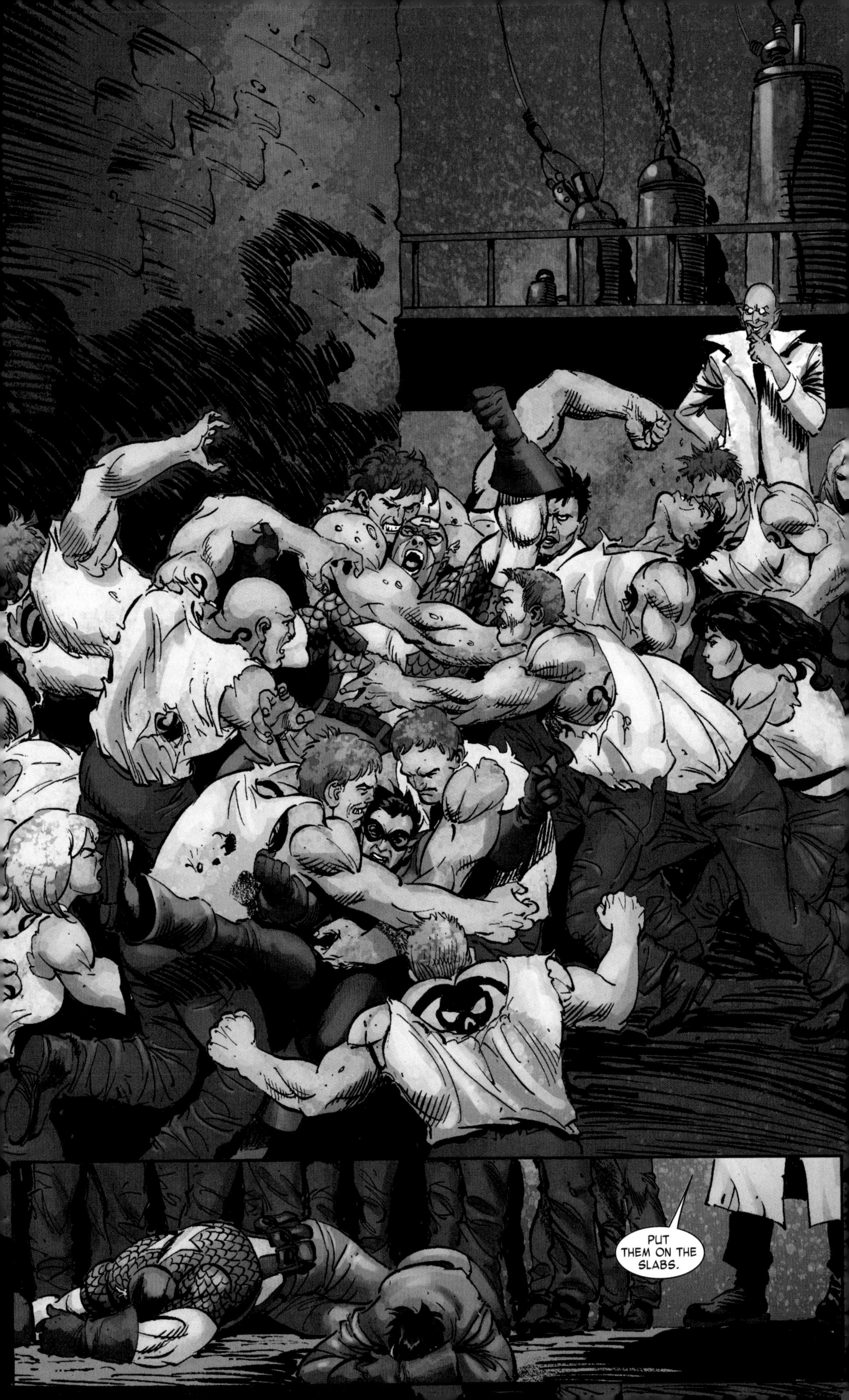
PUT THEM ON THE SLABS.

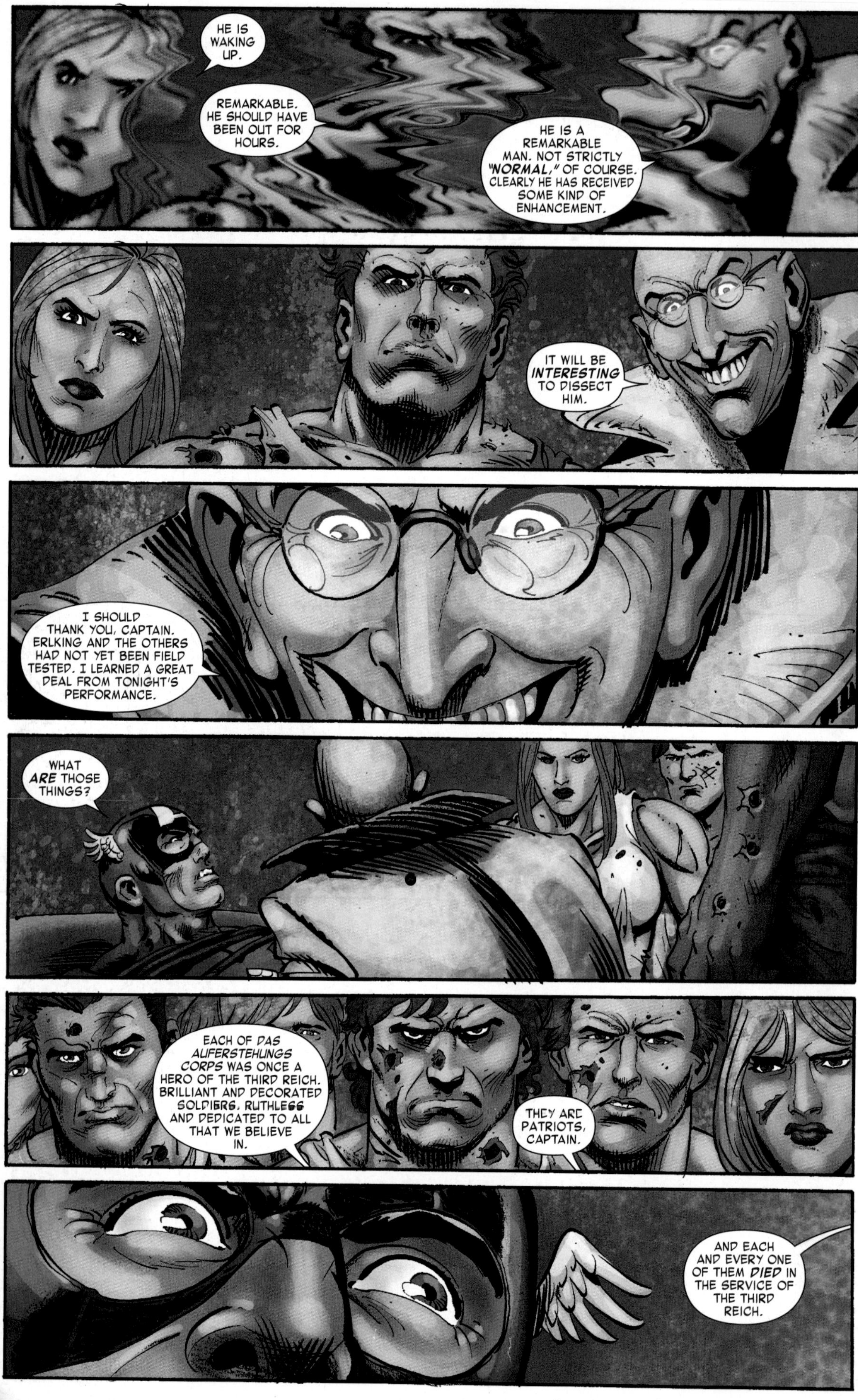
HE IS WAKING UP.
REMARKABLE. HE SHOULD HAVE BEEN OUT FOR HOURS.
HE IS A REMARKABLE MAN. NOT STRICTLY "NORMAL," OF COURSE. CLEARLY HE HAS RECEIVED SOME KIND OF ENHANCEMENT.
IT WILL BE INTERESTING TO DISSECT HIM.
I SHOULD THANK YOU, CAPTAIN. ERLKING AND THE OTHERS HAD NOT YET BEEN FIELD TESTED. I LEARNED A GREAT DEAL FROM TONIGHT'S PERFORMANCE.
WHAT ARE THOSE THINGS?
THEY ARE PATRIOTS, CAPTAIN.
EACH OF DAS AUFERSTEHUNGS CORPS WAS ONCE A HERO OF THE THIRD REICH. BRILLIANT AND DECORATED SOLDIERS. RUTHLESS AND DEDICATED TO ALL THAT WE BELIEVE IN.
AND EACH AND EVERY ONE OF THEM DIED IN THE SERVICE OF THE THIRD REICH.

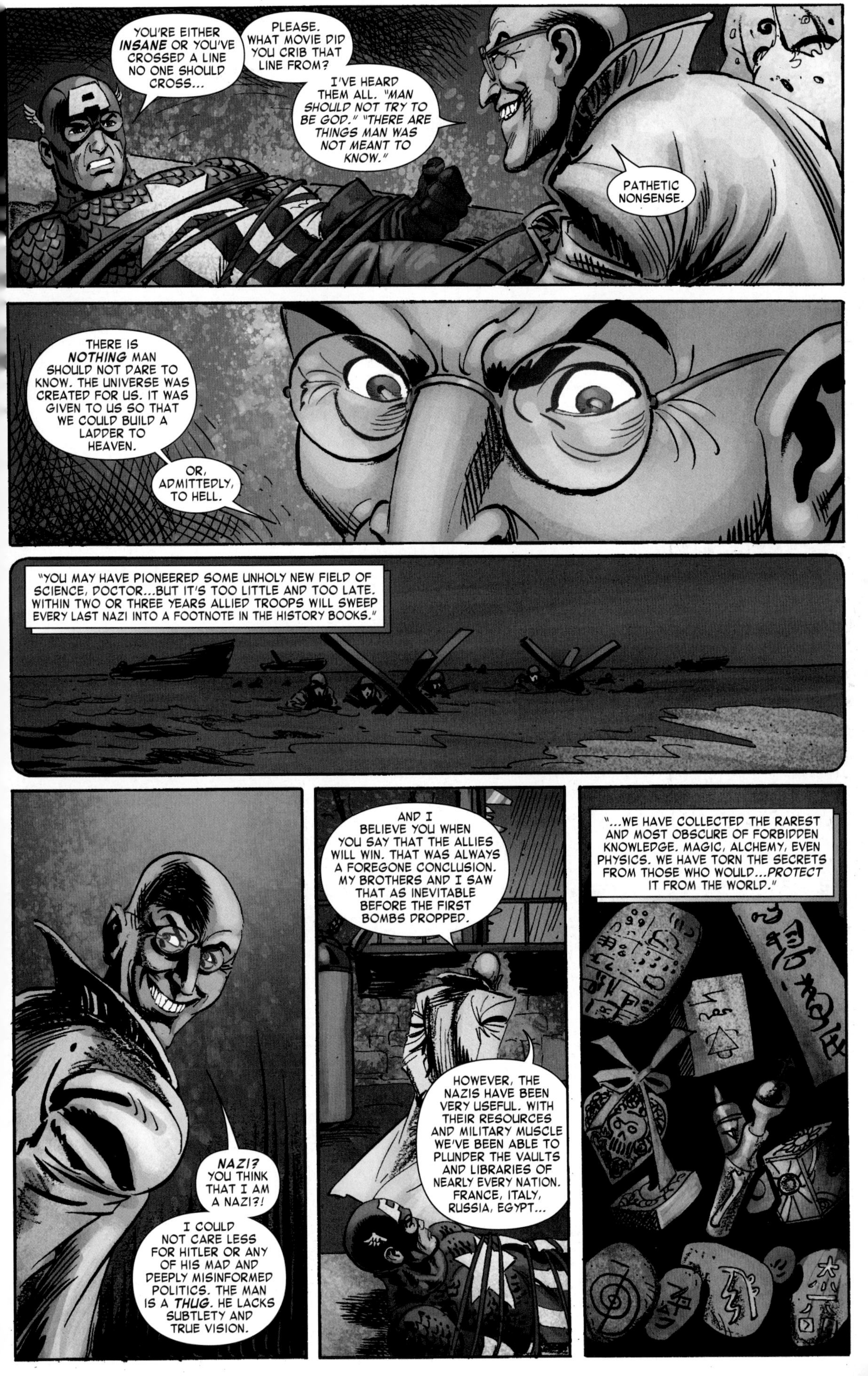
YOU'RE EITHER INSANE OR YOU'VE CROSSED A LINE NO ONE SHOULD CROSS...
PLEASE. WHAT MOVIE DID YOU CRIB THAT LINE FROM?
I'VE HEARD THEM ALL. "MAN SHOULD NOT TRY TO BE GOD." "THERE ARE THINGS MAN WAS NOT MEANT TO KNOW."
PATHETIC NONSENSE.
THERE IS NOTHING MAN SHOULD NOT DARE TO KNOW. THE UNIVERSE WAS CREATED FOR US. IT WAS GIVEN TO US SO THAT WE COULD BUILD A LADDER TO HEAVEN.
OR, ADMITTEDLY, TO HELL.
"YOU MAY HAVE PIONEERED SOME UNHOLY NEW FIELD OF SCIENCE, DOCTOR...BUT IT'S TOO LITTLE AND TOO LATE. WITHIN TWO OR THREE YEARS ALLIED TROOPS WILL SWEEP EVERY LAST NAZI INTO A FOOTNOTE IN THE HISTORY BOOKS."
NAZI? YOU THINK THAT I AM A NAZI?!
I COULD NOT CARE LESS FOR HITLER OR ANY OF HIS MAD AND DEEPLY MISINFORMED POLITICS. THE MAN IS A THUG. HE LACKS SUBTLETY AND TRUE VISION.
AND I BELIEVE YOU WHEN YOU SAY THAT THE ALLIES WILL WIN. THAT WAS ALWAYS A FOREGONE CONCLUSION. MY BROTHERS AND I SAW THAT AS INEVITABLE BEFORE THE FIRST BOMBS DROPPED.
HOWEVER, THE NAZIS HAVE BEEN VERY USEFUL. WITH THEIR RESOURCES AND MILITARY MUSCLE WE'VE BEEN ABLE TO PLUNDER THE VAULTS AND LIBRARIES OF NEARLY EVERY NATION. FRANCE, ITALY, RUSSIA, EGYPT...
"...WE HAVE COLLECTED THE RAREST AND MOST OBSCURE OF FORBIDDEN KNOWLEDGE. MAGIC, ALCHEMY, EVEN PHYSICS. WE HAVE TORN THE SECRETS FROM THOSE WHO WOULD...PROTECT IT FROM THE WORLD."

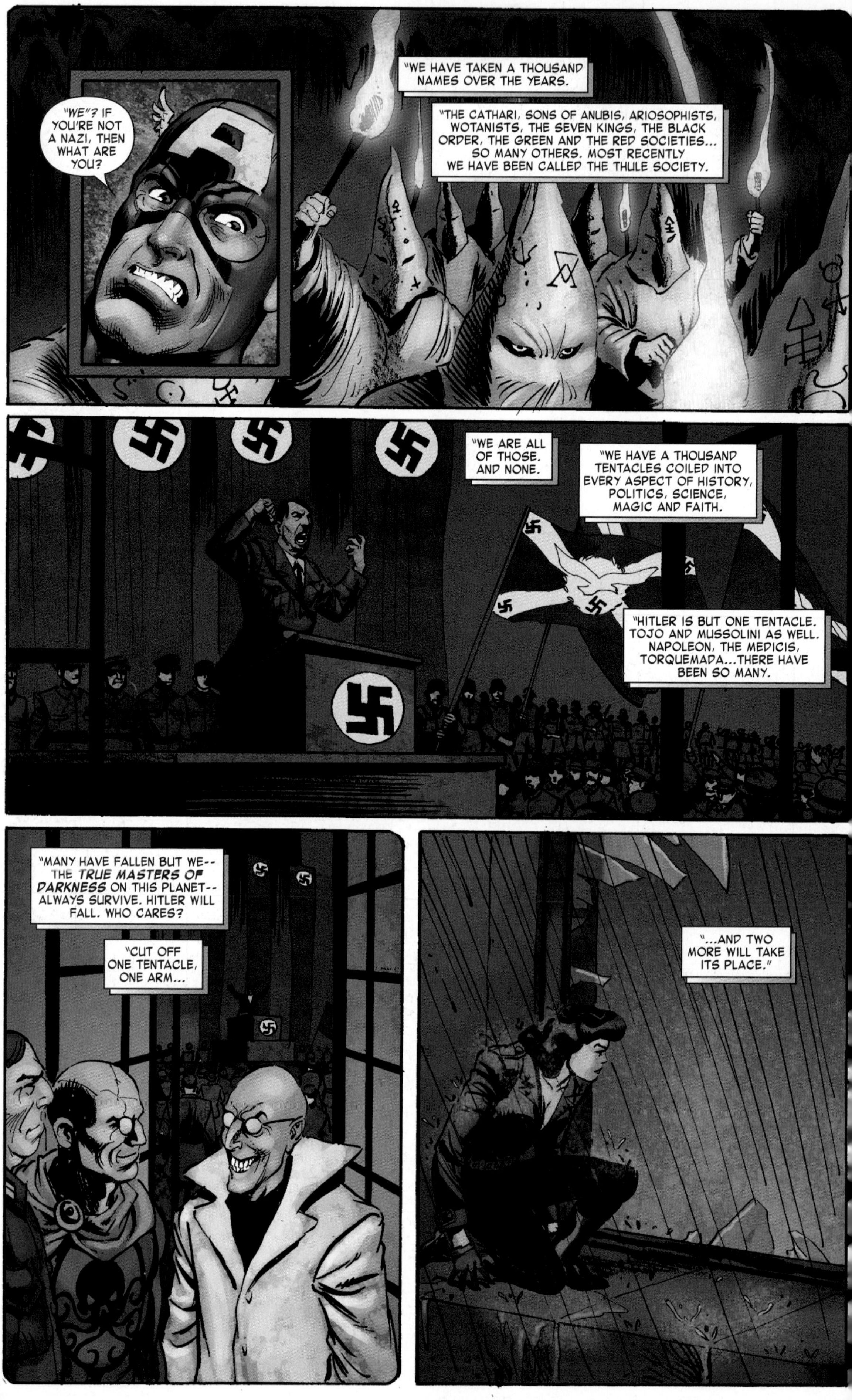
"WE"? IF YOU'RE NOT A NAZI, THEN WHAT ARE YOU?
"WE HAVE TAKEN A THOUSAND NAMES OVER THE YEARS.
"THE CATHARI, SONS OF ANUBIS, ARIOSOPHISTS, WOTANISTS, THE SEVEN KINGS, THE BLACK ORDER, THE GREEN AND THE RED SOCIETIES... SO MANY OTHERS. MOST RECENTLY WE HAVE BEEN CALLED THE THULE SOCIETY.
"WE ARE ALL OF THOSE. AND NONE.
"WE HAVE A THOUSAND TENTACLES COILED INTO EVERY ASPECT OF HISTORY, POLITICS, SCIENCE, MAGIC AND FAITH.
"HITLER IS BUT ONE TENTACLE. TOJO AND MUSSOLINI AS WELL. NAPOLEON, THE MEDICIS, TORQUEMADA...THERE HAVE BEEN SO MANY.
"MANY HAVE FALLEN BUT WE-- THE TRUE MASTERS OF DARKNESS ON THIS PLANET-- ALWAYS SURVIVE. HITLER WILL FALL. WHO CARES?
"CUT OFF ONE TENTACLE, ONE ARM...
"...AND TWO MORE WILL TAKE ITS PLACE."

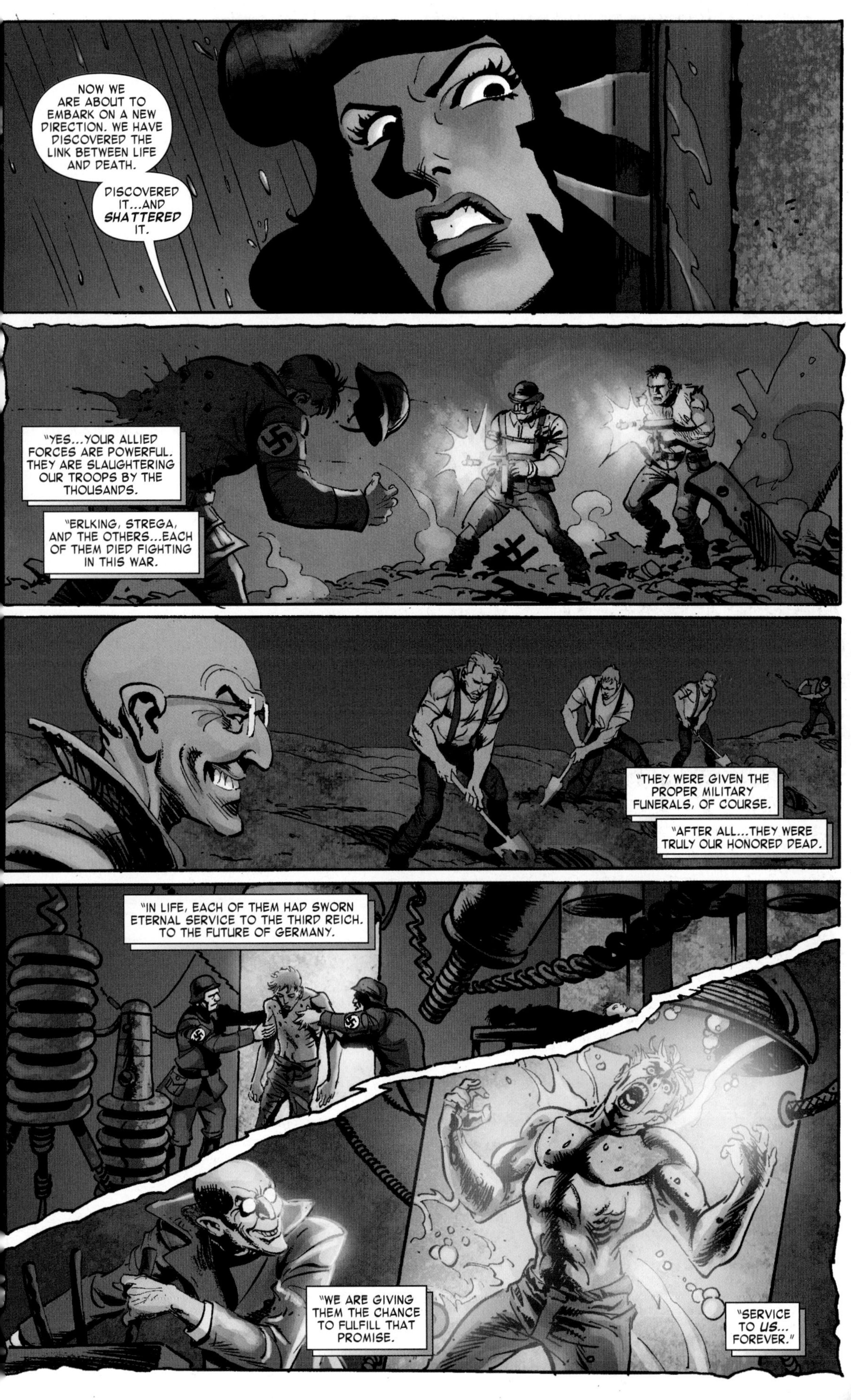
NOW WE ARE ABOUT TO EMBARK ON A NEW DIRECTION. WE HAVE DISCOVERED THE LINK BETWEEN LIFE AND DEATH.
DISCOVERED IT...AND *SHATTERED* IT.
"YES...YOUR ALLIED FORCES ARE POWERFUL. THEY ARE SLAUGHTERING OUR TROOPS BY THE THOUSANDS.
"ERLKING, STREGA, AND THE OTHERS...EACH OF THEM DIED FIGHTING IN THIS WAR.
"THEY WERE GIVEN THE PROPER MILITARY FUNERALS, OF COURSE.
"AFTER ALL...THEY WERE TRULY OUR HONORED DEAD.
"IN LIFE, EACH OF THEM HAD SWORN ETERNAL SERVICE TO THE THIRD REICH. TO THE FUTURE OF GERMANY.
"WE ARE GIVING THEM THE CHANCE TO FULFILL THAT PROMISE.
"SERVICE TO *US*... FOREVER."

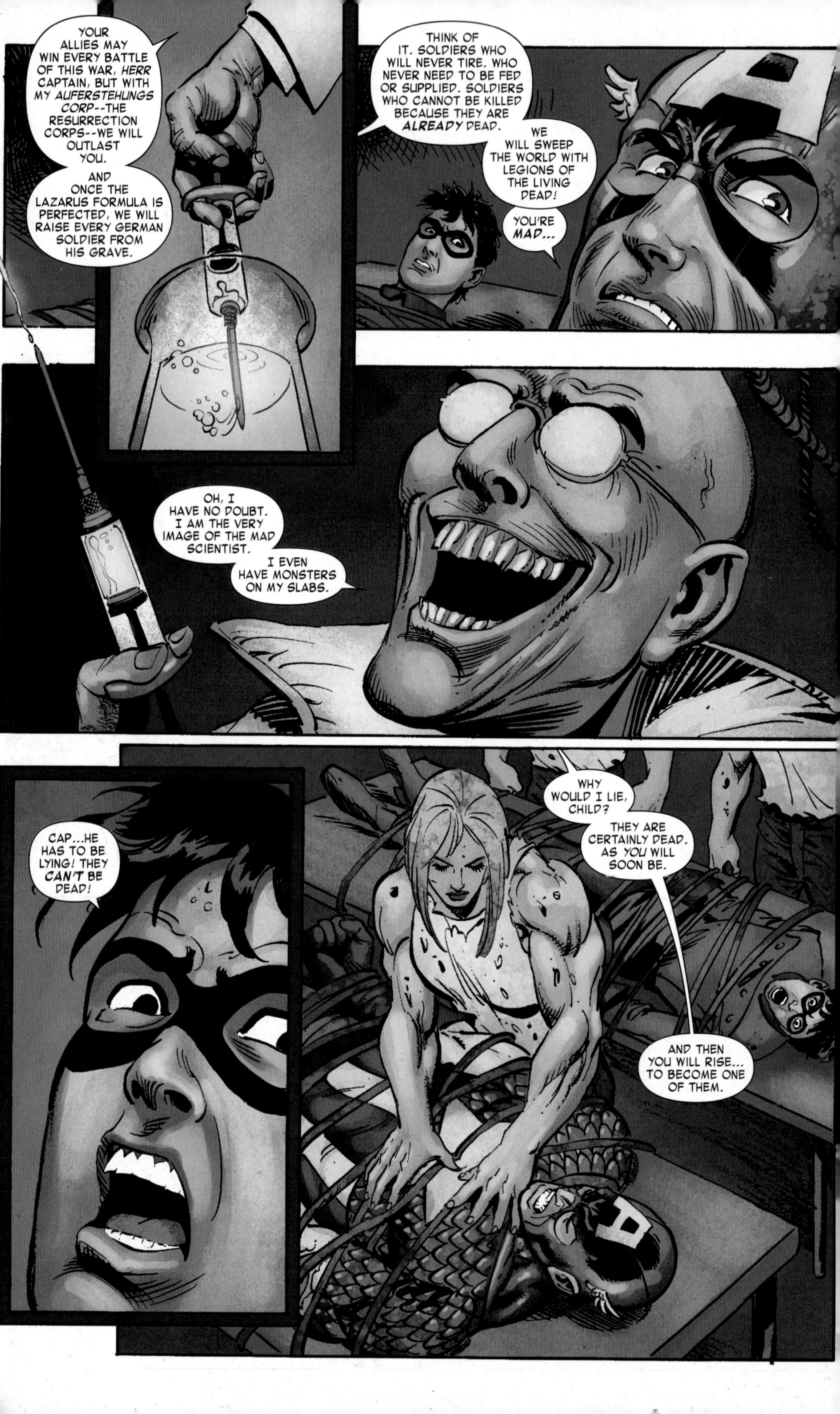
YOUR ALLIES MAY WIN EVERY BATTLE OF THIS WAR, *HERR* CAPTAIN, BUT WITH MY *AUFERSTEHUNGS CORP*--THE RESURRECTION CORPS--WE WILL OUTLAST YOU.
AND ONCE THE LAZARUS FORMULA IS PERFECTED, WE WILL RAISE EVERY GERMAN SOLDIER FROM HIS GRAVE.
THINK OF IT. SOLDIERS WHO WILL NEVER TIRE. WHO NEVER NEED TO BE FED OR SUPPLIED. SOLDIERS WHO CANNOT BE KILLED BECAUSE THEY ARE *ALREADY* DEAD.
WE WILL SWEEP THE WORLD WITH LEGIONS OF THE LIVING DEAD!
YOU'RE *MAD...*
OH, I HAVE NO DOUBT. I AM THE VERY IMAGE OF THE MAD SCIENTIST.
I EVEN HAVE MONSTERS ON MY SLABS.
CAP...HE HAS TO BE LYING! THEY *CAN'T* BE DEAD!
WHY WOULD I LIE, CHILD?
THEY ARE CERTAINLY DEAD. AS *YOU* WILL SOON BE.
AND THEN YOU WILL RISE... TO BECOME ONE OF THEM.

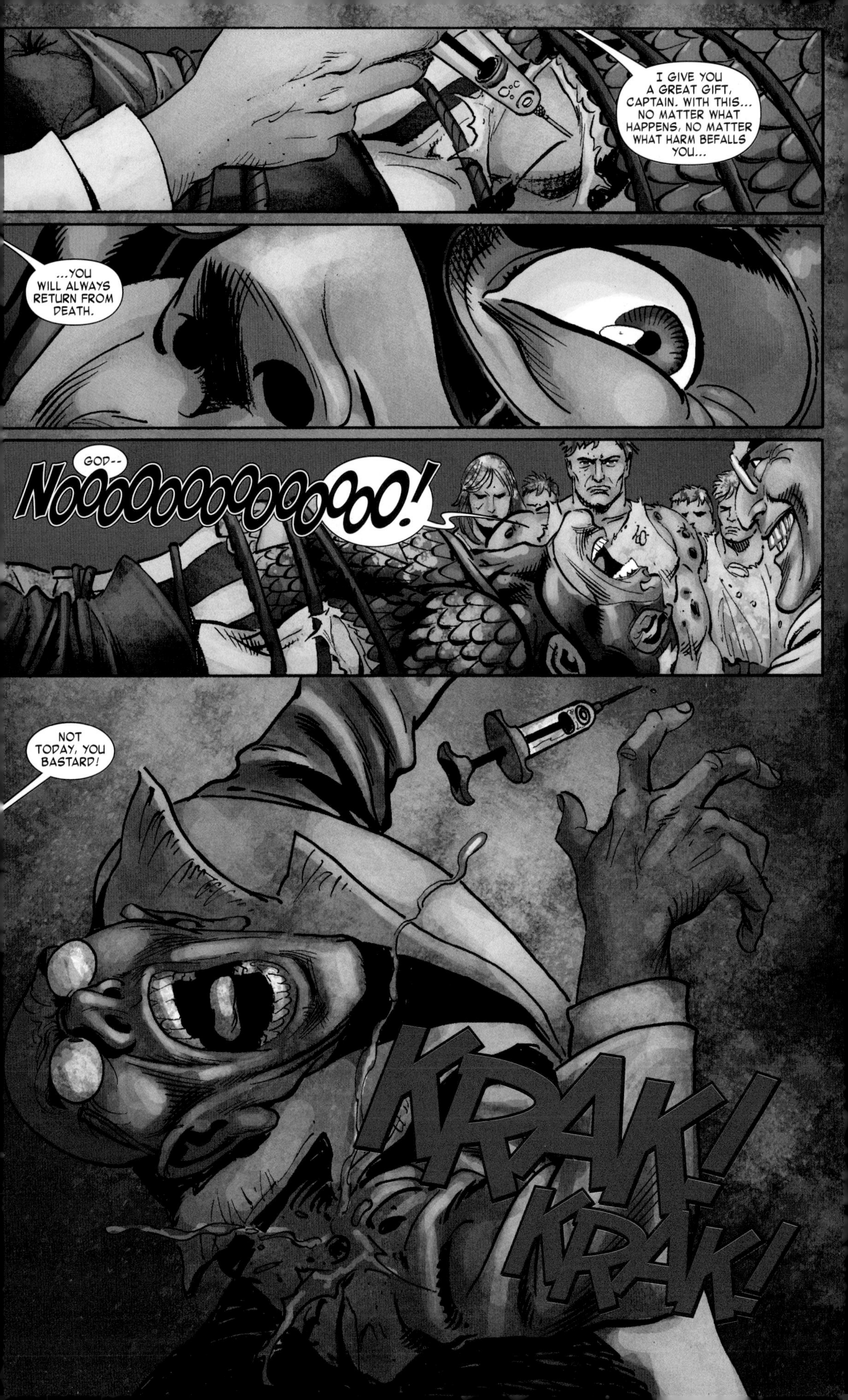
I GIVE YOU A GREAT GIFT, CAPTAIN. WITH THIS... NO MATTER WHAT HAPPENS, NO MATTER WHAT HARM BEFALLS YOU...
...YOU WILL ALWAYS RETURN FROM DEATH.
GOD--
NOOOOOOOOOOOOOOO!
NOT TODAY, YOU BASTARD!
KRAK!
KRAK!

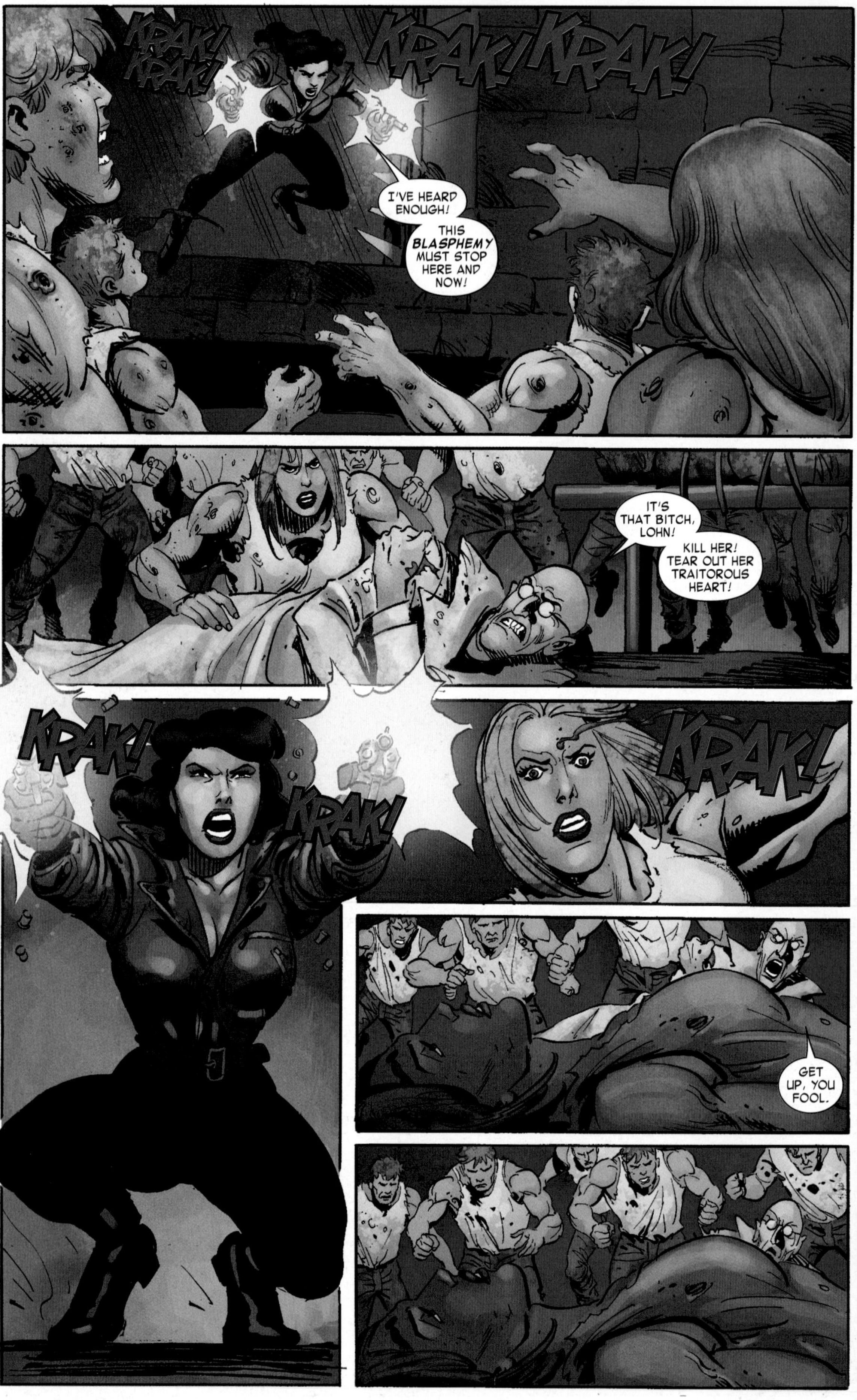
KRAK! KRAK!
KRAK! KRAK!
I'VE HEARD ENOUGH!
THIS BLASPHEMY MUST STOP HERE AND NOW!
IT'S THAT BITCH, LOHN!
KILL HER! TEAR OUT HER TRAITOROUS HEART!
KRAK!
KRAK!
KRAK!
GET UP, YOU FOOL.

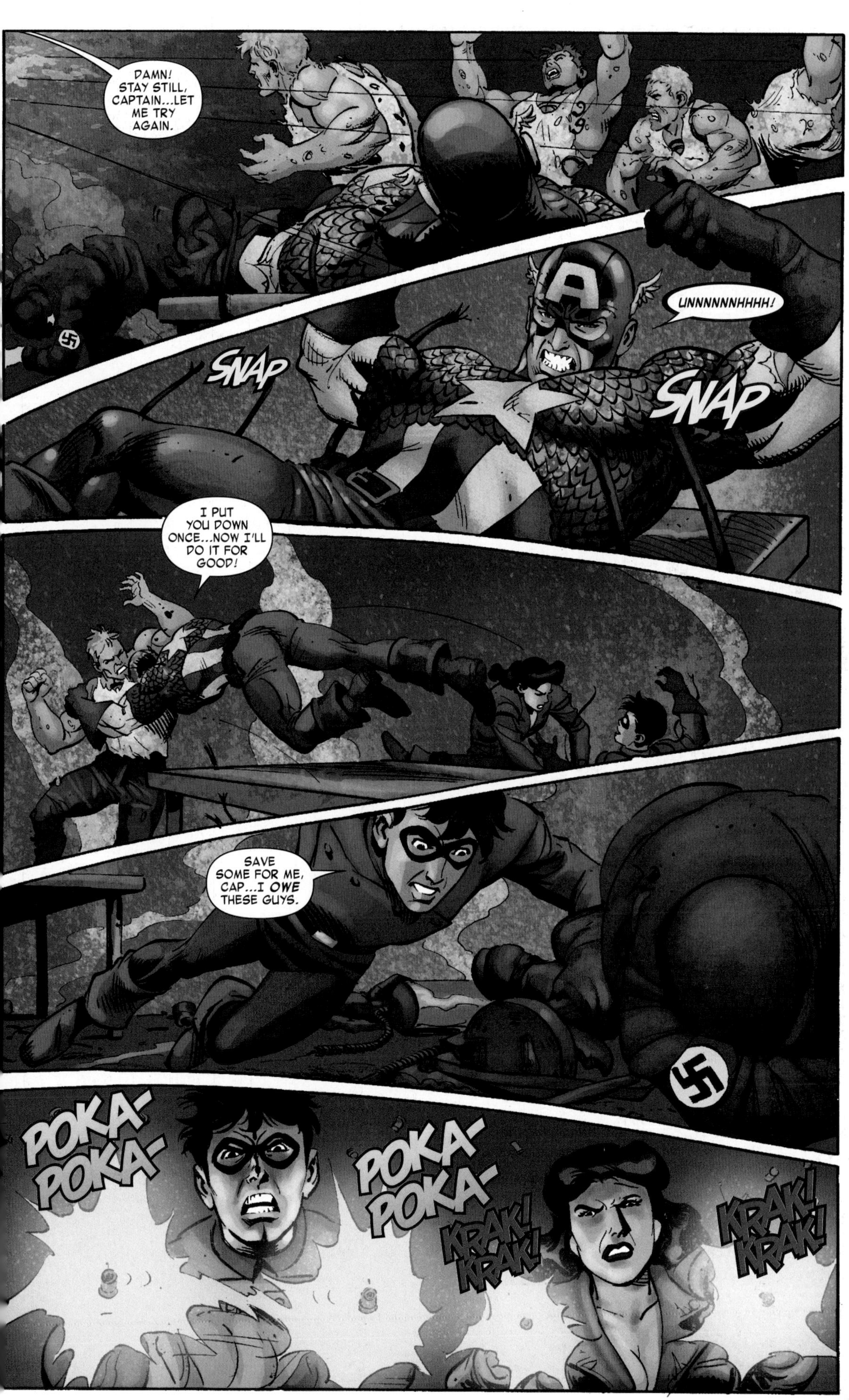
DAMN! STAY STILL, CAPTAIN...LET ME TRY AGAIN.
UNNNNNNHHHH!
SNAP
SNAP
I PUT YOU DOWN ONCE...NOW I'LL DO IT FOR GOOD!
SAVE SOME FOR ME, CAP...I OWE THESE GUYS.
POKA-POKA-
POKA-POKA-
KRAK! KRAK!
KRAK! KRAK!

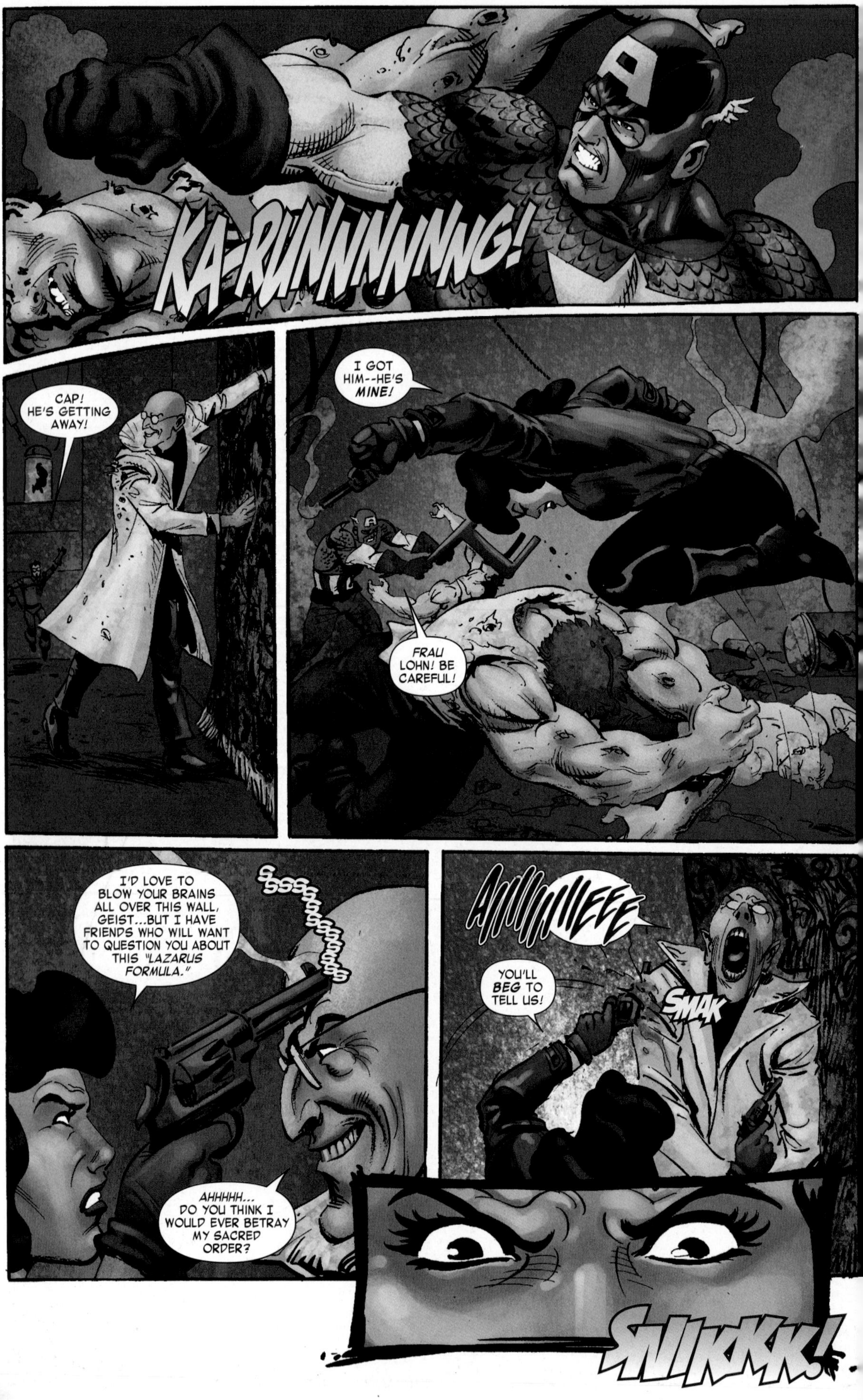
KA-RUNNNNNNG!
CAP! HE'S GETTING AWAY!
I GOT HIM--HE'S MINE!
FRAU LOHN! BE CAREFUL!
I'D LOVE TO BLOW YOUR BRAINS ALL OVER THIS WALL, GEIST...BUT I HAVE FRIENDS WHO WILL WANT TO QUESTION YOU ABOUT THIS "LAZARUS FORMULA."
AHHHHH... DO YOU THINK I WOULD EVER BETRAY MY SACRED ORDER?
AIIIIIIIEEEE
YOU'LL BEG TO TELL US!
SMAK
SHLIKKK!

OH MY GOD!

LOHN!

CAP--GET OUT OF THE WAY, I DON'T HAVE A CLEAN SHOT!

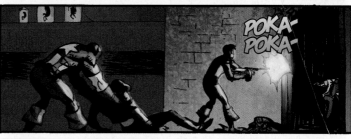

POKA-POKA-

GRENADE! DUCK!

FFOOSH

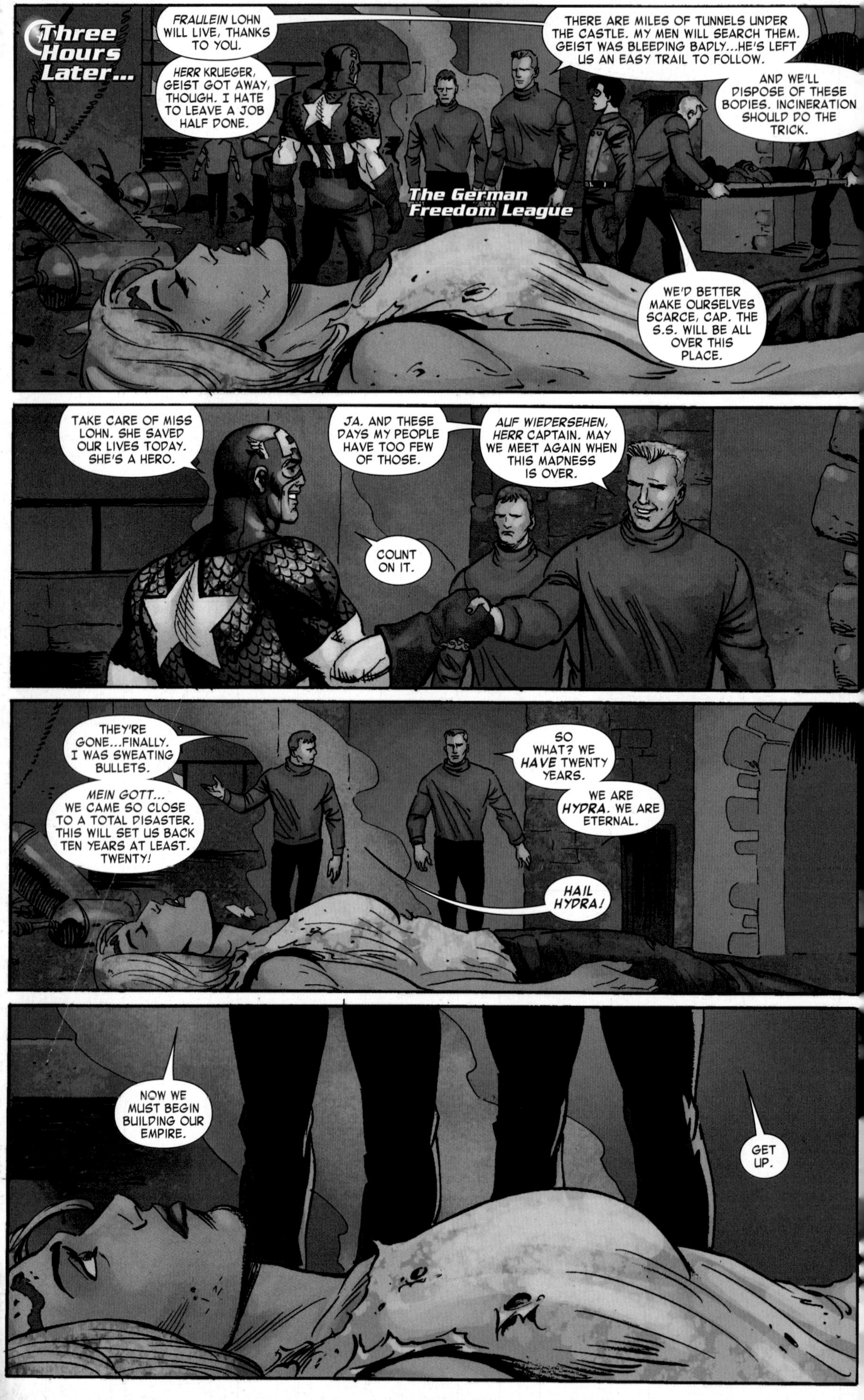
Three Hours Later...
FRAULEIN LOHN WILL LIVE, THANKS TO YOU.
HERR KRUEGER, GEIST GOT AWAY, THOUGH. I HATE TO LEAVE A JOB HALF DONE.
THERE ARE MILES OF TUNNELS UNDER THE CASTLE. MY MEN WILL SEARCH THEM. GEIST WAS BLEEDING BADLY...HE'S LEFT US AN EASY TRAIL TO FOLLOW.
AND WE'LL DISPOSE OF THESE BODIES. INCINERATION SHOULD DO THE TRICK.
The German Freedom League
WE'D BETTER MAKE OURSELVES SCARCE, CAP. THE S.S. WILL BE ALL OVER THIS PLACE.
TAKE CARE OF MISS LOHN. SHE SAVED OUR LIVES TODAY. SHE'S A HERO.
JA. AND THESE DAYS MY PEOPLE HAVE TOO FEW OF THOSE.
AUF WIEDERSEHEN, HERR CAPTAIN. MAY WE MEET AGAIN WHEN THIS MADNESS IS OVER.
COUNT ON IT.
THEY'RE GONE...FINALLY. I WAS SWEATING BULLETS.
MEIN GOTT... WE CAME SO CLOSE TO A TOTAL DISASTER. THIS WILL SET US BACK TEN YEARS AT LEAST. TWENTY!
SO WHAT? WE HAVE TWENTY YEARS.
WE ARE HYDRA. WE ARE ETERNAL.
HAIL HYDRA!
NOW WE MUST BEGIN BUILDING OUR EMPIRE.
GET UP.

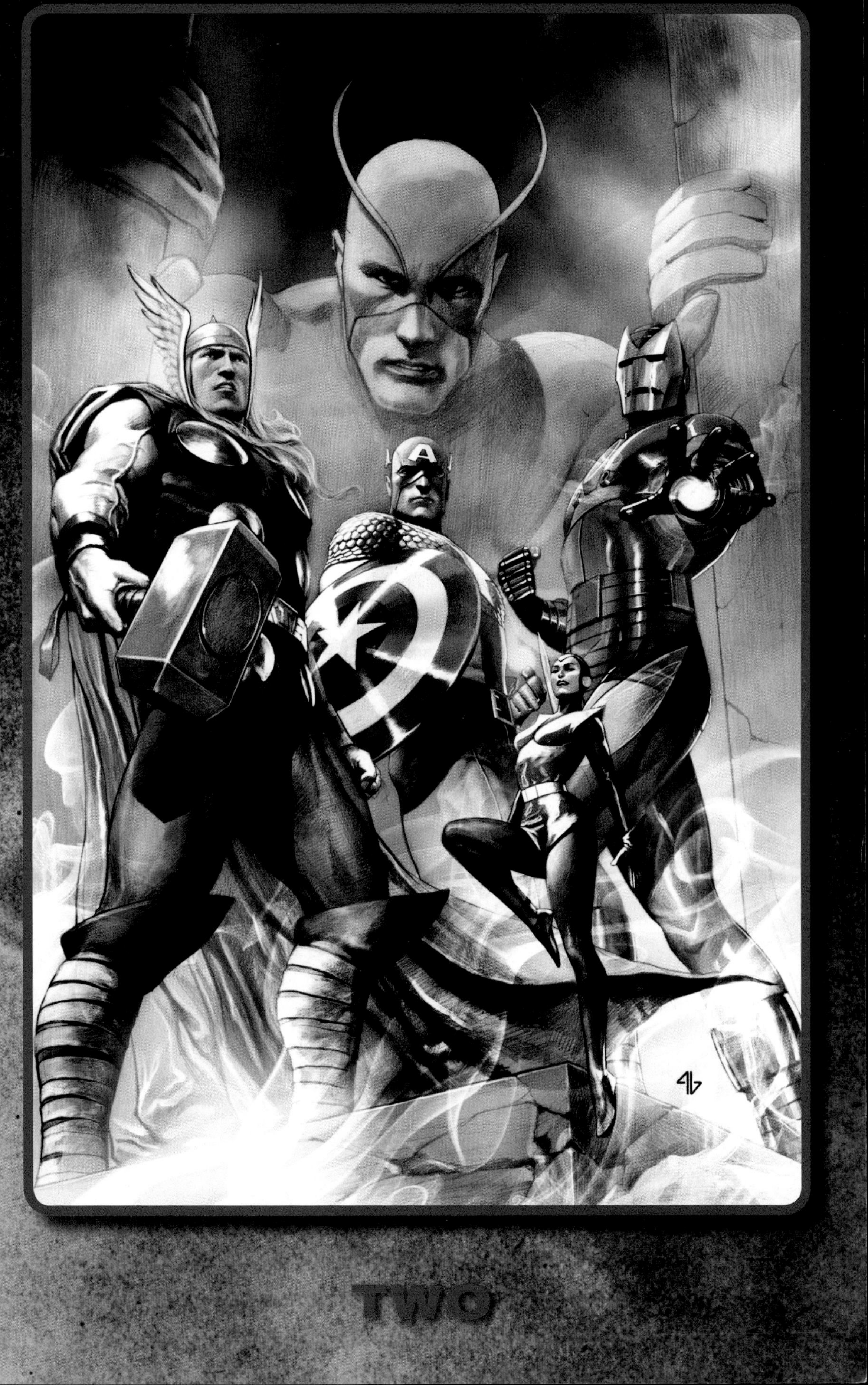

TWO

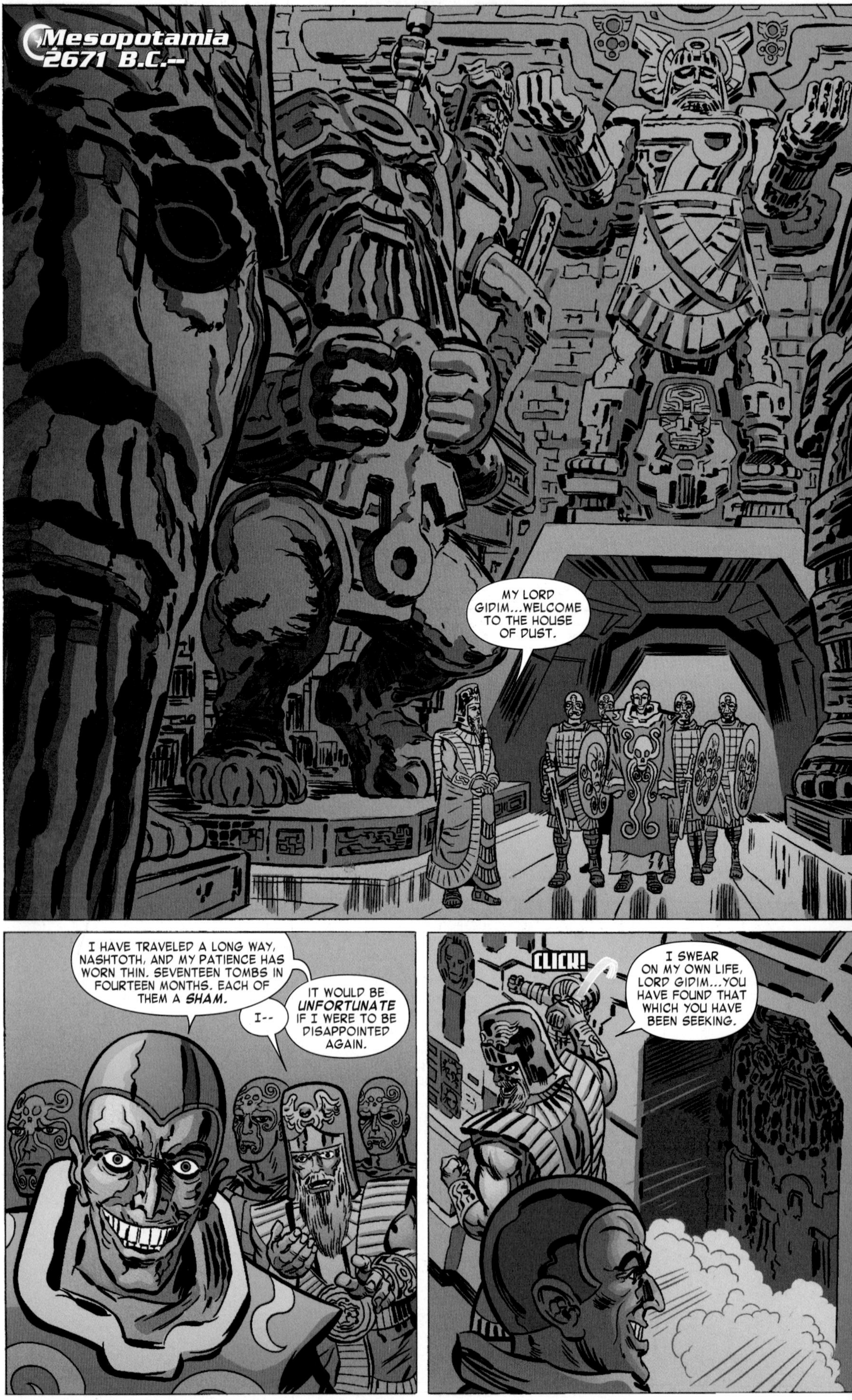
Mesopotamia 2671 B.C.--
MY LORD GIDIM...WELCOME TO THE HOUSE OF DUST.
I HAVE TRAVELED A LONG WAY, NASHTOTH, AND MY PATIENCE HAS WORN THIN. SEVENTEEN TOMBS IN FOURTEEN MONTHS. EACH OF THEM A SHAM.
I--
IT WOULD BE UNFORTUNATE IF I WERE TO BE DISAPPOINTED AGAIN.
CLICK!
I SWEAR ON MY OWN LIFE, LORD GIDIM...YOU HAVE FOUND THAT WHICH YOU HAVE BEEN SEEKING.

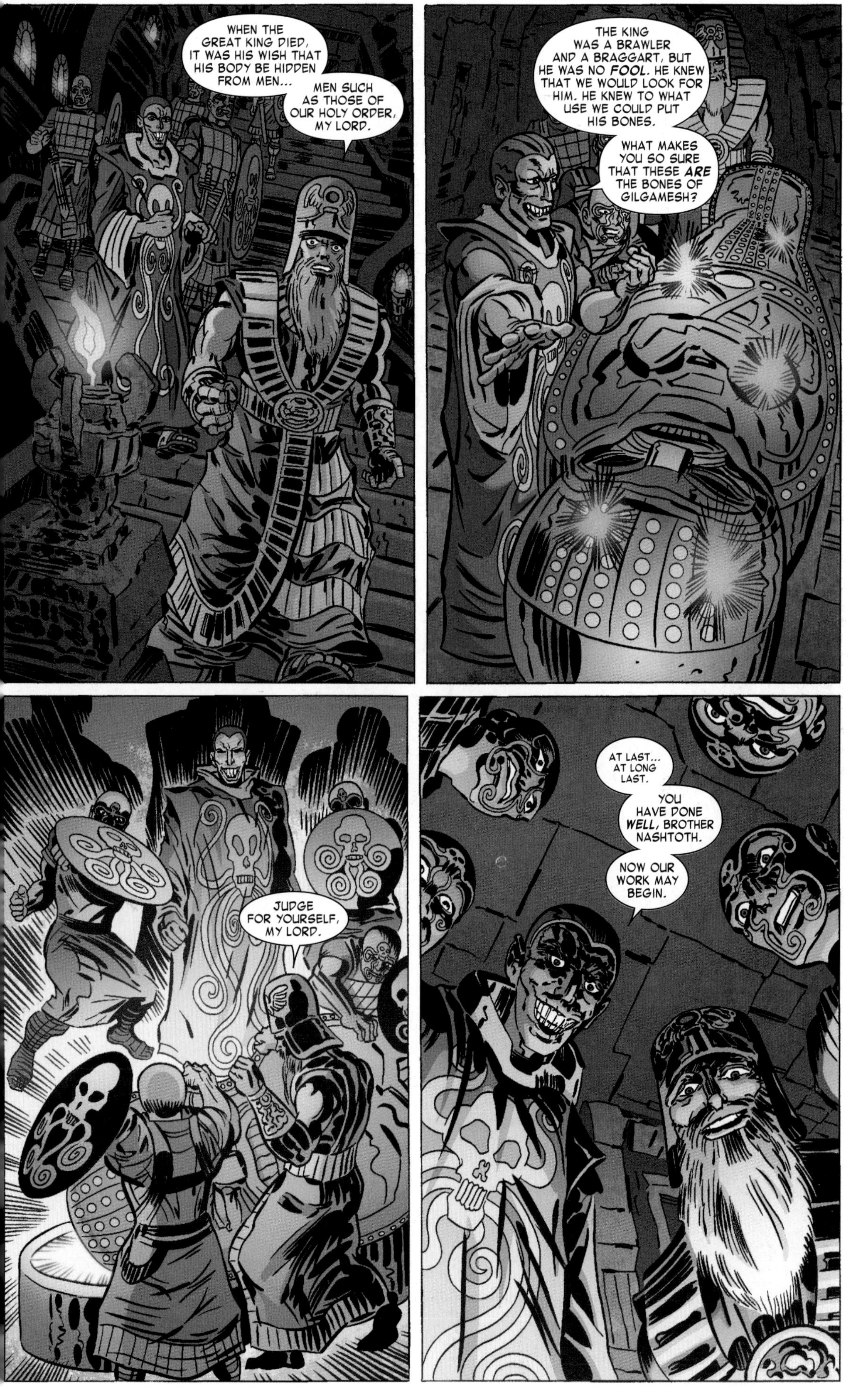
WHEN THE GREAT KING DIED, IT WAS HIS WISH THAT HIS BODY BE HIDDEN FROM MEN...
MEN SUCH AS THOSE OF OUR HOLY ORDER, MY LORD.
THE KING WAS A BRAWLER AND A BRAGGART, BUT HE WAS NO FOOL. HE KNEW THAT WE WOULD LOOK FOR HIM. HE KNEW TO WHAT USE WE COULD PUT HIS BONES.
WHAT MAKES YOU SO SURE THAT THESE ARE THE BONES OF GILGAMESH?
JUDGE FOR YOURSELF, MY LORD.
AT LAST... AT LONG LAST.
YOU HAVE DONE WELL, BROTHER NASHTOTH.
NOW OUR WORK MAY BEGIN.

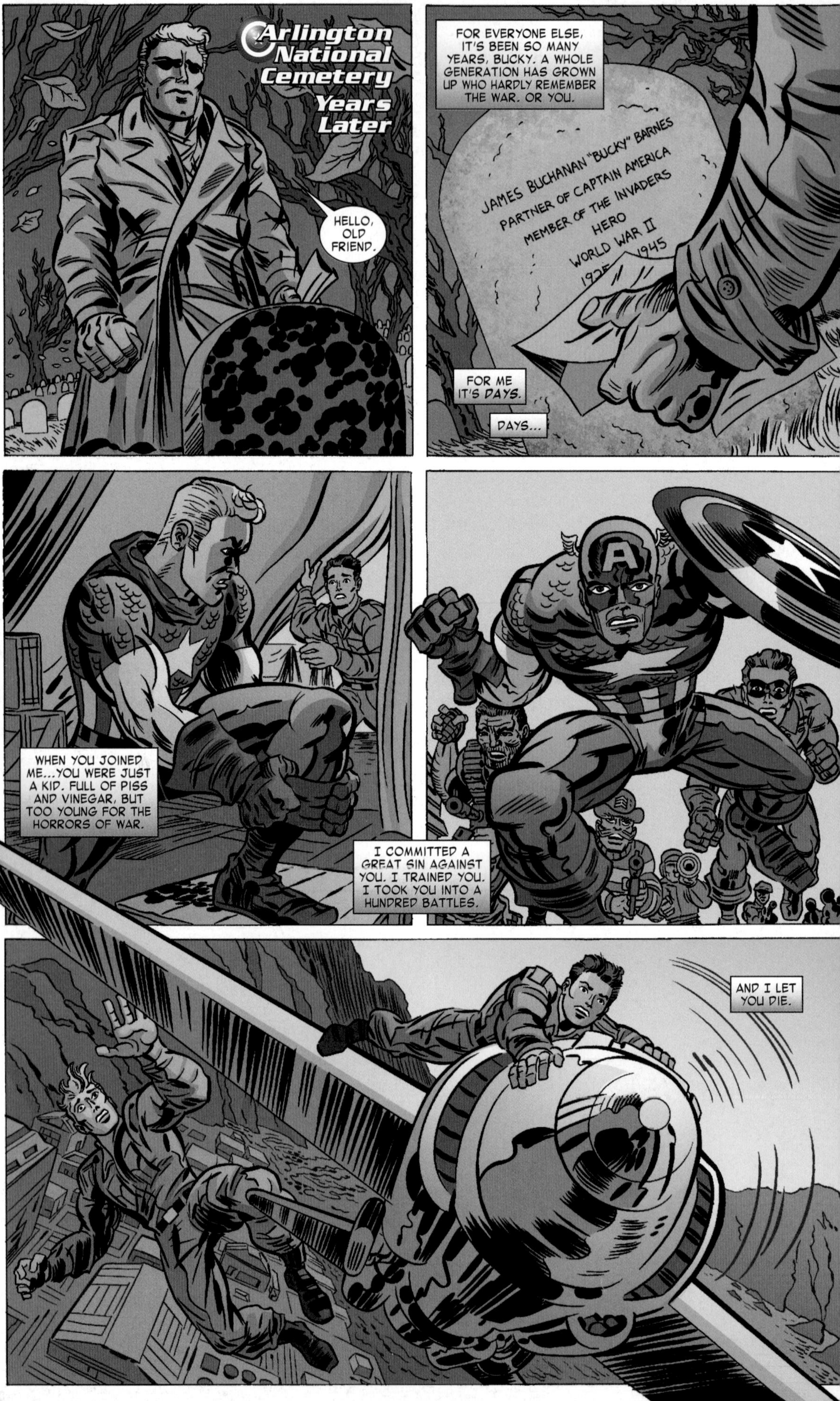
Arlington National Cemetery Years Later
HELLO, OLD FRIEND.
FOR EVERYONE ELSE, IT'S BEEN SO MANY YEARS, BUCKY. A WHOLE GENERATION HAS GROWN UP WHO HARDLY REMEMBER THE WAR. OR YOU.
JAMES BUCHANAN "BUCKY" BARNES
PARTNER OF CAPTAIN AMERICA
MEMBER OF THE INVADERS
HERO
WORLD WAR II
FOR ME IT'S DAYS.
DAYS...
WHEN YOU JOINED ME...YOU WERE JUST A KID. FULL OF PISS AND VINEGAR, BUT TOO YOUNG FOR THE HORRORS OF WAR.
I COMMITTED A GREAT SIN AGAINST YOU. I TRAINED YOU. I TOOK YOU INTO A HUNDRED BATTLES.
AND I LET YOU DIE.

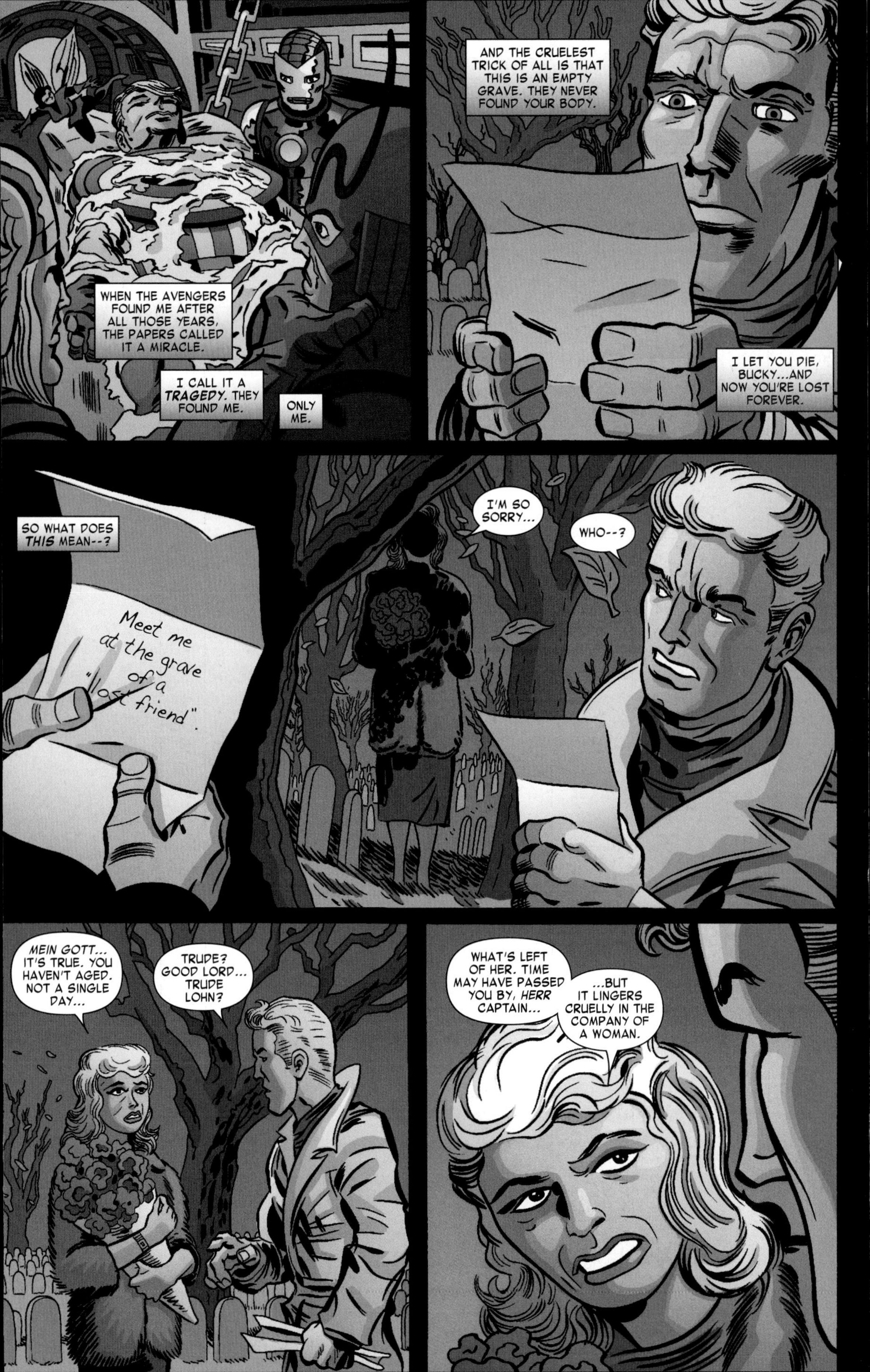
WHEN THE AVENGERS FOUND ME AFTER ALL THOSE YEARS, THE PAPERS CALLED IT A MIRACLE.
I CALL IT A TRAGEDY. THEY FOUND ME.
ONLY ME.
AND THE CRUELEST TRICK OF ALL IS THAT THIS IS AN EMPTY GRAVE. THEY NEVER FOUND YOUR BODY.
I LET YOU DIE, BUCKY...AND NOW YOU'RE LOST FOREVER.
SO WHAT DOES THIS MEAN--?
Meet me at the grave of a "lost friend".
I'M SO SORRY...
WHO--?
MEIN GOTT... IT'S TRUE. YOU HAVEN'T AGED. NOT A SINGLE DAY...
TRUDE? GOOD LORD... TRUDE LOHN?
WHAT'S LEFT OF HER. TIME MAY HAVE PASSED YOU BY, HERR CAPTAIN...
...BUT IT LINGERS CRUELLY IN THE COMPANY OF A WOMAN.

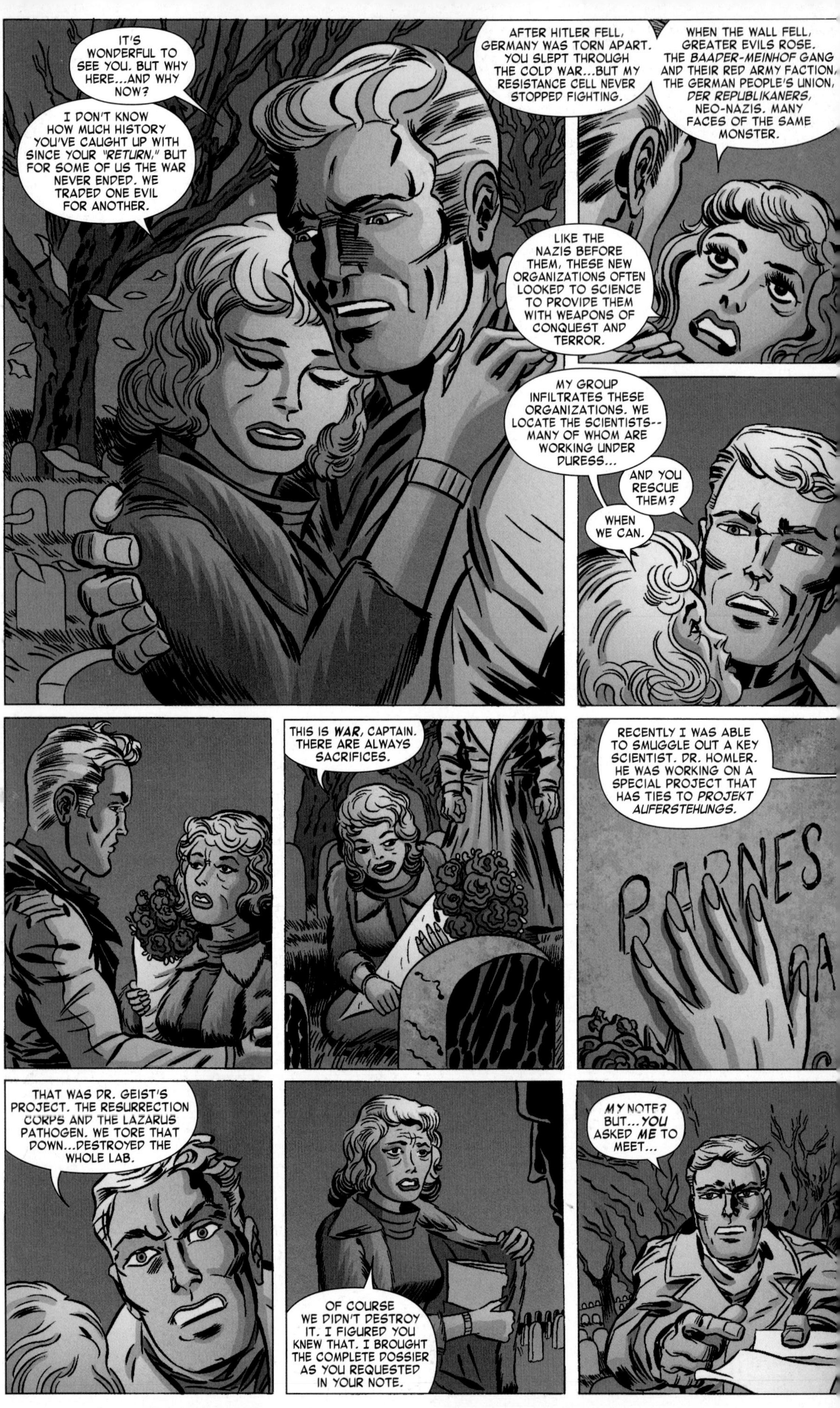
IT'S WONDERFUL TO SEE YOU. BUT WHY HERE...AND WHY NOW?
I DON'T KNOW HOW MUCH HISTORY YOU'VE CAUGHT UP WITH SINCE YOUR "RETURN," BUT FOR SOME OF US THE WAR NEVER ENDED. WE TRADED ONE EVIL FOR ANOTHER.
AFTER HITLER FELL, GERMANY WAS TORN APART. YOU SLEPT THROUGH THE COLD WAR...BUT MY RESISTANCE CELL NEVER STOPPED FIGHTING.
WHEN THE WALL FELL, GREATER EVILS ROSE. THE *BAADER-MEINHOF* GANG AND THEIR RED ARMY FACTION, THE GERMAN PEOPLE'S UNION, *DER REPUBLIKANERS*, NEO-NAZIS. MANY FACES OF THE SAME MONSTER.
LIKE THE NAZIS BEFORE THEM, THESE NEW ORGANIZATIONS OFTEN LOOKED TO SCIENCE TO PROVIDE THEM WITH WEAPONS OF CONQUEST AND TERROR.
MY GROUP INFILTRATES THESE ORGANIZATIONS. WE LOCATE THE SCIENTISTS--MANY OF WHOM ARE WORKING UNDER DURESS...
AND YOU RESCUE THEM?
WHEN WE CAN.
THIS IS **WAR**, CAPTAIN. THERE ARE ALWAYS SACRIFICES.
RECENTLY I WAS ABLE TO SMUGGLE OUT A KEY SCIENTIST. DR. HOMLER. HE WAS WORKING ON A SPECIAL PROJECT THAT HAS TIES TO *PROJEKT AUFERSTEHUNGS.*
BARNES
THAT WAS DR. GEIST'S PROJECT. THE RESURRECTION CORPS AND THE LAZARUS PATHOGEN. WE TORE THAT DOWN...DESTROYED THE WHOLE LAB.
OF COURSE WE DIDN'T DESTROY IT. I FIGURED YOU KNEW THAT. I BROUGHT THE COMPLETE DOSSIER AS YOU REQUESTED IN YOUR NOTE.
MY NOTE? BUT...*YOU* ASKED *ME* TO MEET...

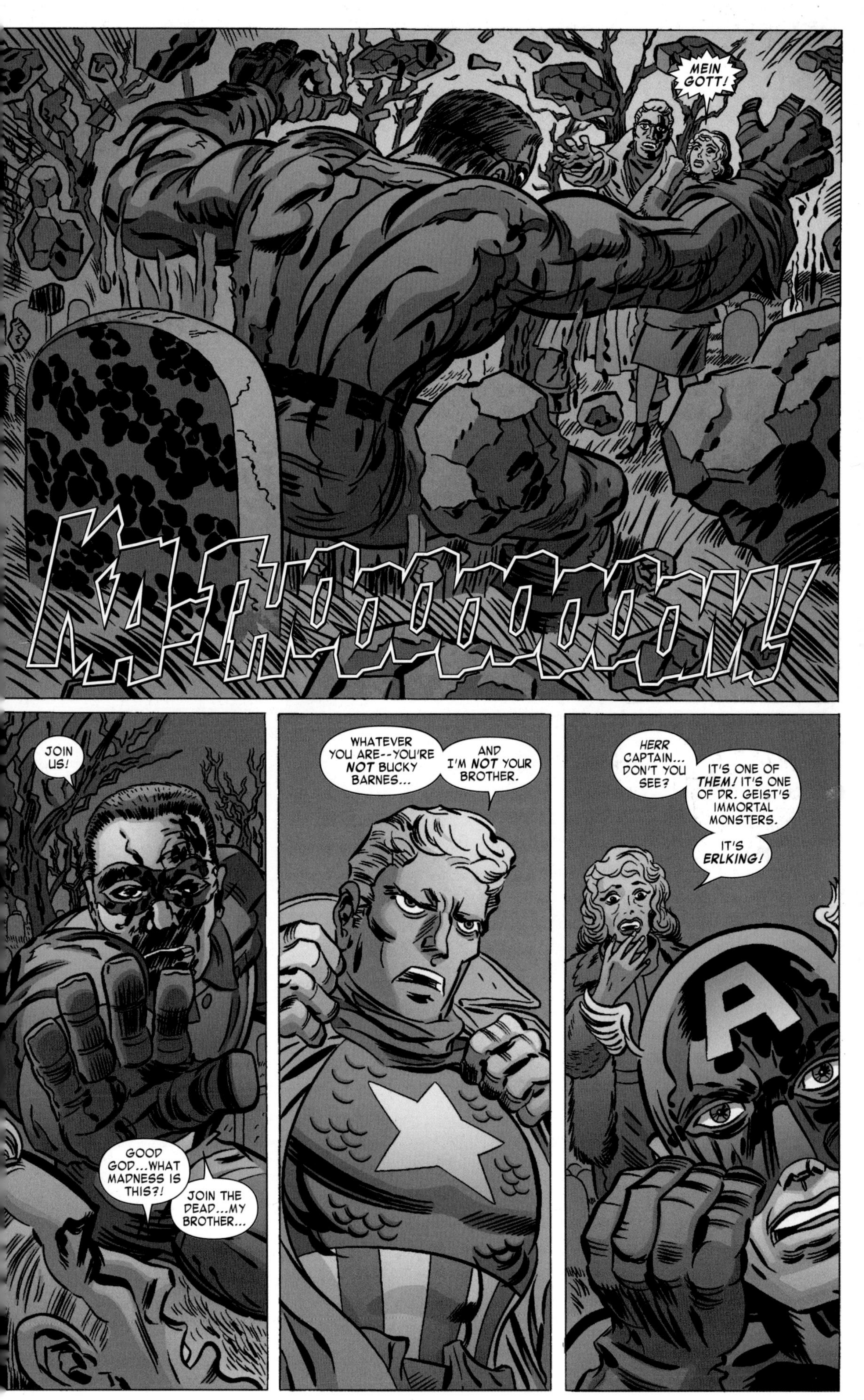
MEIN GOTT!
KA-THOOOOOOOOOM!
JOIN US!
GOOD GOD...WHAT MADNESS IS THIS?!
JOIN THE DEAD...MY BROTHER...
WHATEVER YOU ARE--YOU'RE NOT BUCKY BARNES...
AND I'M NOT YOUR BROTHER.
HERR CAPTAIN... DON'T YOU SEE?
IT'S ONE OF THEM! IT'S ONE OF DR. GEIST'S IMMORTAL MONSTERS.
IT'S ERLKING!

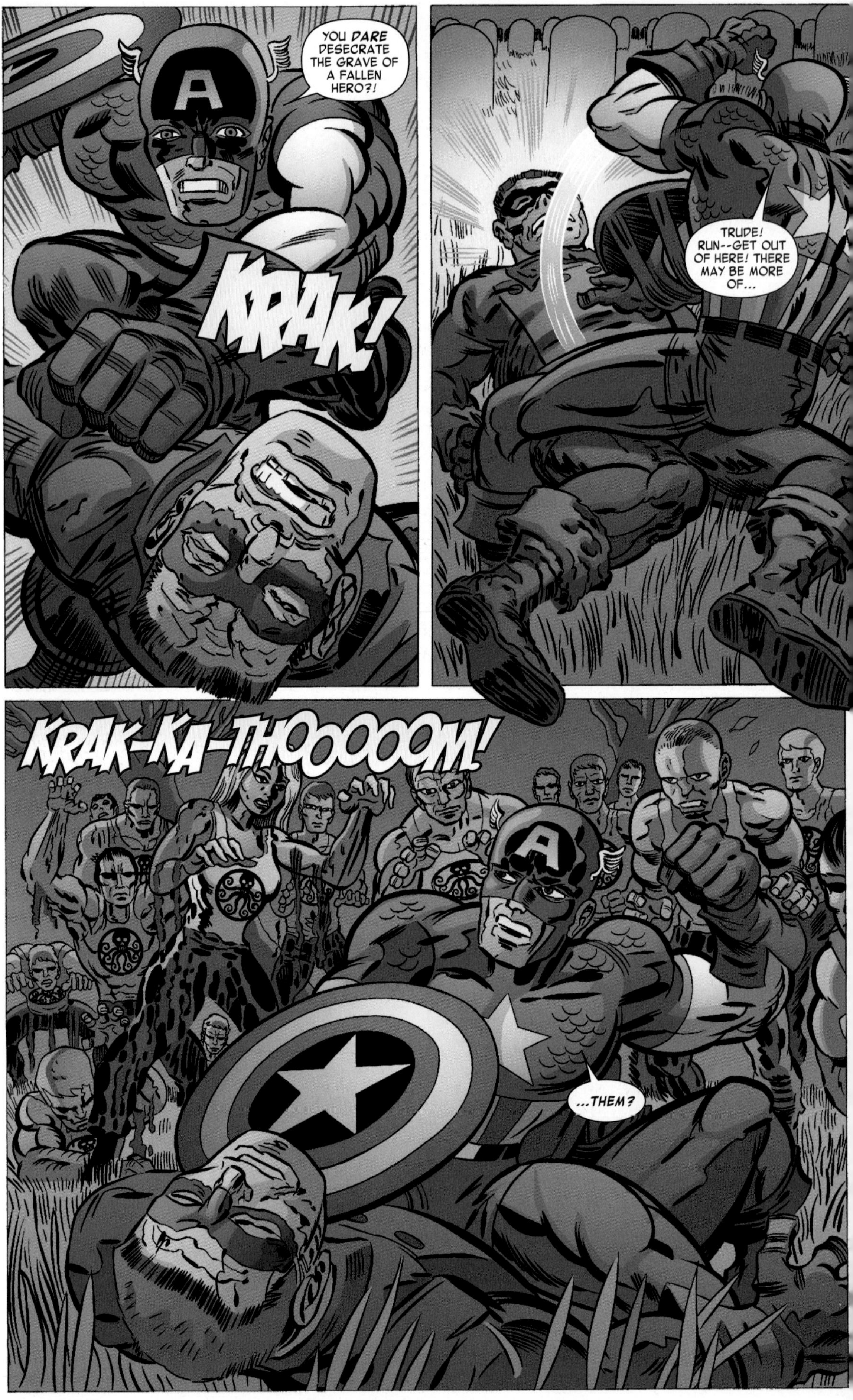
YOU DARE DESECRATE THE GRAVE OF A FALLEN HERO?!
KRAK!
TRUDE! RUN--GET OUT OF HERE! THERE MAY BE MORE OF...
KRAK-KA-THOOOOOM!
...THEM?

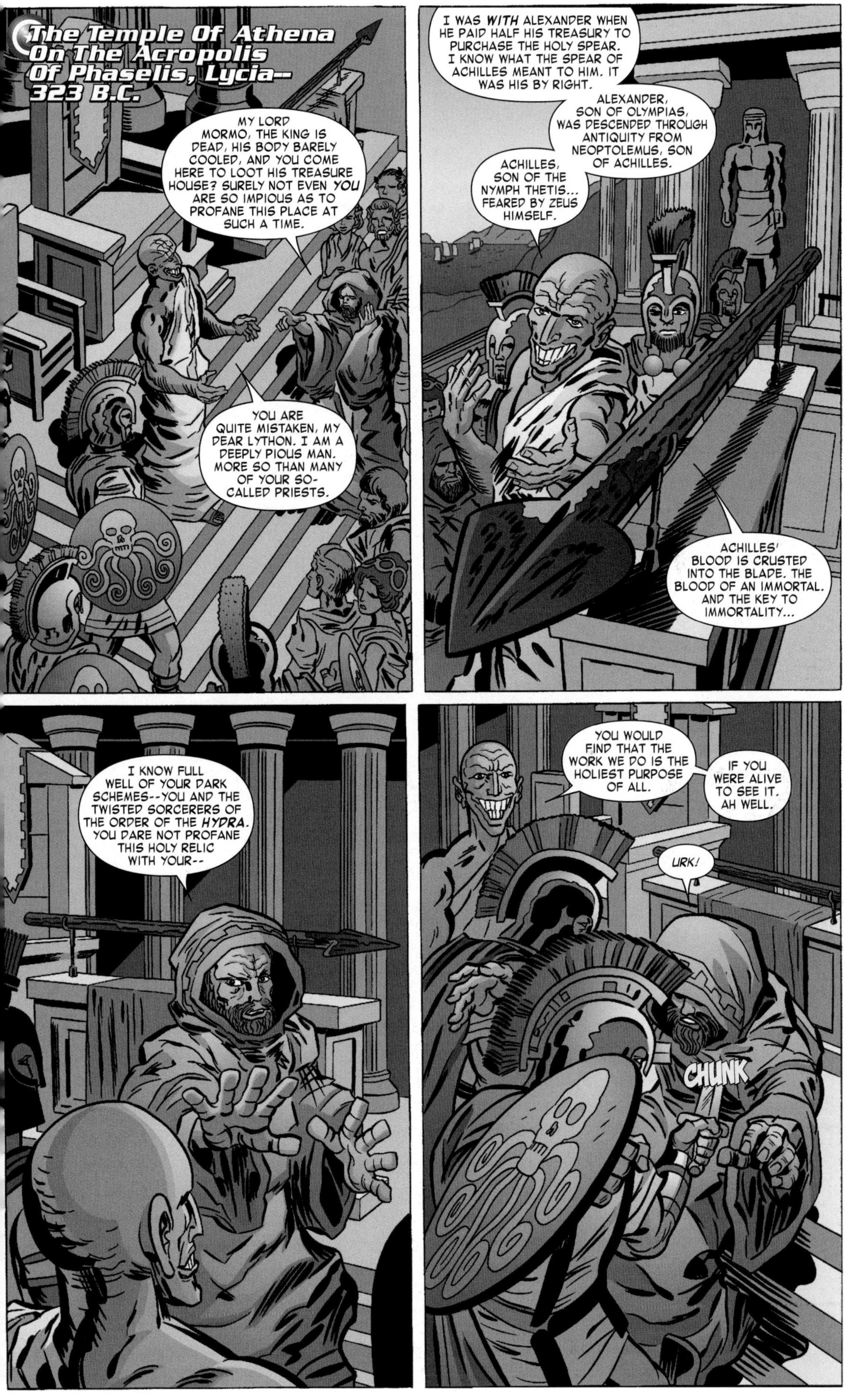
The Temple Of Athena On The Acropolis Of Phaselis, Lycia-- 323 B.C.
MY LORD MORMO, THE KING IS DEAD, HIS BODY BARELY COOLED, AND YOU COME HERE TO LOOT HIS TREASURE HOUSE? SURELY NOT EVEN YOU ARE SO IMPIOUS AS TO PROFANE THIS PLACE AT SUCH A TIME.
YOU ARE QUITE MISTAKEN, MY DEAR LYTHON. I AM A DEEPLY PIOUS MAN. MORE SO THAN MANY OF YOUR SO-CALLED PRIESTS.
I WAS WITH ALEXANDER WHEN HE PAID HALF HIS TREASURY TO PURCHASE THE HOLY SPEAR. I KNOW WHAT THE SPEAR OF ACHILLES MEANT TO HIM. IT WAS HIS BY RIGHT.
ALEXANDER, SON OF OLYMPIAS, WAS DESCENDED THROUGH ANTIQUITY FROM NEOPTOLEMUS, SON OF ACHILLES.
ACHILLES, SON OF THE NYMPH THETIS... FEARED BY ZEUS HIMSELF.
ACHILLES' BLOOD IS CRUSTED INTO THE BLADE. THE BLOOD OF AN IMMORTAL. AND THE KEY TO IMMORTALITY...
I KNOW FULL WELL OF YOUR DARK SCHEMES--YOU AND THE TWISTED SORCERERS OF THE ORDER OF THE HYDRA. YOU DARE NOT PROFANE THIS HOLY RELIC WITH YOUR--
YOU WOULD FIND THAT THE WORK WE DO IS THE HOLIEST PURPOSE OF ALL.
IF YOU WERE ALIVE TO SEE IT. AH WELL.
URK!
CHUNK

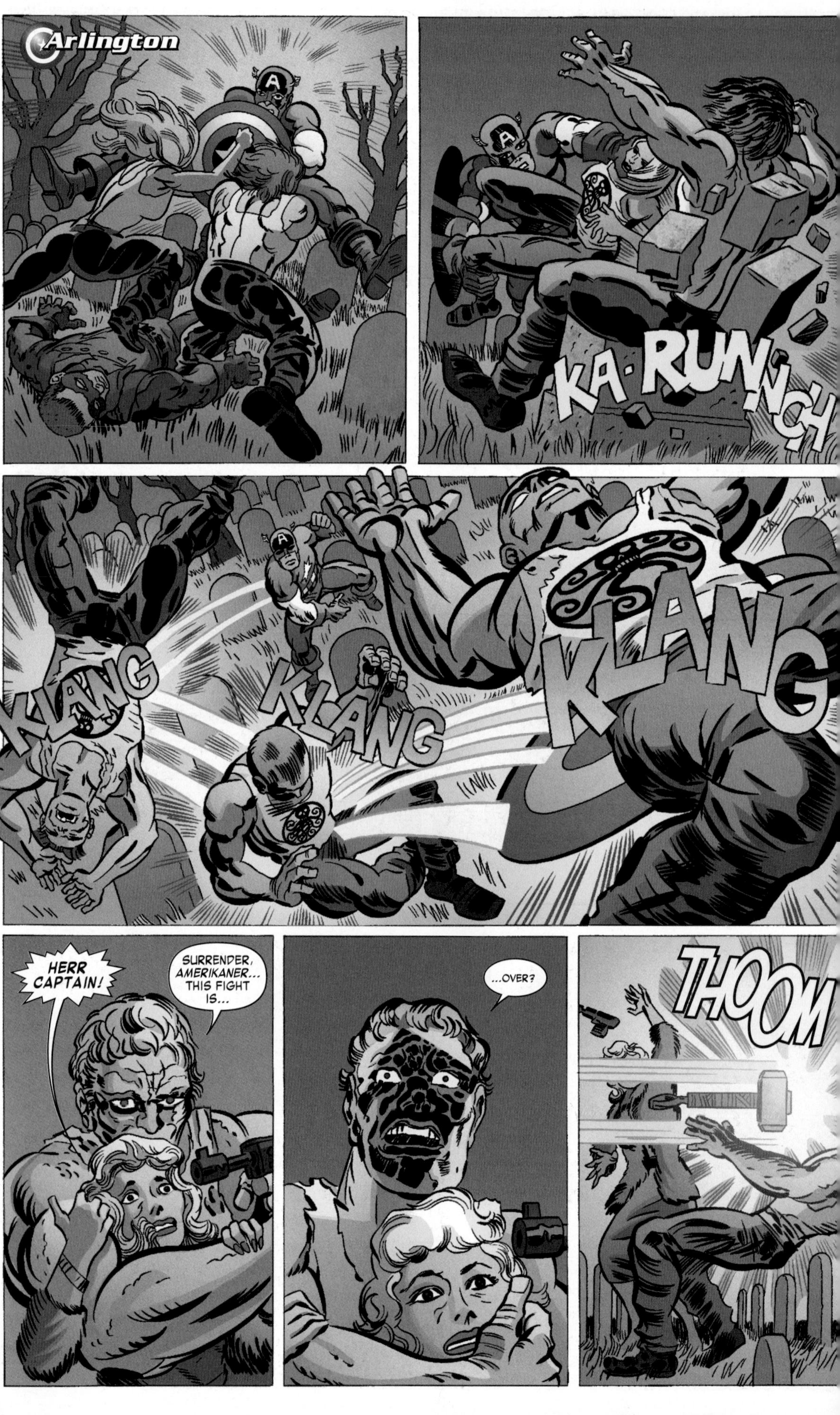

Arlington
KA-RUNNCH
KLANG
KLANG
KLANG
HERR CAPTAIN!
SURRENDER, AMERIKANER... THIS FIGHT IS...
...OVER?
THOOM

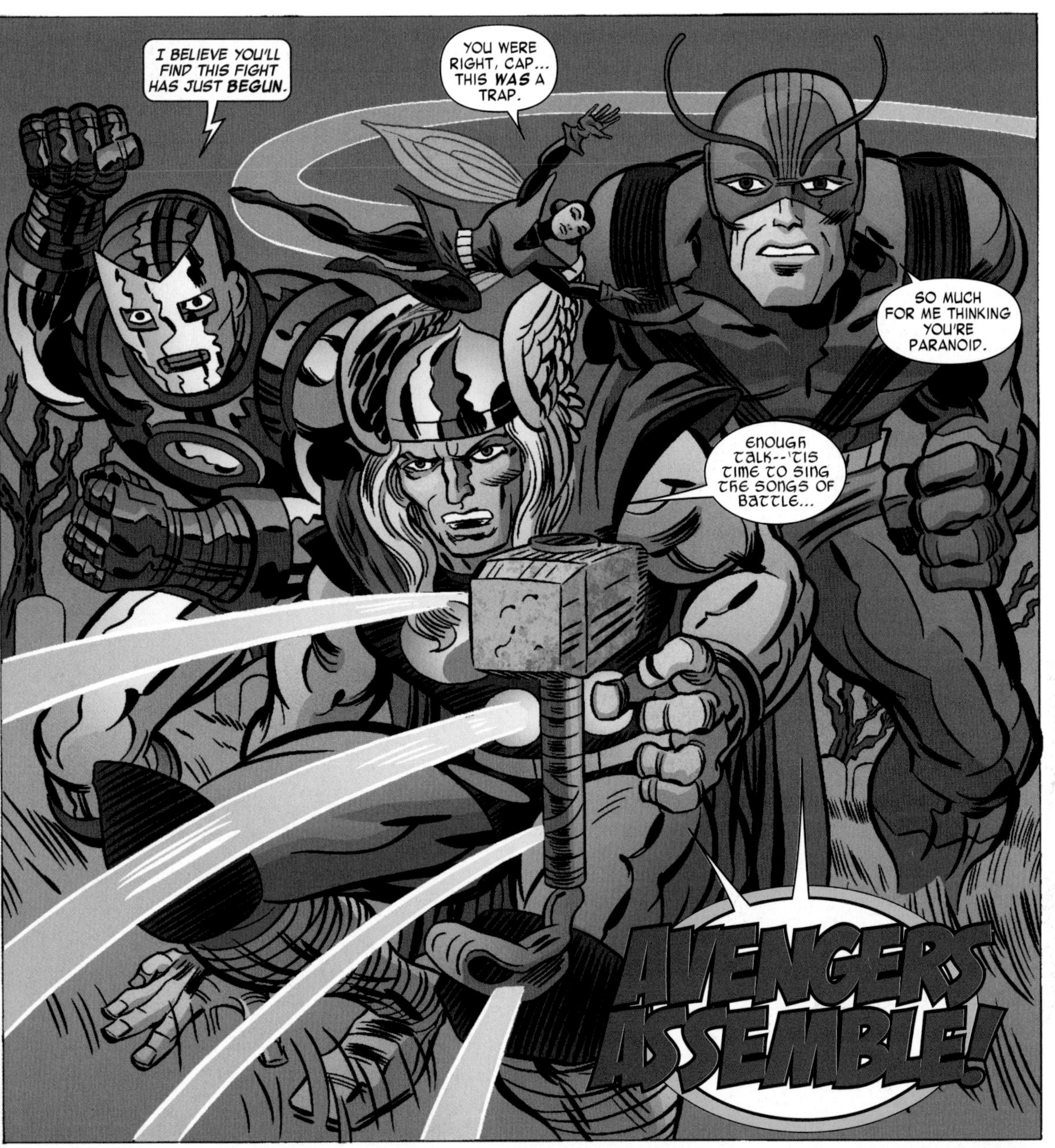
I BELIEVE YOU'LL FIND THIS FIGHT HAS JUST BEGUN.
YOU WERE RIGHT, CAP... THIS WAS A TRAP.
SO MUCH FOR ME THINKING YOU'RE PARANOID.
ENOUGH TALK--'TIS TIME TO SING THE SONGS OF BATTLE...
AVENGERS ASSEMBLE!

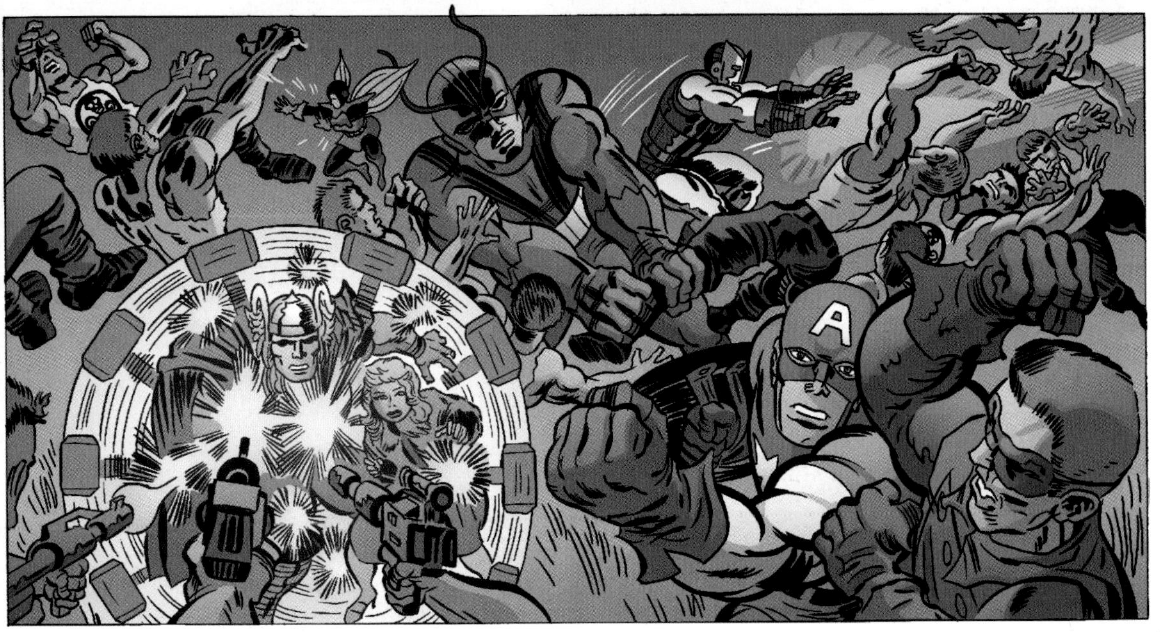

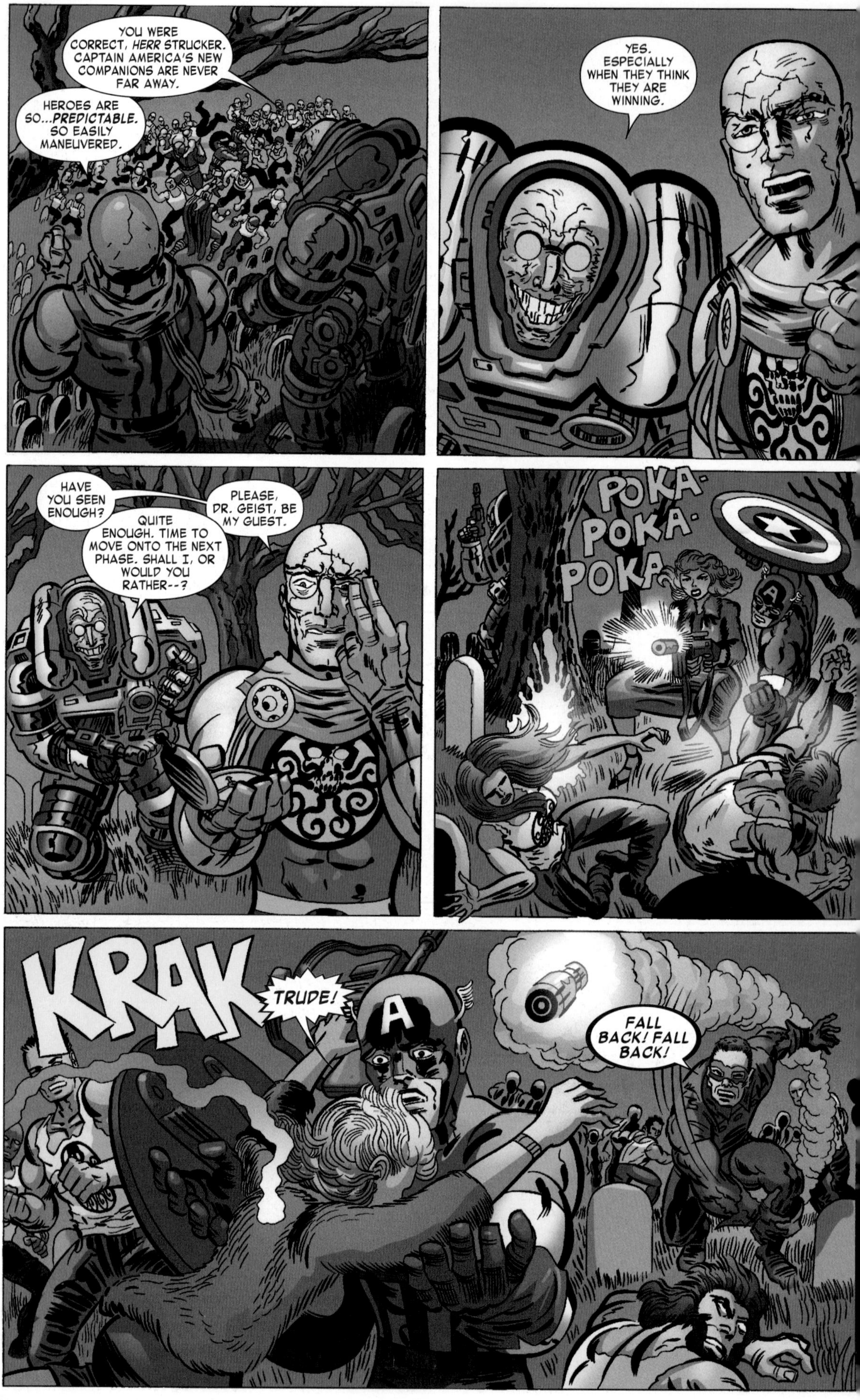

YOU WERE CORRECT, *HERR* STRUCKER. CAPTAIN AMERICA'S NEW COMPANIONS ARE NEVER FAR AWAY.
HEROES ARE SO...**PREDICTABLE.** SO EASILY MANEUVERED.
YES. ESPECIALLY WHEN THEY THINK THEY ARE WINNING.
HAVE YOU SEEN ENOUGH?
QUITE ENOUGH. TIME TO MOVE ONTO THE NEXT PHASE. SHALL I, OR WOULD YOU RATHER--?
PLEASE, DR. GEIST, BE MY GUEST.
POKA-POKA-POKA
KRAK
TRUDE!
FALL BACK! FALL BACK!

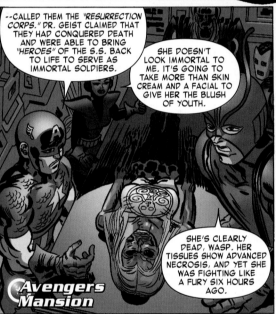

--CALLED THEM THE "RESURRECTION CORPS." DR. GEIST CLAIMED THAT THEY HAD CONQUERED DEATH AND WERE ABLE TO BRING "HEROES" OF THE S.S. BACK TO LIFE TO SERVE AS IMMORTAL SOLDIERS.

SHE DOESN'T LOOK IMMORTAL TO ME. IT'S GOING TO TAKE MORE THAN SKIN CREAM AND A FACIAL TO GIVE HER THE BLUSH OF YOUTH.

SHE'S CLEARLY DEAD, WASP. HER TISSUES SHOW ADVANCED NECROSIS, AND YET SHE WAS FIGHTING LIKE A FURY SIX HOURS AGO.

Avengers Mansion

IMMORTALITY IS NOT BORN IN A LABORATORY, GIANT-MAN. SORCERERS AND ALCHEMISTS HAVE LONG SOUGHT ITS SECRET... AND NEVER HAVE THEY SUCCEEDED.

THEY'RE MAKING SOME INROADS INTO IT WITH GENETICS, THOR, BUT WE'RE DECADES AWAY FROM CRACKING IT. MAYBE CENTURIES.

I'LL DO FULL BLOOD AND TISSUE ANALYSIS, SEE IF I CAN GET A HANDLE ON THE SCIENCE...BUT THESE NOTES--DR. HOMLER'S RESEARCH--THEY'RE MUCH MORE INTERESTING.

BRRRINNING! BRRRINNING!

RIGHT AWAY, DOCTOR. CAP...MISS LOHN IS AWAKE AND SHE'S ASKING TO SEE YOU...BUT THE DOCTOR SAYS TO HURRY.

C'MON, CAP...WE CAN GET YOU THERE FASTER THAN ANY CAB.

246.

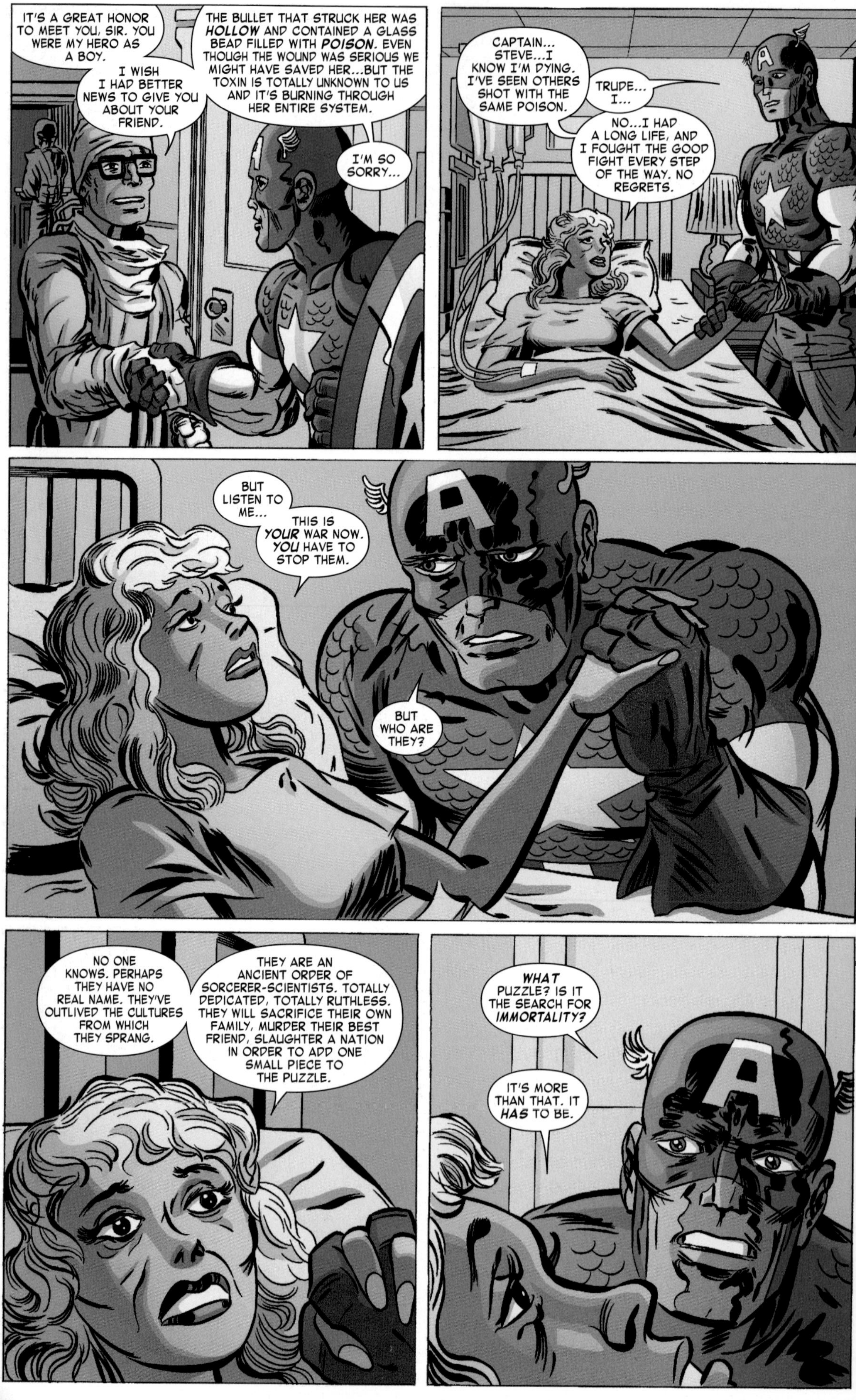

IT'S A GREAT HONOR TO MEET YOU, SIR. YOU WERE MY HERO AS A BOY.
I WISH I HAD BETTER NEWS TO GIVE YOU ABOUT YOUR FRIEND.
THE BULLET THAT STRUCK HER WAS HOLLOW AND CONTAINED A GLASS BEAD FILLED WITH POISON. EVEN THOUGH THE WOUND WAS SERIOUS WE MIGHT HAVE SAVED HER...BUT THE TOXIN IS TOTALLY UNKNOWN TO US AND IT'S BURNING THROUGH HER ENTIRE SYSTEM.
I'M SO SORRY...
CAPTAIN... STEVE...I KNOW I'M DYING. I'VE SEEN OTHERS SHOT WITH THE SAME POISON.
TRUDE... I...
NO...I HAD A LONG LIFE, AND I FOUGHT THE GOOD FIGHT EVERY STEP OF THE WAY. NO REGRETS.
BUT LISTEN TO ME...
THIS IS YOUR WAR NOW. YOU HAVE TO STOP THEM.
BUT WHO ARE THEY?
NO ONE KNOWS. PERHAPS THEY HAVE NO REAL NAME. THEY'VE OUTLIVED THE CULTURES FROM WHICH THEY SPRANG.
THEY ARE AN ANCIENT ORDER OF SORCERER-SCIENTISTS. TOTALLY DEDICATED, TOTALLY RUTHLESS. THEY WILL SACRIFICE THEIR OWN FAMILY, MURDER THEIR BEST FRIEND, SLAUGHTER A NATION IN ORDER TO ADD ONE SMALL PIECE TO THE PUZZLE.
WHAT PUZZLE? IS IT THE SEARCH FOR IMMORTALITY?
IT'S MORE THAN THAT. IT HAS TO BE.

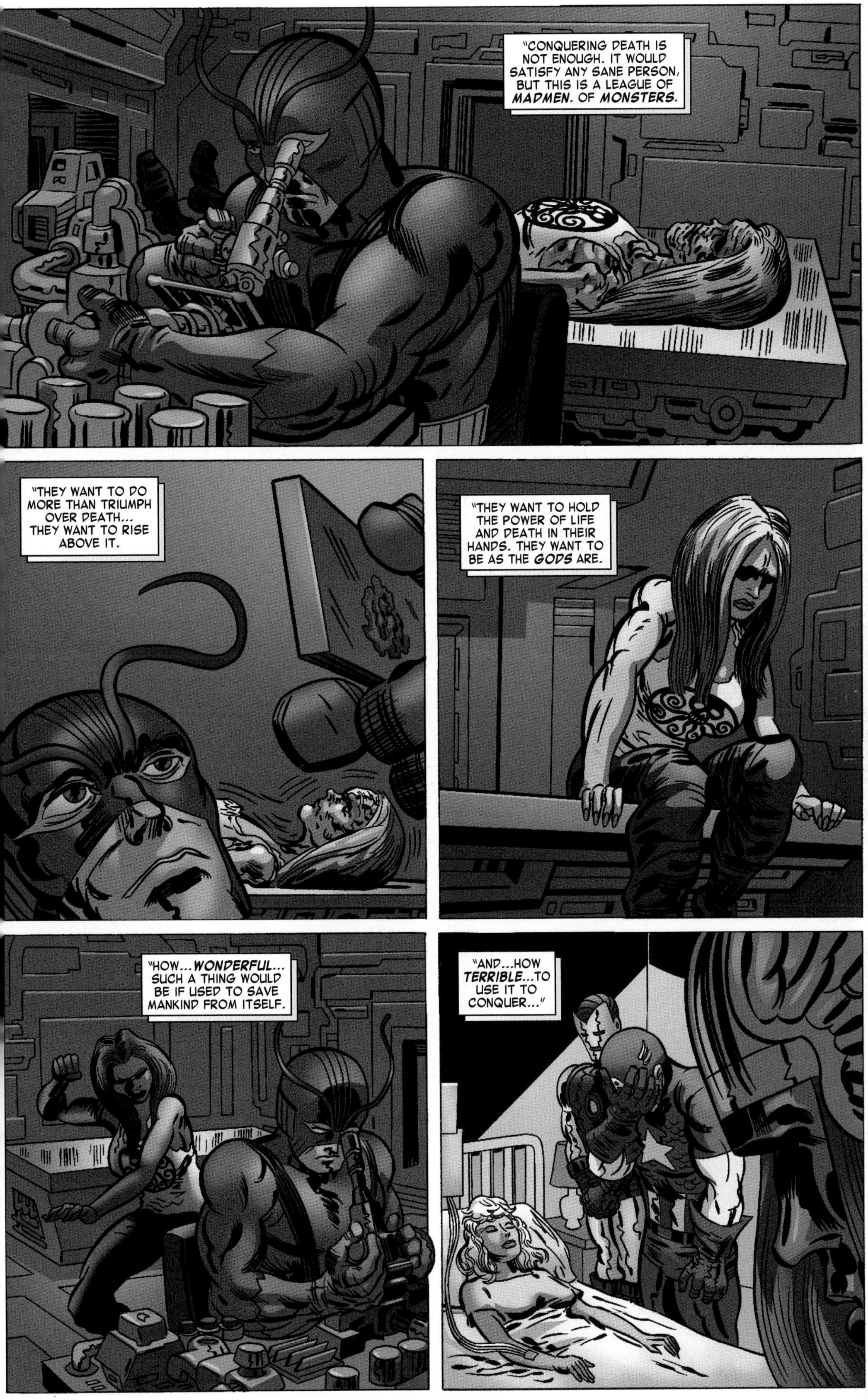
"CONQUERING DEATH IS NOT ENOUGH. IT WOULD SATISFY ANY SANE PERSON, BUT THIS IS A LEAGUE OF MADMEN. OF MONSTERS.
"THEY WANT TO DO MORE THAN TRIUMPH OVER DEATH... THEY WANT TO RISE ABOVE IT.
"THEY WANT TO HOLD THE POWER OF LIFE AND DEATH IN THEIR HANDS. THEY WANT TO BE AS THE GODS ARE.
"HOW...WONDERFUL... SUCH A THING WOULD BE IF USED TO SAVE MANKIND FROM ITSELF.
"AND...HOW TERRIBLE...TO USE IT TO CONQUER..."

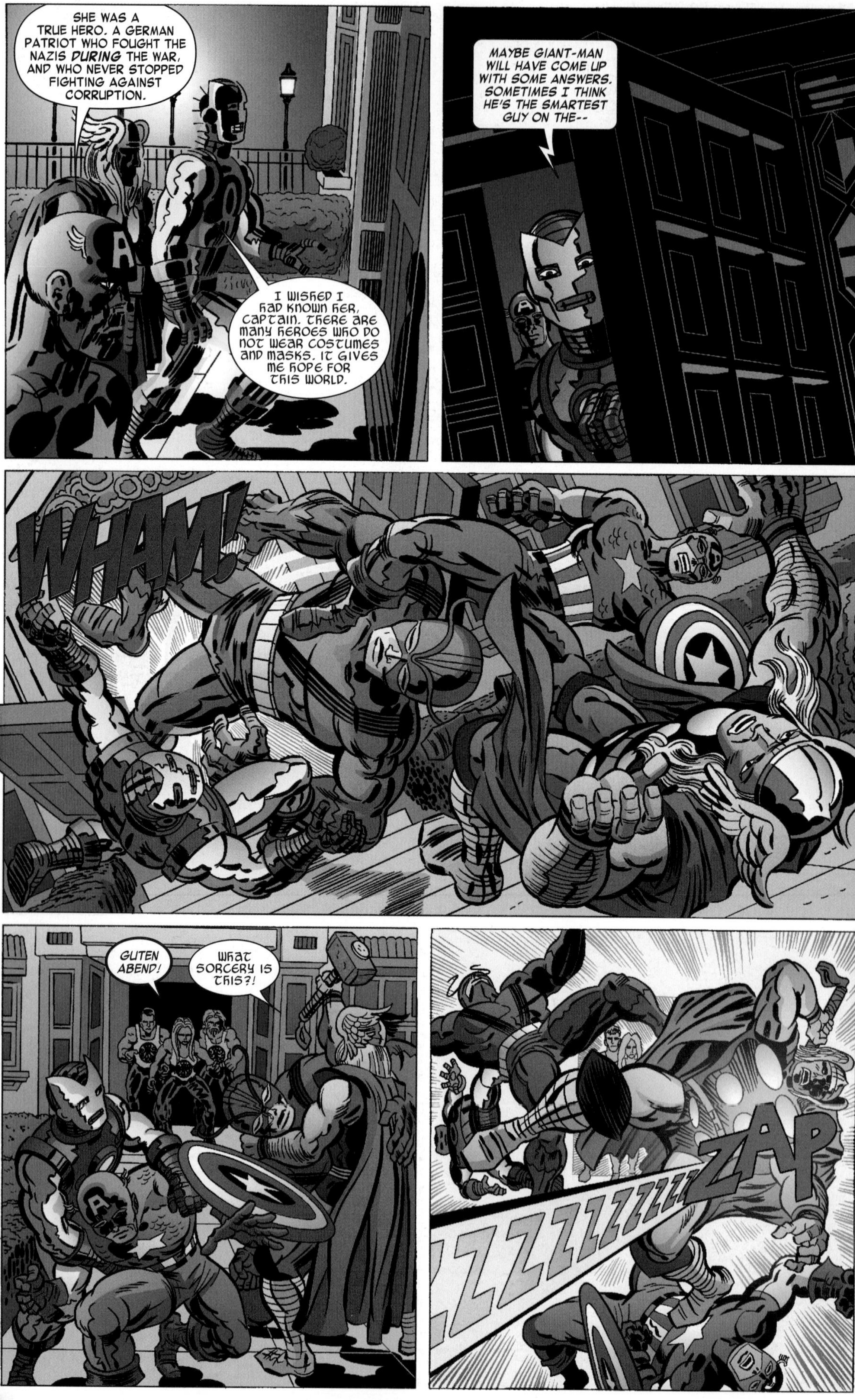
SHE WAS A TRUE HERO. A GERMAN PATRIOT WHO FOUGHT THE NAZIS *DURING* THE WAR, AND WHO NEVER STOPPED FIGHTING AGAINST CORRUPTION.
I WISHED I HAD KNOWN HER, CAPTAIN. THERE ARE MANY HEROES WHO DO NOT WEAR COSTUMES AND MASKS. IT GIVES ME HOPE FOR THIS WORLD.
MAYBE GIANT-MAN WILL HAVE COME UP WITH SOME ANSWERS. SOMETIMES I THINK HE'S THE SMARTEST GUY ON THE--
WHAM!
GUTEN ABEND!
WHAT SORCERY IS THIS?!
ZZZZZZZZZZZZZAP

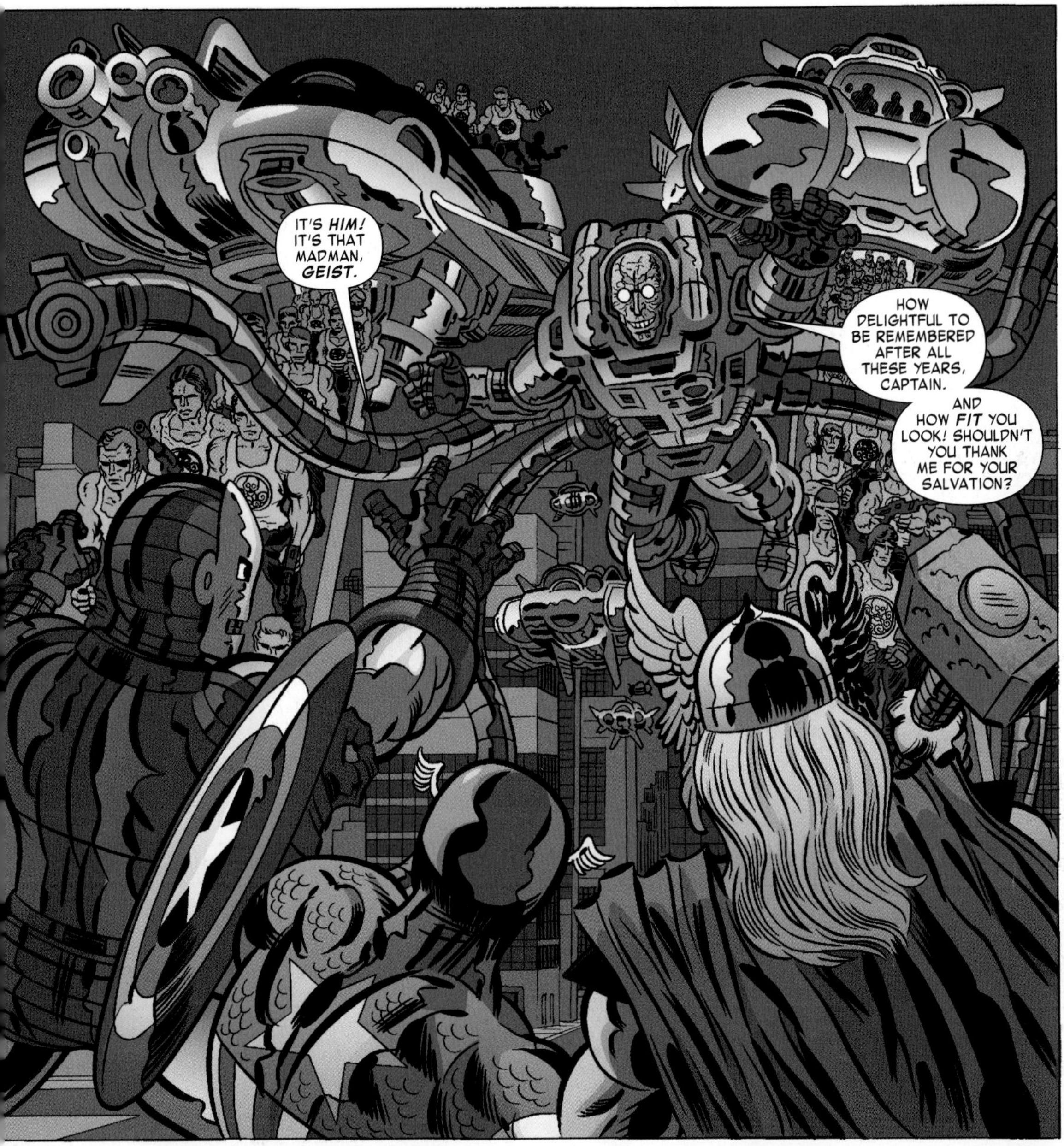
IT'S HIM! IT'S THAT MADMAN, GEIST.
HOW DELIGHTFUL TO BE REMEMBERED AFTER ALL THESE YEARS, CAPTAIN.
AND HOW FIT YOU LOOK! SHOULDN'T YOU THANK ME FOR YOUR SALVATION?

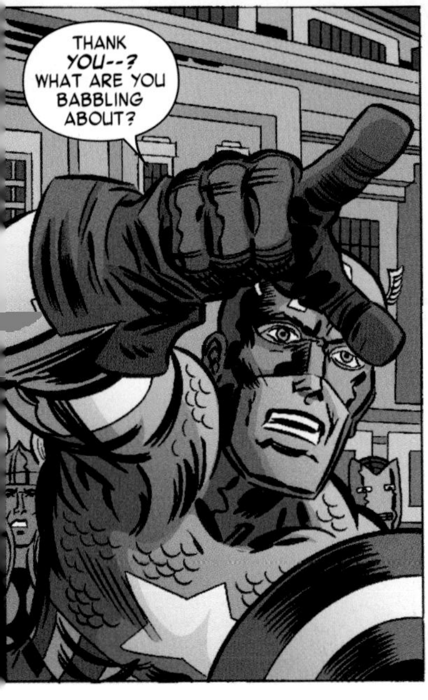
THANK YOU--? WHAT ARE YOU BABBLING ABOUT?

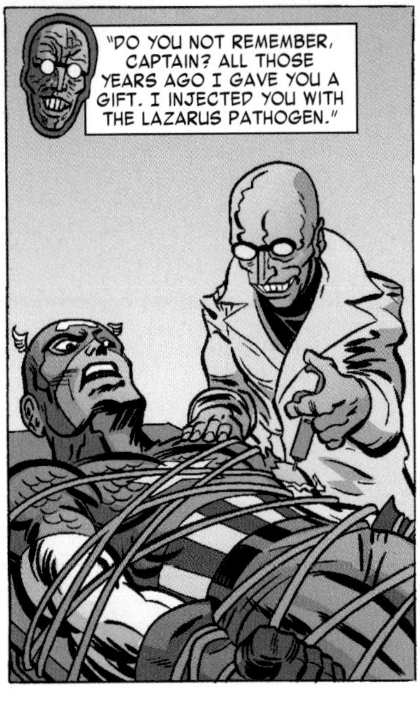
"DO YOU NOT REMEMBER, CAPTAIN? ALL THOSE YEARS AGO I GAVE YOU A GIFT. I INJECTED YOU WITH THE LAZARUS PATHOGEN."

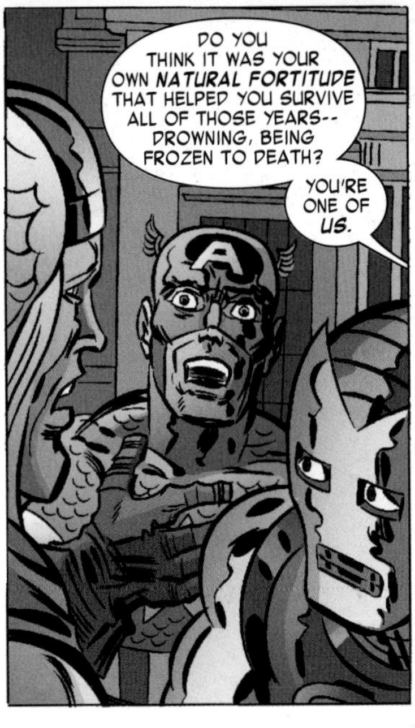
DO YOU THINK IT WAS YOUR OWN NATURAL FORTITUDE THAT HELPED YOU SURVIVE ALL OF THOSE YEARS-- DROWNING, BEING FROZEN TO DEATH?
YOU'RE ONE OF US.

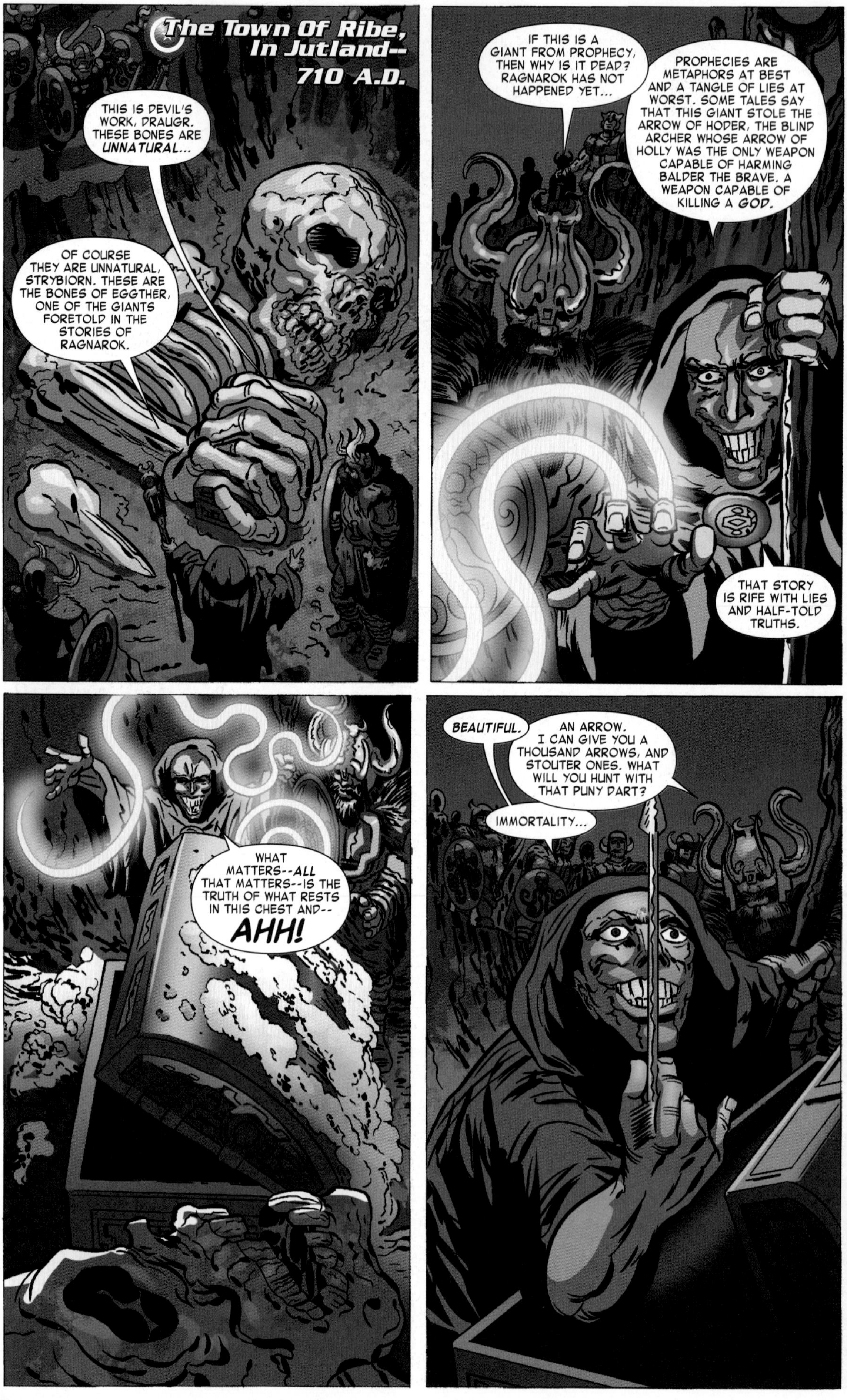
The Town Of Ribe, In Jutland-- 710 A.D.
THIS IS DEVIL'S WORK, DRAUGR. THESE BONES ARE UNNATURAL...
OF COURSE THEY ARE UNNATURAL, STRYBIORN. THESE ARE THE BONES OF EGGTHER, ONE OF THE GIANTS FORETOLD IN THE STORIES OF RAGNAROK.
IF THIS IS A GIANT FROM PROPHECY, THEN WHY IS IT DEAD? RAGNAROK HAS NOT HAPPENED YET...
PROPHECIES ARE METAPHORS AT BEST AND A TANGLE OF LIES AT WORST. SOME TALES SAY THAT THIS GIANT STOLE THE ARROW OF HODER, THE BLIND ARCHER WHOSE ARROW OF HOLLY WAS THE ONLY WEAPON CAPABLE OF HARMING BALDER THE BRAVE. A WEAPON CAPABLE OF KILLING A GOD.
THAT STORY IS RIFE WITH LIES AND HALF-TOLD TRUTHS.
WHAT MATTERS--ALL THAT MATTERS--IS THE TRUTH OF WHAT RESTS IN THIS CHEST AND-- AHH!
BEAUTIFUL.
AN ARROW. I CAN GIVE YOU A THOUSAND ARROWS, AND STOUTER ONES. WHAT WILL YOU HUNT WITH THAT PUNY DART?
IMMORTALITY...

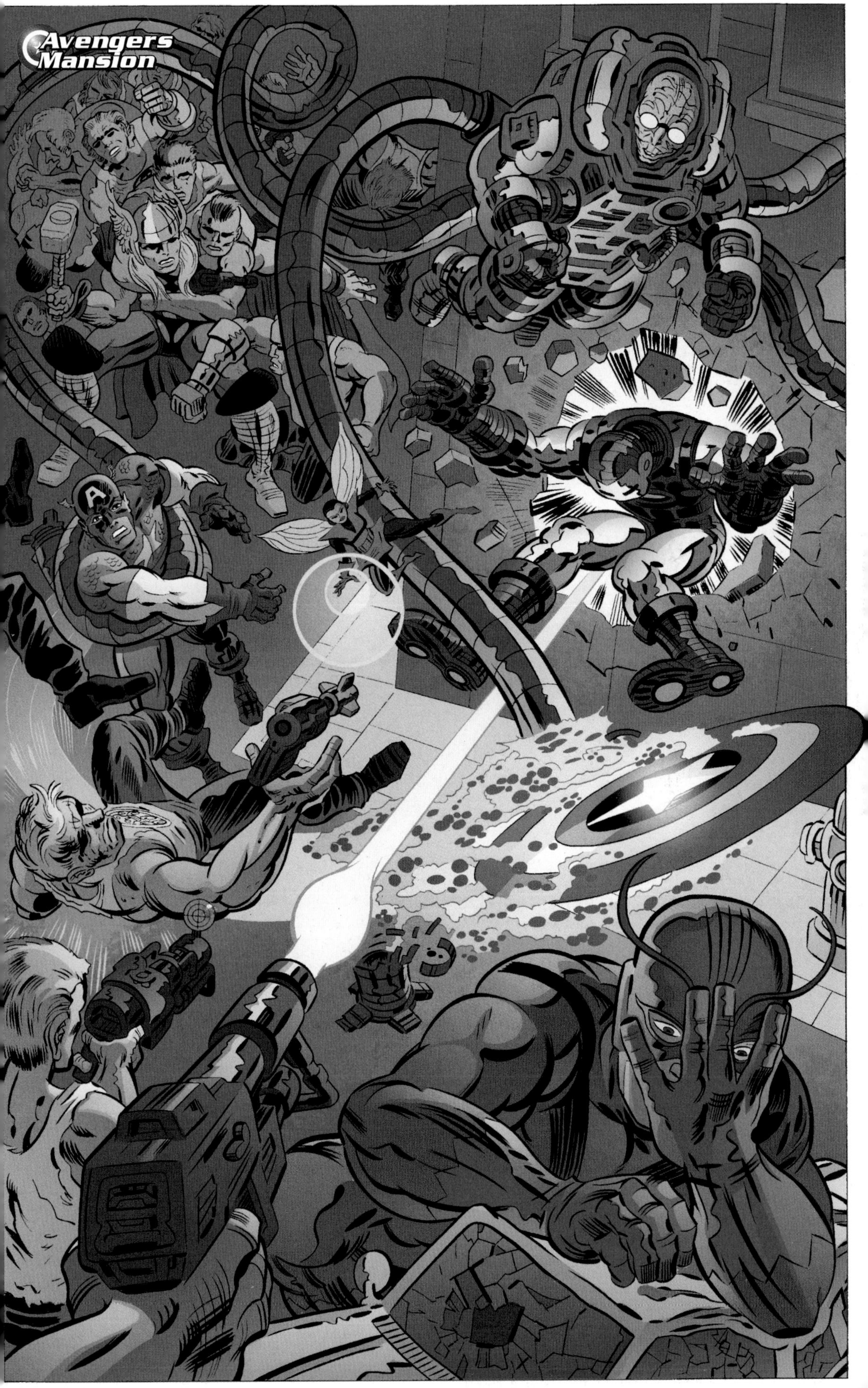
Avengers Mansion

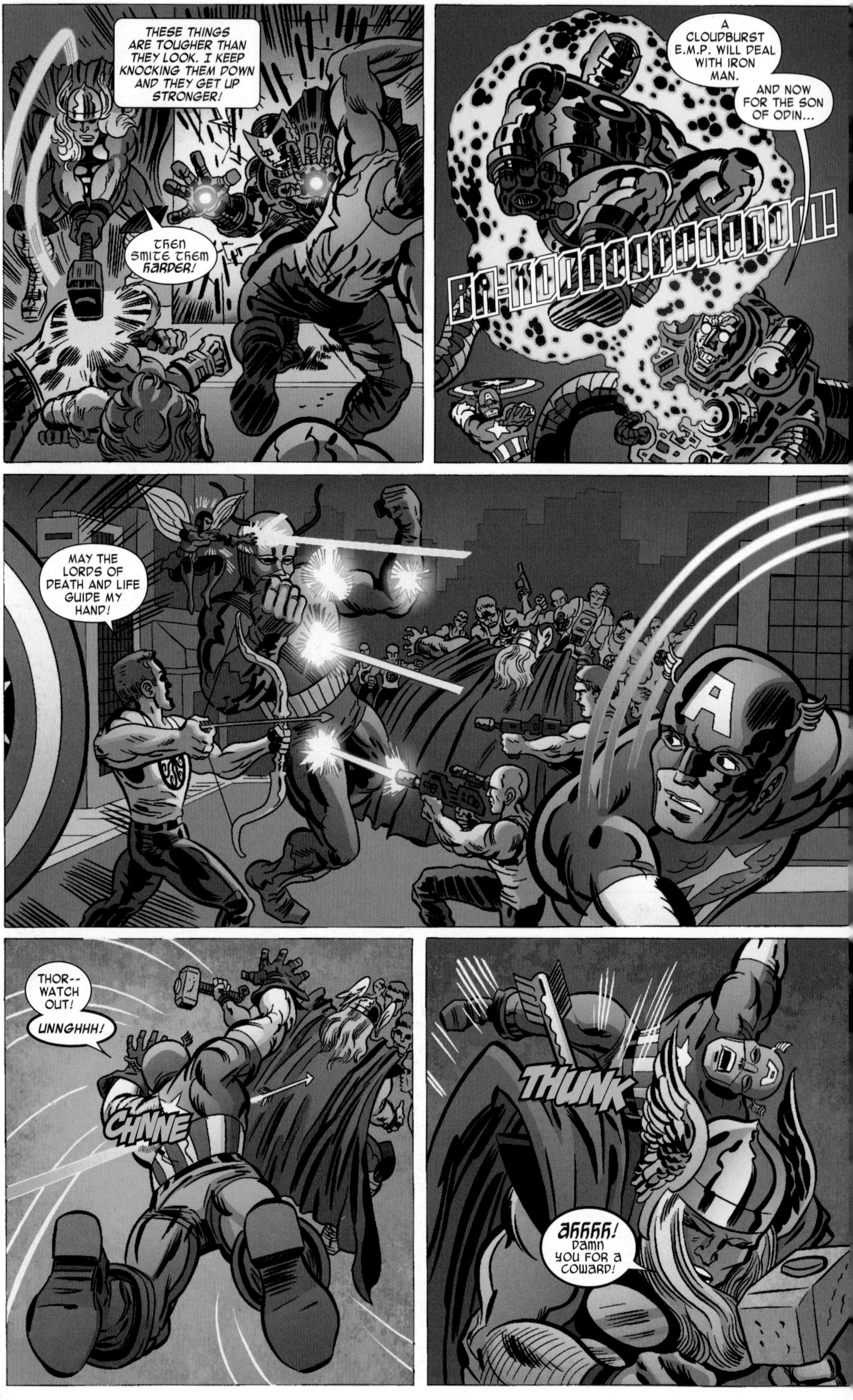
THESE THINGS ARE TOUGHER THAN THEY LOOK. I KEEP KNOCKING THEM DOWN AND THEY GET UP STRONGER!
THEN SMITE THEM HARDER!
A CLOUDBURST E.M.P. WILL DEAL WITH IRON MAN.
AND NOW FOR THE SON OF ODIN...
BA-KOOOOOOOOOOOOOM!!
MAY THE LORDS OF DEATH AND LIFE GUIDE MY HAND!
THOR-- WATCH OUT!
UNNGHHH!
CHNNE
THUNK
AHHHH! DAMN YOU FOR A COWARD!

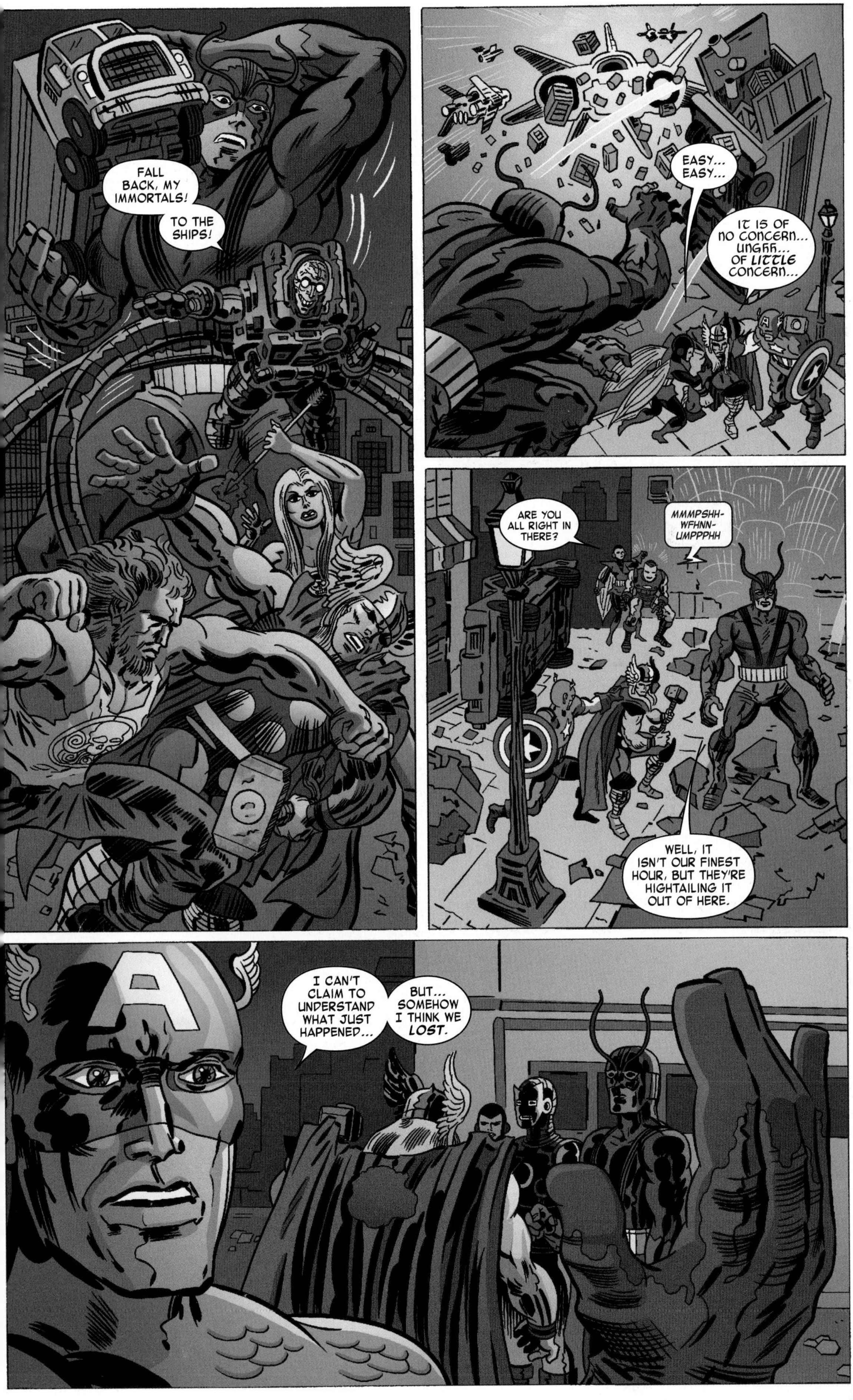
FALL BACK, MY IMMORTALS!
TO THE SHIPS!
EASY... EASY...
IT IS OF NO CONCERN... UNGHH... OF LITTLE CONCERN...
ARE YOU ALL RIGHT IN THERE?
MMMPSHH-WFHNN-UMPPPHH
WELL, IT ISN'T OUR FINEST HOUR, BUT THEY'RE HIGHTAILING IT OUT OF HERE.
I CAN'T CLAIM TO UNDERSTAND WHAT JUST HAPPENED...
BUT... SOMEHOW I THINK WE LOST.

YOU TOOK AN AWFUL CHANCE, GEIST. REVEALING OURSELVES TO THE AVENGERS HAS SENT SHUDDERS OF APPREHENSION THROUGH THE COUNCIL.

I HOPE IT WAS WORTH THE RISK, BECAUSE IT'S *YOUR HEAD* ON THE BLOCK.

RISK, *HERR* STRUCKER?

THERE WAS NEVER ANY RISK. AT WORST, CAPTAIN AMERICA AND THE AVENGERS WOULD HAVE DESTROYED MY RESURRECTION CORPS.

"AT WORST"? YOU FORGET, *HERR* DOCTOR, THAT ERLKING AND THE REST OF THE *AUFERSTEHUNGS CORPS* ARE OUR MOST PRIZED ASSETS. THEY ARE THE VANGUARD OF HYDRA'S ARMY. THEY ARE--

NOTHING.

THEY ARE NOTHING AT ALL...

...COMPARED TO WHAT *IS* TO COME.

THIS IS THE BLOOD OF A *GOD*, HERR STRUCKER. AND THE BLOOD OF CAPTAIN AMERICA.

FROM ONE WE WILL UNLOCK THE TRUE SECRET OF IMMORTALITY...AND FROM THE OTHER, FROM THE LOST SUPER-SOLDIER FORMULA THAT COURSES THROUGH HIS VEINS, WE WILL FINALLY--AND TRULY-- CREATE *DAS HERRENVOLK.*

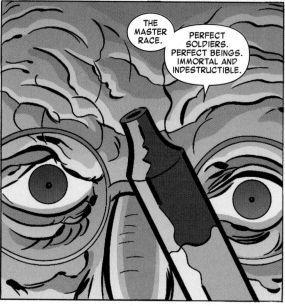

THE MASTER RACE.

PERFECT SOLDIERS. PERFECT BEINGS. IMMORTAL AND INDESTRUCTIBLE.

GRAND DREAMS, DR. GEIST...BUT EVEN YOU MUST ADMIT THAT WE DO NOT YET HAVE THE TECHNOLOGY TO EXPLOIT THESE RICHES.

WHAT DOES THAT MATTER? WHEN HAS IT *EVER* MATTERED? HYDRA HAS SPENT MILLENNIA ON THIS PROJECT. IF WE HAVE TO WAIT A FEW DECADES FOR THE SCIENCE OF GENETICS TO GROW OUT OF ITS INFANCY, THEN SO BE IT.

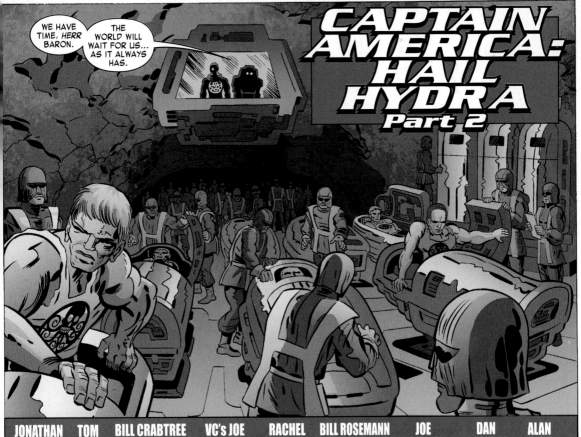

WE HAVE TIME, *HERR* BARON.

THE WORLD WILL WAIT FOR US... AS IT ALWAYS HAS.

CAPTAIN AMERICA: HAIL HYDRA
Part 2

JONATHAN MABERRY
Writer

TOM SCIOLI
Artist

BILL CRABTREE w/ SOTO
Colorists

VC's JOE CARAMAGNA
Letterer

RACHEL PINNELAS
Asst. Editor

BILL ROSEMANN TOM BRENNAN
Editors

JOE QUESADA
Editor in Chief

DAN BUCKLEY
Publisher

ALAN FINE
Exec. Producer

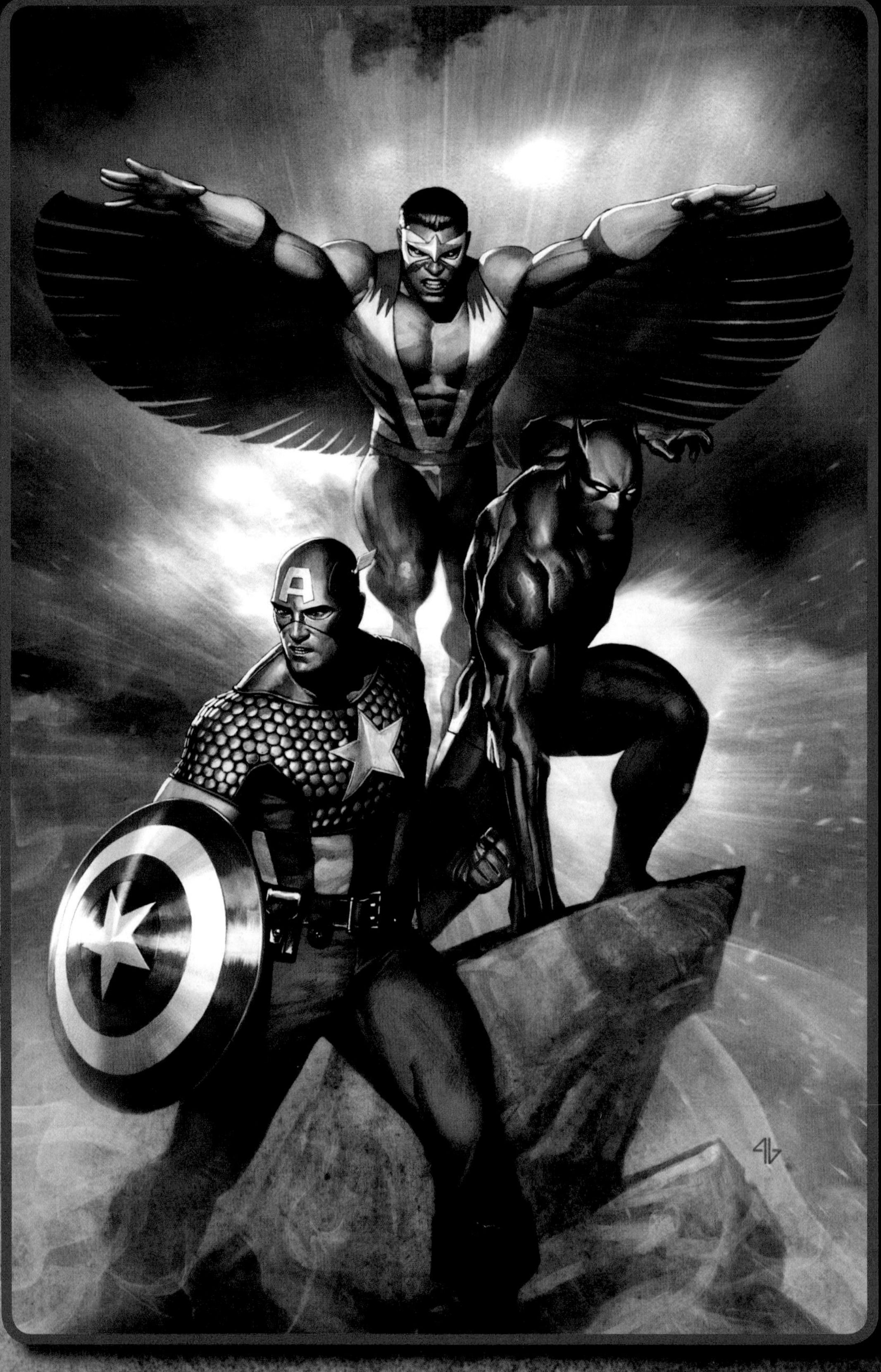

THREE

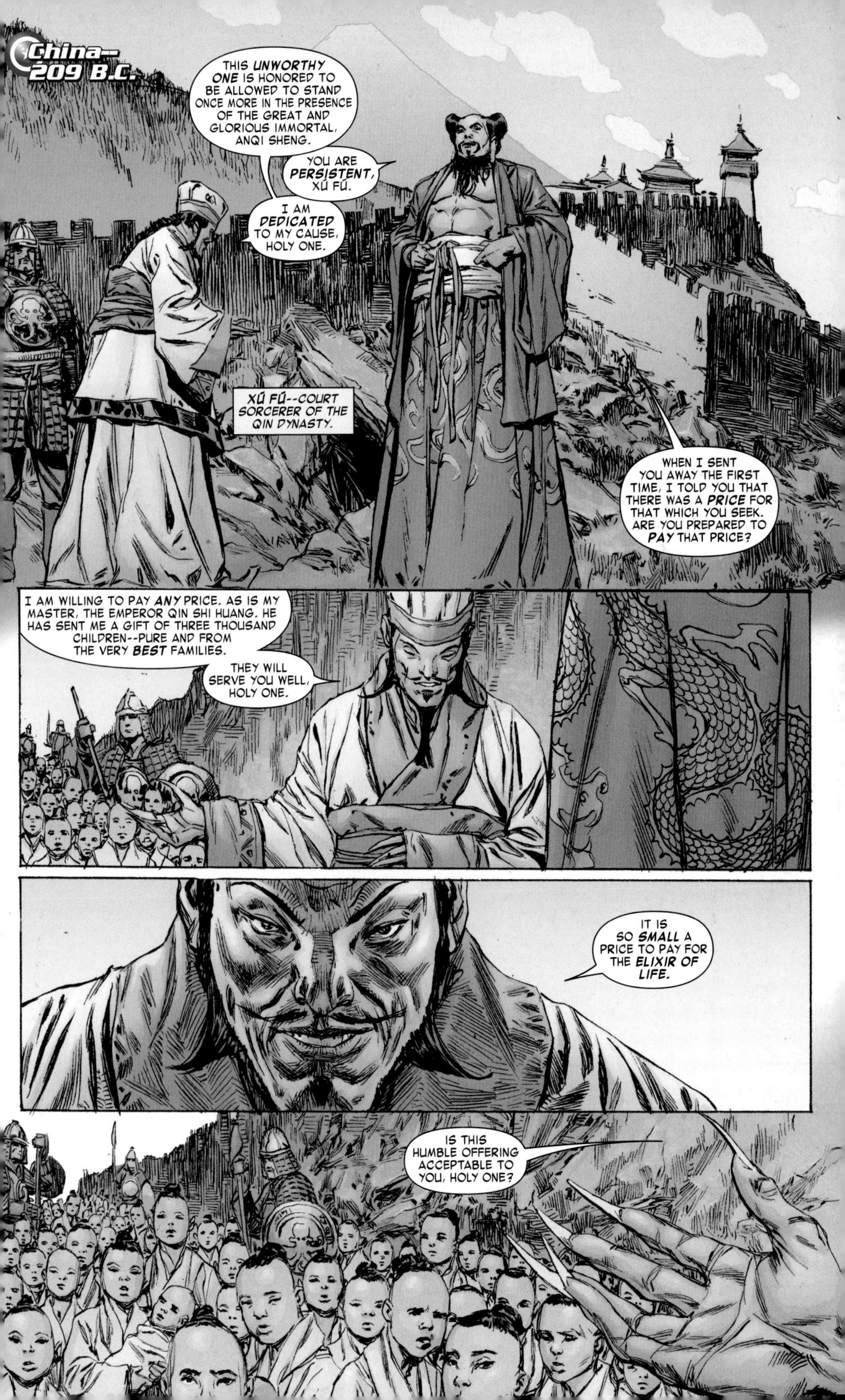
China--209 B.C.
THIS UNWORTHY ONE IS HONORED TO BE ALLOWED TO STAND ONCE MORE IN THE PRESENCE OF THE GREAT AND GLORIOUS IMMORTAL, ANQI SHENG.
YOU ARE PERSISTENT, XŬ FŬ.
I AM DEDICATED TO MY CAUSE, HOLY ONE.
XŬ FŬ--COURT SORCERER OF THE QIN DYNASTY.
WHEN I SENT YOU AWAY THE FIRST TIME, I TOLD YOU THAT THERE WAS A PRICE FOR THAT WHICH YOU SEEK. ARE YOU PREPARED TO PAY THAT PRICE?
I AM WILLING TO PAY ANY PRICE. AS IS MY MASTER, THE EMPEROR QIN SHI HUANG. HE HAS SENT ME A GIFT OF THREE THOUSAND CHILDREN--PURE AND FROM THE VERY BEST FAMILIES.
THEY WILL SERVE YOU WELL, HOLY ONE.
IT IS SO SMALL A PRICE TO PAY FOR THE ELIXIR OF LIFE.
IS THIS HUMBLE OFFERING ACCEPTABLE TO YOU, HOLY ONE?

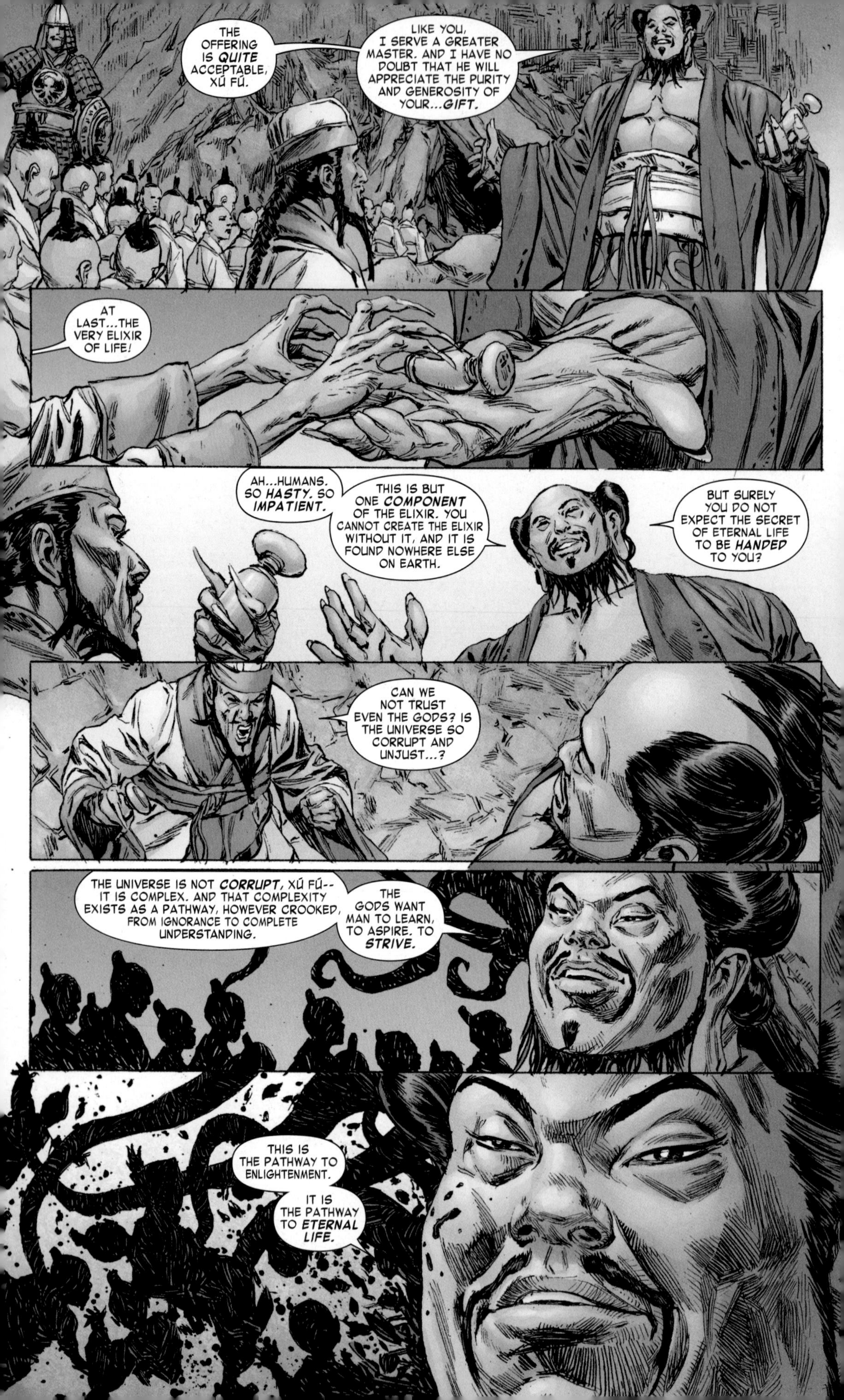
THE OFFERING IS QUITE ACCEPTABLE, XÚ FÚ.
LIKE YOU, I SERVE A GREATER MASTER. AND I HAVE NO DOUBT THAT HE WILL APPRECIATE THE PURITY AND GENEROSITY OF YOUR...GIFT.
AT LAST...THE VERY ELIXIR OF LIFE!
AH...HUMANS. SO HASTY. SO IMPATIENT.
THIS IS BUT ONE COMPONENT OF THE ELIXIR. YOU CANNOT CREATE THE ELIXIR WITHOUT IT, AND IT IS FOUND NOWHERE ELSE ON EARTH.
BUT SURELY YOU DO NOT EXPECT THE SECRET OF ETERNAL LIFE TO BE HANDED TO YOU?
CAN WE NOT TRUST EVEN THE GODS? IS THE UNIVERSE SO CORRUPT AND UNJUST...?
THE UNIVERSE IS NOT CORRUPT, XÚ FÚ-- IT IS COMPLEX. AND THAT COMPLEXITY EXISTS AS A PATHWAY, HOWEVER CROOKED, FROM IGNORANCE TO COMPLETE UNDERSTANDING.
THE GODS WANT MAN TO LEARN, TO ASPIRE. TO STRIVE.
THIS IS THE PATHWAY TO ENLIGHTENMENT.
IT IS THE PATHWAY TO ETERNAL LIFE.

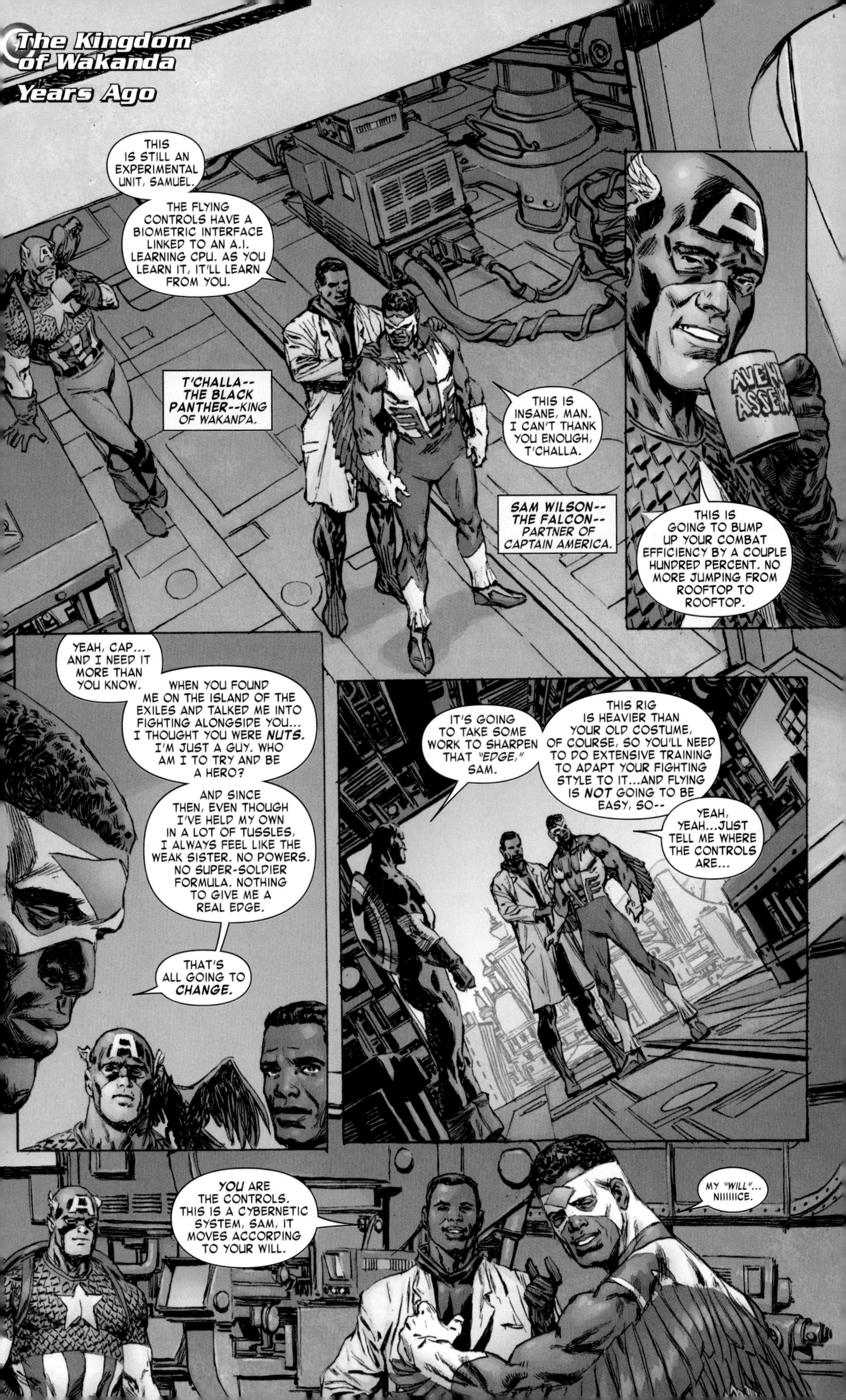
The Kingdom of Wakanda
Years Ago
THIS IS STILL AN EXPERIMENTAL UNIT, SAMUEL.
THE FLYING CONTROLS HAVE A BIOMETRIC INTERFACE LINKED TO AN A.I. LEARNING CPU. AS YOU LEARN IT, IT'LL LEARN FROM YOU.
T'CHALLA-- THE BLACK PANTHER--KING OF WAKANDA.
THIS IS INSANE, MAN. I CAN'T THANK YOU ENOUGH, T'CHALLA.
SAM WILSON-- THE FALCON-- PARTNER OF CAPTAIN AMERICA.
THIS IS GOING TO BUMP UP YOUR COMBAT EFFICIENCY BY A COUPLE HUNDRED PERCENT. NO MORE JUMPING FROM ROOFTOP TO ROOFTOP.
YEAH, CAP... AND I NEED IT MORE THAN YOU KNOW.
WHEN YOU FOUND ME ON THE ISLAND OF THE EXILES AND TALKED ME INTO FIGHTING ALONGSIDE YOU... I THOUGHT YOU WERE NUTS. I'M JUST A GUY. WHO AM I TO TRY AND BE A HERO?
AND SINCE THEN, EVEN THOUGH I'VE HELD MY OWN IN A LOT OF TUSSLES, I ALWAYS FEEL LIKE THE WEAK SISTER. NO POWERS. NO SUPER-SOLDIER FORMULA. NOTHING TO GIVE ME A REAL EDGE.
THAT'S ALL GOING TO CHANGE.
IT'S GOING TO TAKE SOME WORK TO SHARPEN THAT "EDGE," SAM.
THIS RIG IS HEAVIER THAN YOUR OLD COSTUME, OF COURSE, SO YOU'LL NEED TO DO EXTENSIVE TRAINING TO ADAPT YOUR FIGHTING STYLE TO IT...AND FLYING IS NOT GOING TO BE EASY, SO--
YEAH, YEAH...JUST TELL ME WHERE THE CONTROLS ARE...
YOU ARE THE CONTROLS. THIS IS A CYBERNETIC SYSTEM, SAM, IT MOVES ACCORDING TO YOUR WILL.
MY "WILL"... NIIIIICE.

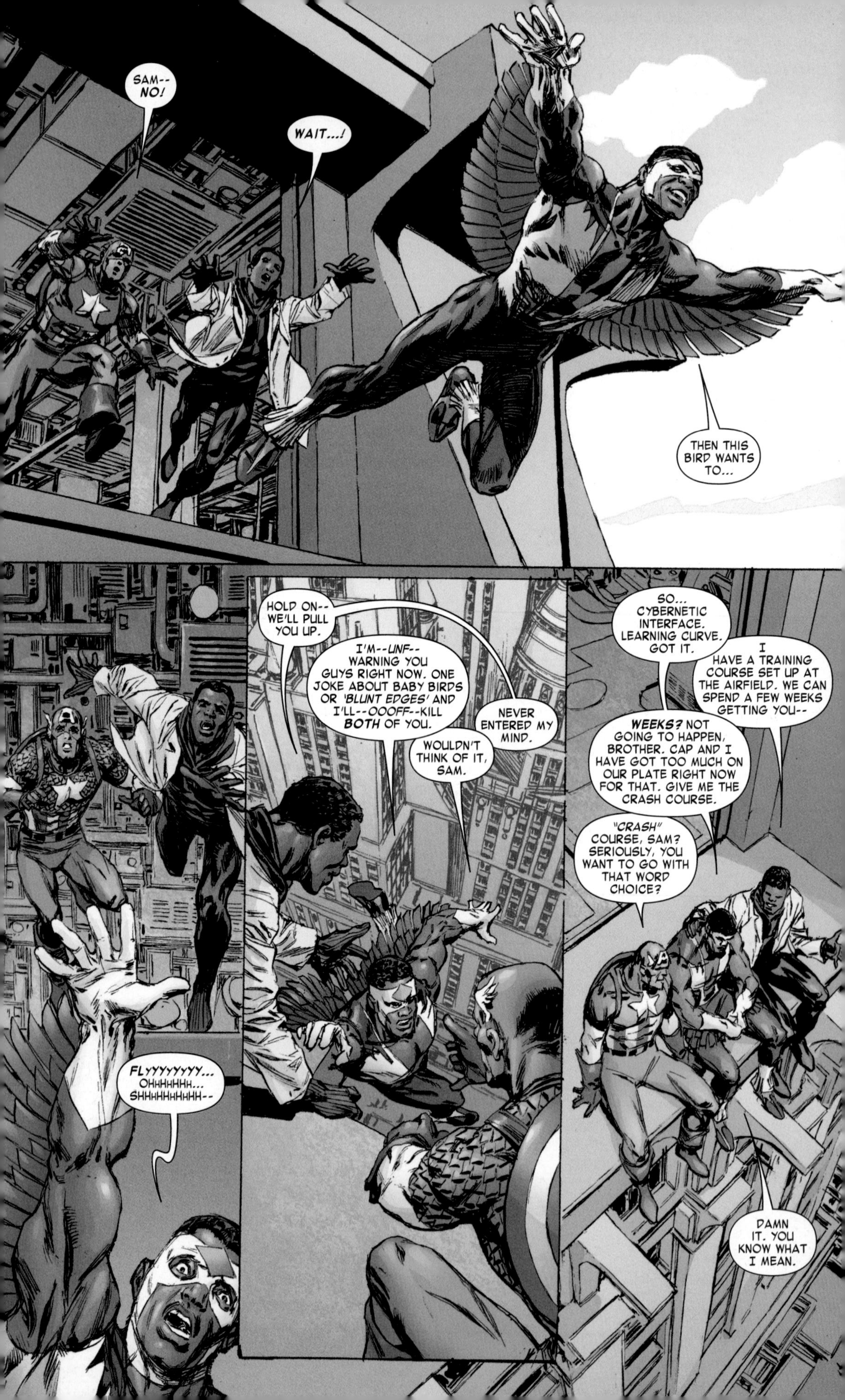
SAM-- NO!
WAIT...!
THEN THIS BIRD WANTS TO...
FLYYYYYYYY... OHHHHHHH... SHHHHHHHHHH--
HOLD ON-- WE'LL PULL YOU UP.
I'M--UNF-- WARNING YOU GUYS RIGHT NOW. ONE JOKE ABOUT BABY BIRDS OR 'BLUNT EDGES' AND I'LL--OOOFF--KILL BOTH OF YOU.
NEVER ENTERED MY MIND.
WOULDN'T THINK OF IT, SAM.
SO... CYBERNETIC INTERFACE. LEARNING CURVE. GOT IT.
I HAVE A TRAINING COURSE SET UP AT THE AIRFIELD. WE CAN SPEND A FEW WEEKS GETTING YOU--
WEEKS? NOT GOING TO HAPPEN, BROTHER. CAP AND I HAVE GOT TOO MUCH ON OUR PLATE RIGHT NOW FOR THAT. GIVE ME THE CRASH COURSE.
"CRASH" COURSE, SAM? SERIOUSLY, YOU WANT TO GO WITH THAT WORD CHOICE?
DAMN IT. YOU KNOW WHAT I MEAN.

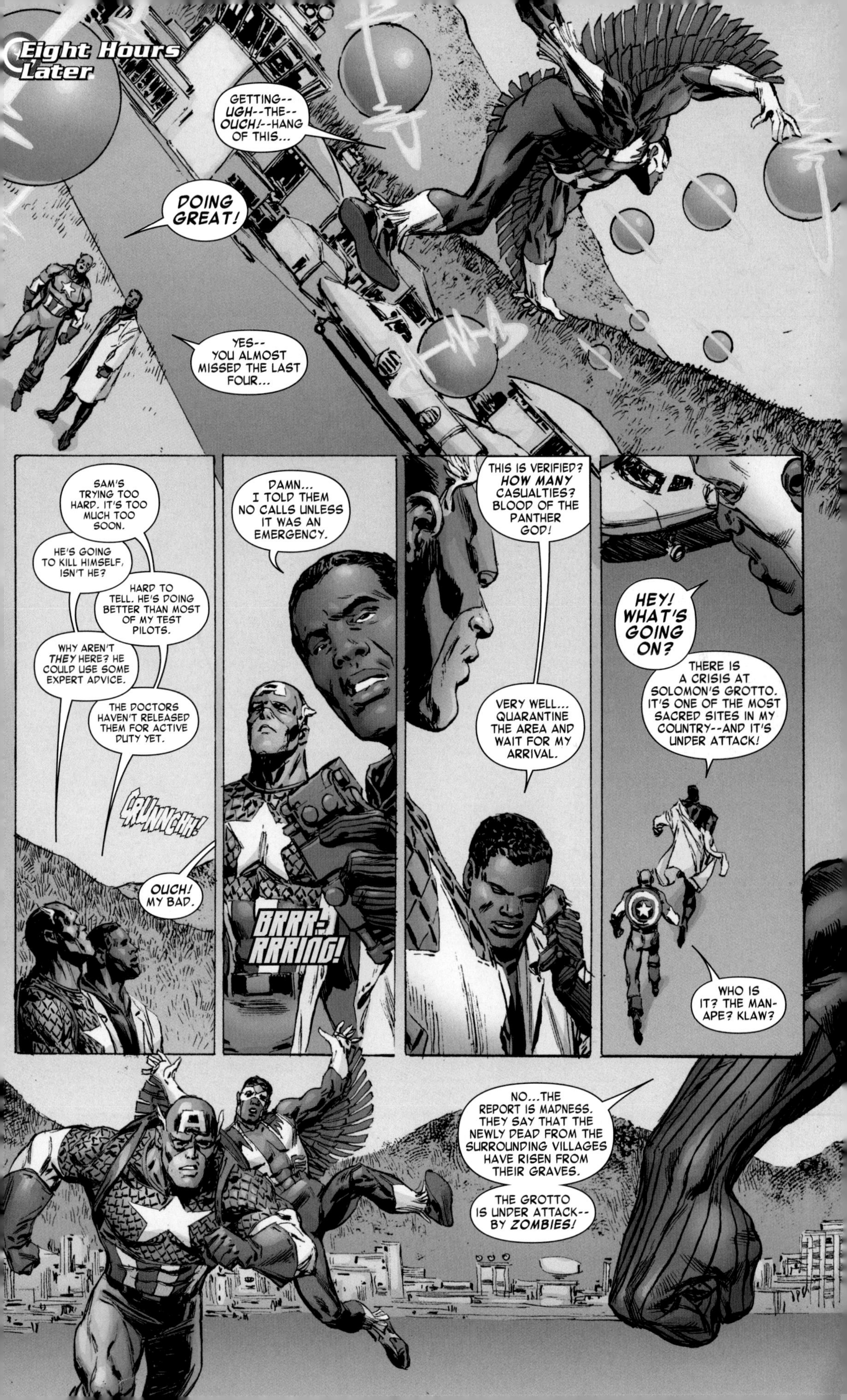
Eight Hours Later
GETTING--UGH--THE--OUCH!--HANG OF THIS...
DOING GREAT!
YES--YOU ALMOST MISSED THE LAST FOUR...
SAM'S TRYING TOO HARD. IT'S TOO MUCH TOO SOON.
HE'S GOING TO KILL HIMSELF, ISN'T HE?
HARD TO TELL. HE'S DOING BETTER THAN MOST OF MY TEST PILOTS.
WHY AREN'T THEY HERE? HE COULD USE SOME EXPERT ADVICE.
THE DOCTORS HAVEN'T RELEASED THEM FOR ACTIVE DUTY YET.
CRUNNCHH!
OUCH! MY BAD.
DAMN... I TOLD THEM NO CALLS UNLESS IT WAS AN EMERGENCY.
BRRR-RRRING!
THIS IS VERIFIED? HOW MANY CASUALTIES? BLOOD OF THE PANTHER GOD!
VERY WELL... QUARANTINE THE AREA AND WAIT FOR MY ARRIVAL.
HEY! WHAT'S GOING ON?
THERE IS A CRISIS AT SOLOMON'S GROTTO. IT'S ONE OF THE MOST SACRED SITES IN MY COUNTRY--AND IT'S UNDER ATTACK!
WHO IS IT? THE MAN-APE? KLAW?
NO...THE REPORT IS MADNESS. THEY SAY THAT THE NEWLY DEAD FROM THE SURROUNDING VILLAGES HAVE RISEN FROM THEIR GRAVES.
THE GROTTO IS UNDER ATTACK--BY ZOMBIES!

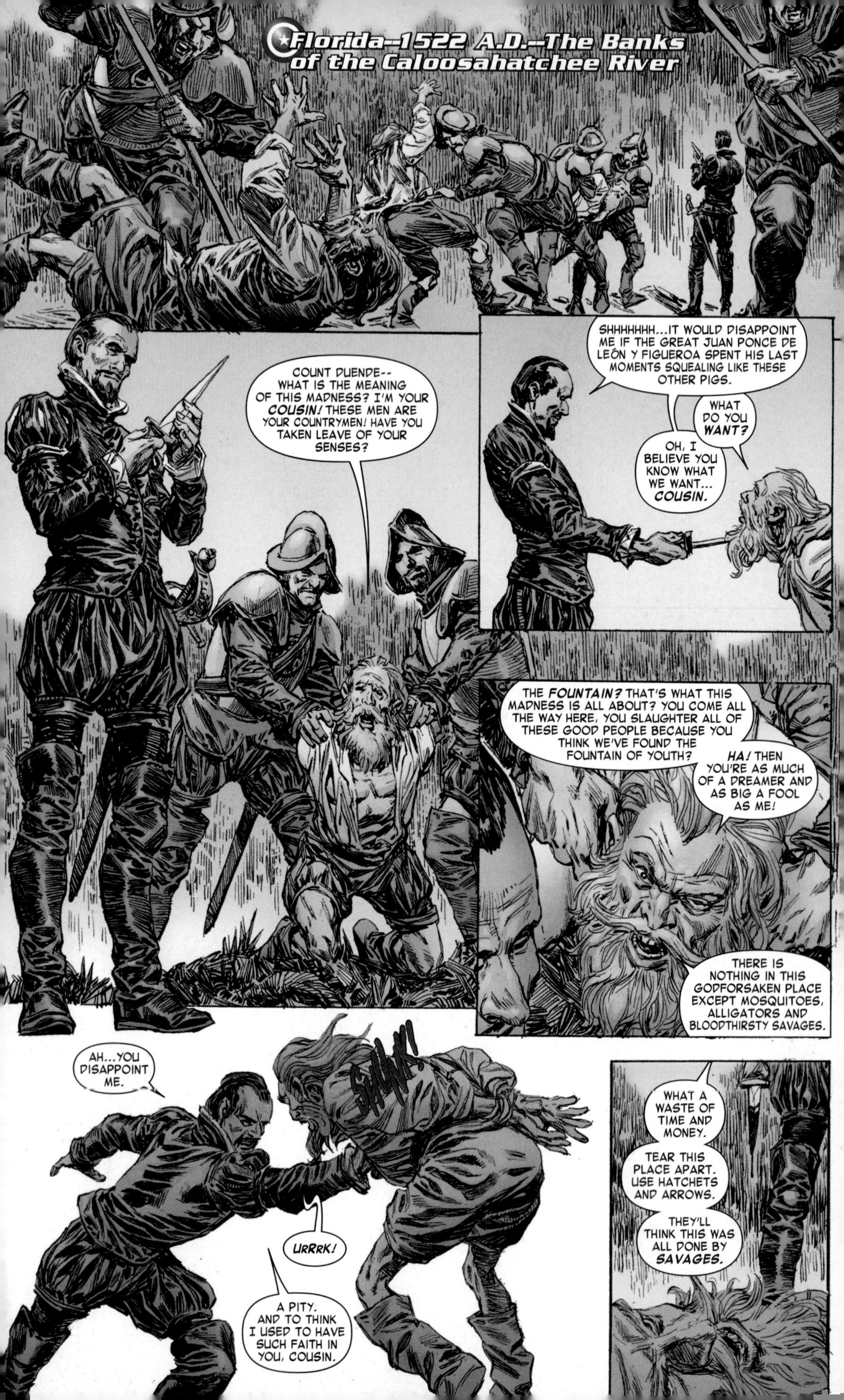

Florida--1522 A.D.--The Banks of the Caloosahatchee River
COUNT DUENDE-- WHAT IS THE MEANING OF THIS MADNESS? I'M YOUR COUSIN! THESE MEN ARE YOUR COUNTRYMEN! HAVE YOU TAKEN LEAVE OF YOUR SENSES?
SHHHHHHH...IT WOULD DISAPPOINT ME IF THE GREAT JUAN PONCE DE LEÓN Y FIGUEROA SPENT HIS LAST MOMENTS SQUEALING LIKE THESE OTHER PIGS.
WHAT DO YOU WANT?
OH, I BELIEVE YOU KNOW WHAT WE WANT... COUSIN.
THE FOUNTAIN? THAT'S WHAT THIS MADNESS IS ALL ABOUT? YOU COME ALL THE WAY HERE, YOU SLAUGHTER ALL OF THESE GOOD PEOPLE BECAUSE YOU THINK WE'VE FOUND THE FOUNTAIN OF YOUTH?
HA! THEN YOU'RE AS MUCH OF A DREAMER AND AS BIG A FOOL AS ME!
THERE IS NOTHING IN THIS GODFORSAKEN PLACE EXCEPT MOSQUITOES, ALLIGATORS AND BLOODTHIRSTY SAVAGES.
AH...YOU DISAPPOINT ME.
SHLIK!
URRRK!
A PITY. AND TO THINK I USED TO HAVE SUCH FAITH IN YOU, COUSIN.
WHAT A WASTE OF TIME AND MONEY.
TEAR THIS PLACE APART. USE HATCHETS AND ARROWS.
THEY'LL THINK THIS WAS ALL DONE BY SAVAGES.

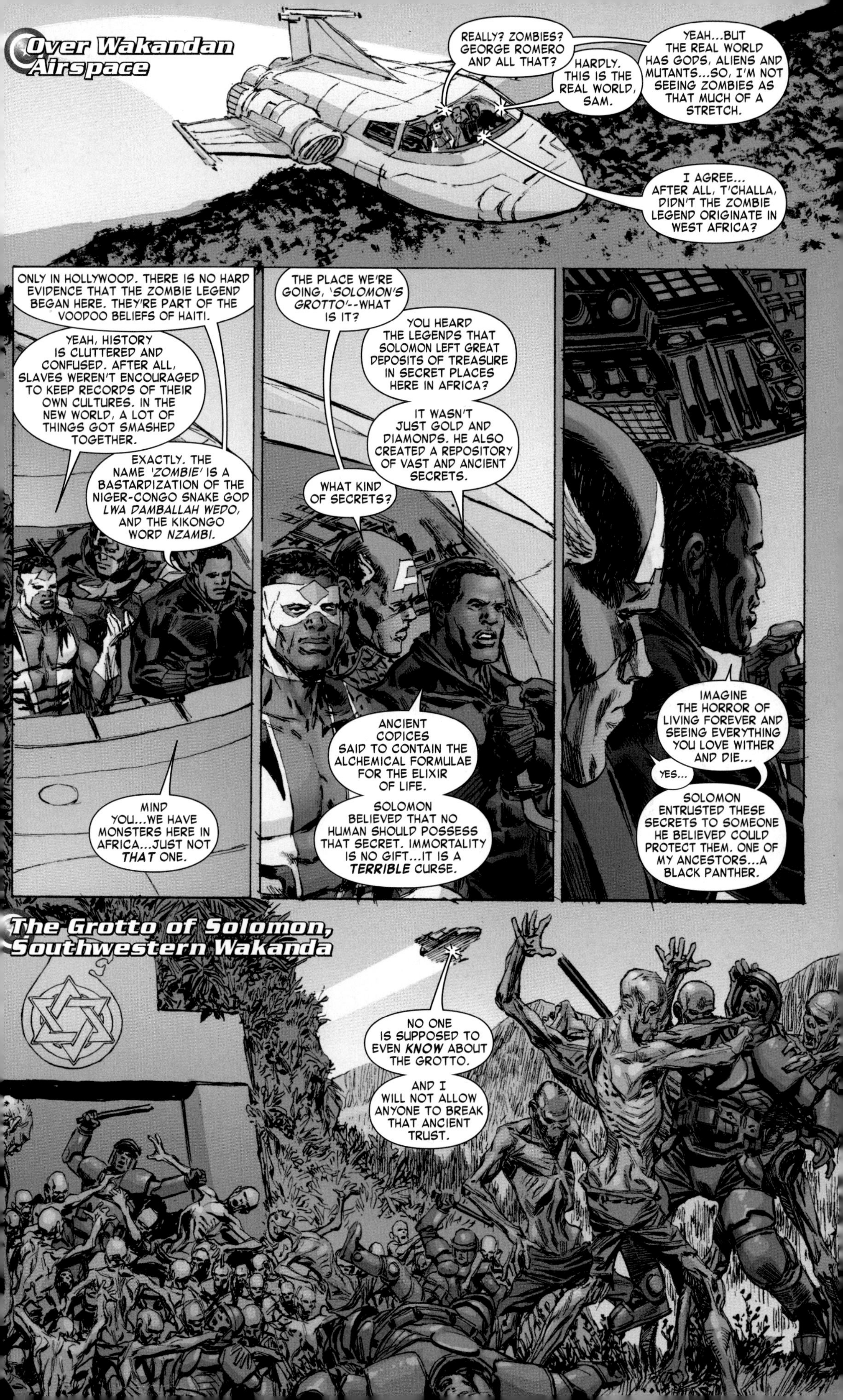
Over Wakandan Airspace
REALLY? ZOMBIES? GEORGE ROMERO AND ALL THAT?
HARDLY. THIS IS THE REAL WORLD, SAM.
YEAH...BUT THE REAL WORLD HAS GODS, ALIENS AND MUTANTS...SO, I'M NOT SEEING ZOMBIES AS THAT MUCH OF A STRETCH.
I AGREE... AFTER ALL, T'CHALLA, DIDN'T THE ZOMBIE LEGEND ORIGINATE IN WEST AFRICA?
ONLY IN HOLLYWOOD. THERE IS NO HARD EVIDENCE THAT THE ZOMBIE LEGEND BEGAN HERE. THEY'RE PART OF THE VOODOO BELIEFS OF HAITI.
YEAH, HISTORY IS CLUTTERED AND CONFUSED. AFTER ALL, SLAVES WEREN'T ENCOURAGED TO KEEP RECORDS OF THEIR OWN CULTURES. IN THE NEW WORLD, A LOT OF THINGS GOT SMASHED TOGETHER.
EXACTLY. THE NAME *'ZOMBIE'* IS A BASTARDIZATION OF THE NIGER-CONGO SNAKE GOD *LWA DAMBALLAH WEDO*, AND THE KIKONGO WORD *NZAMBI*.
MIND YOU...WE HAVE MONSTERS HERE IN AFRICA...JUST NOT *THAT* ONE.
THE PLACE WE'RE GOING, *'SOLOMON'S GROTTO'*--WHAT IS IT?
YOU HEARD THE LEGENDS THAT SOLOMON LEFT GREAT DEPOSITS OF TREASURE IN SECRET PLACES HERE IN AFRICA?
IT WASN'T JUST GOLD AND DIAMONDS. HE ALSO CREATED A REPOSITORY OF VAST AND ANCIENT SECRETS.
WHAT KIND OF SECRETS?
ANCIENT CODICES SAID TO CONTAIN THE ALCHEMICAL FORMULAE FOR THE ELIXIR OF LIFE.
SOLOMON BELIEVED THAT NO HUMAN SHOULD POSSESS THAT SECRET. IMMORTALITY IS NO GIFT...IT IS A ***TERRIBLE*** CURSE.
IMAGINE THE HORROR OF LIVING FOREVER AND SEEING EVERYTHING YOU LOVE WITHER AND DIE...
YES...
SOLOMON ENTRUSTED THESE SECRETS TO SOMEONE HE BELIEVED COULD PROTECT THEM. ONE OF MY ANCESTORS...A BLACK PANTHER.
The Grotto of Solomon, Southwestern Wakanda
NO ONE IS SUPPOSED TO EVEN ***KNOW*** ABOUT THE GROTTO.
AND I WILL NOT ALLOW ANYONE TO BREAK THAT ANCIENT TRUST.

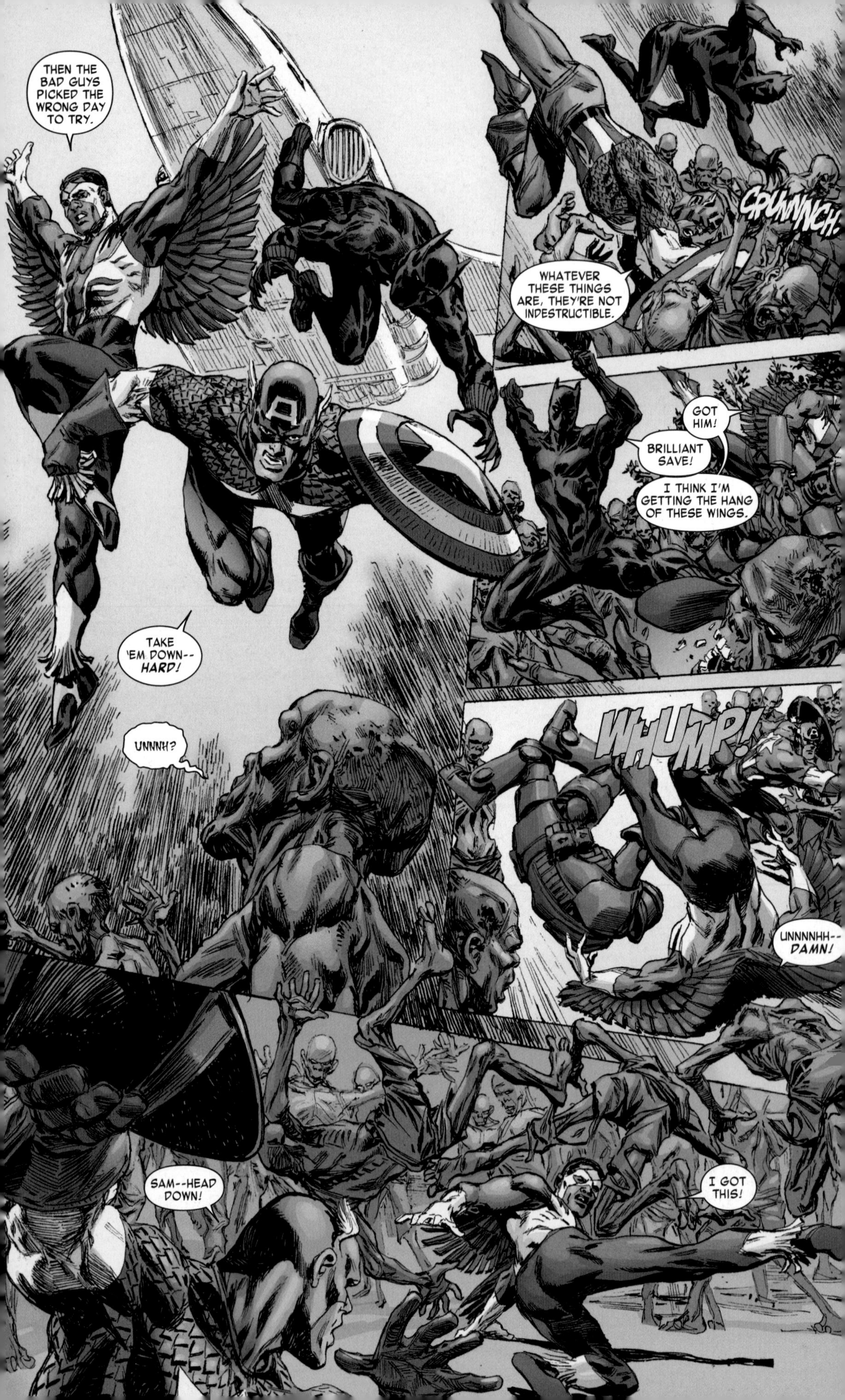
THEN THE BAD GUYS PICKED THE WRONG DAY TO TRY.
TAKE 'EM DOWN--HARD!
CRUNNNCH!
WHATEVER THESE THINGS ARE, THEY'RE NOT INDESTRUCTIBLE.
GOT HIM!
BRILLIANT SAVE!
I THINK I'M GETTING THE HANG OF THESE WINGS.
UNNNH?
WHUMP!
UNNNNHH--DAMN!
SAM--HEAD DOWN!
I GOT THIS!

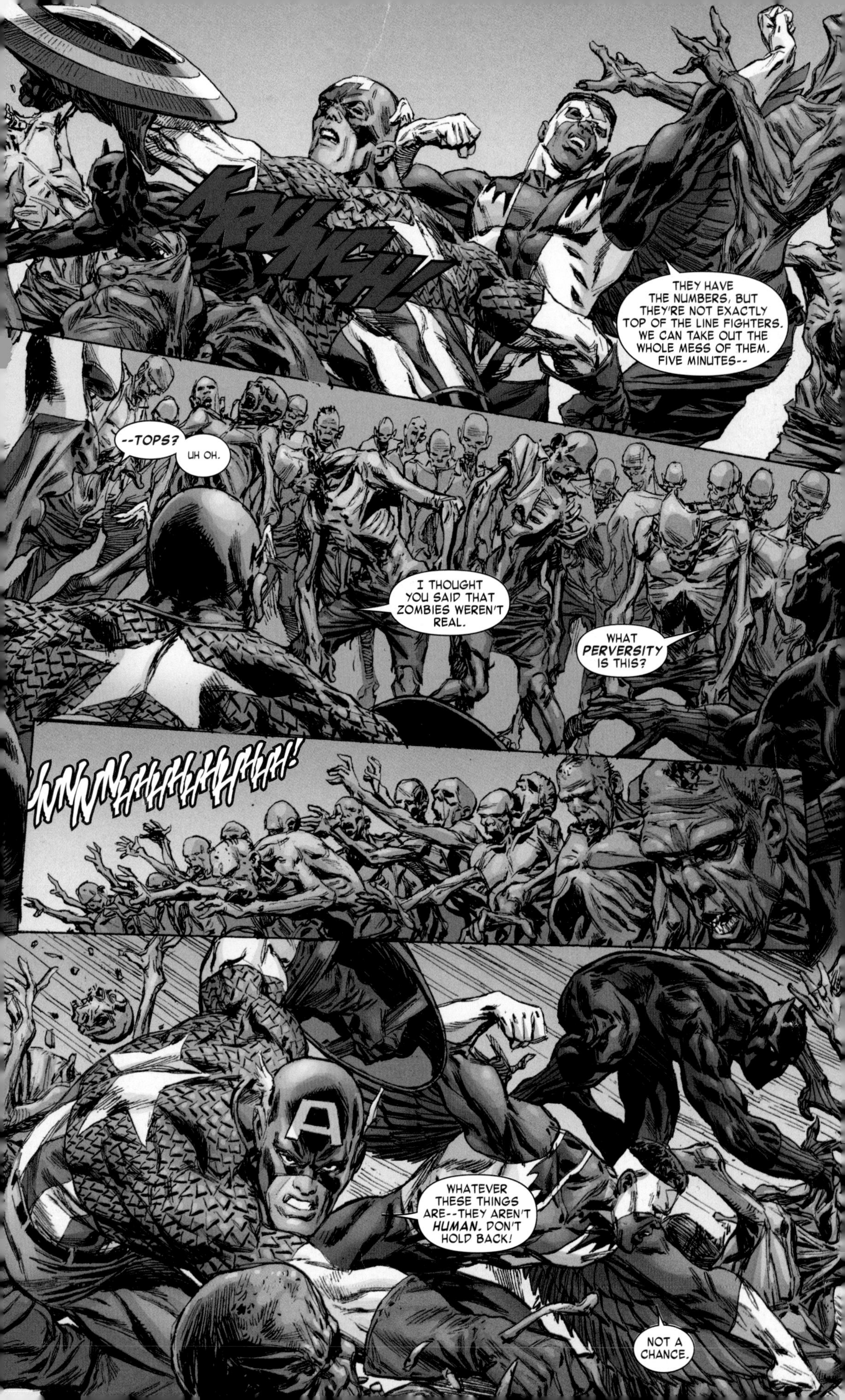
KRUNCH!
THEY HAVE THE NUMBERS, BUT THEY'RE NOT EXACTLY TOP OF THE LINE FIGHTERS. WE CAN TAKE OUT THE WHOLE MESS OF THEM. FIVE MINUTES--
--TOPS?
UH OH.
I THOUGHT YOU SAID THAT ZOMBIES WEREN'T REAL.
WHAT PERVERSITY IS THIS?
HNNNNHHHHHHHHHH!
WHATEVER THESE THINGS ARE--THEY AREN'T HUMAN. DON'T HOLD BACK!
NOT A CHANCE.

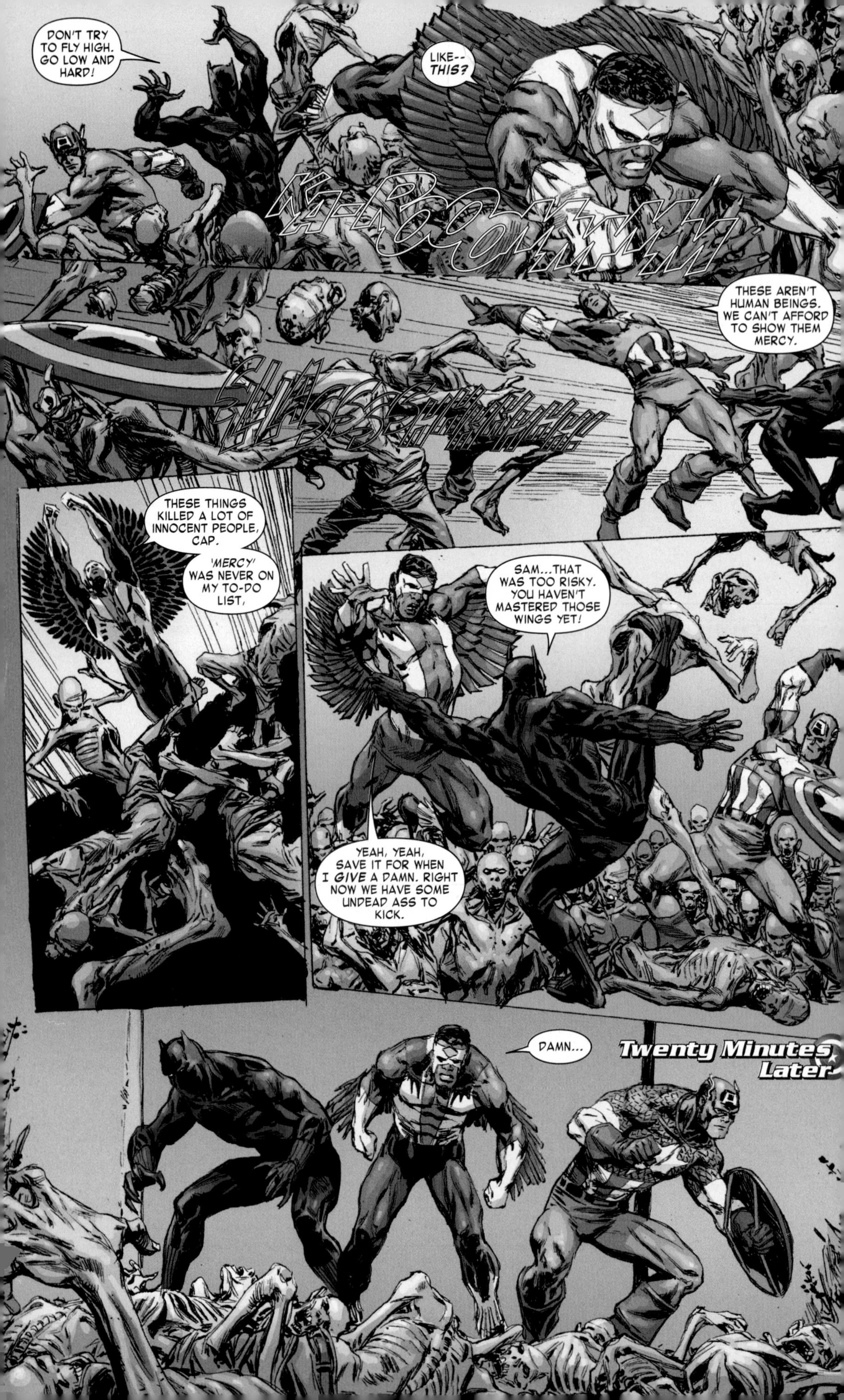

DON'T TRY TO FLY HIGH. GO LOW AND HARD!
LIKE-- *THIS?*
THESE AREN'T HUMAN BEINGS. WE CAN'T AFFORD TO SHOW THEM MERCY.
THESE THINGS KILLED A LOT OF INNOCENT PEOPLE, CAP.
'MERCY' WAS NEVER ON MY TO-DO LIST.
SAM...THAT WAS TOO RISKY. YOU HAVEN'T MASTERED THOSE WINGS YET!
YEAH, YEAH, SAVE IT FOR WHEN I *GIVE* A DAMN. RIGHT NOW WE HAVE SOME UNDEAD ASS TO KICK.
Twenty Minutes Later
DAMN...

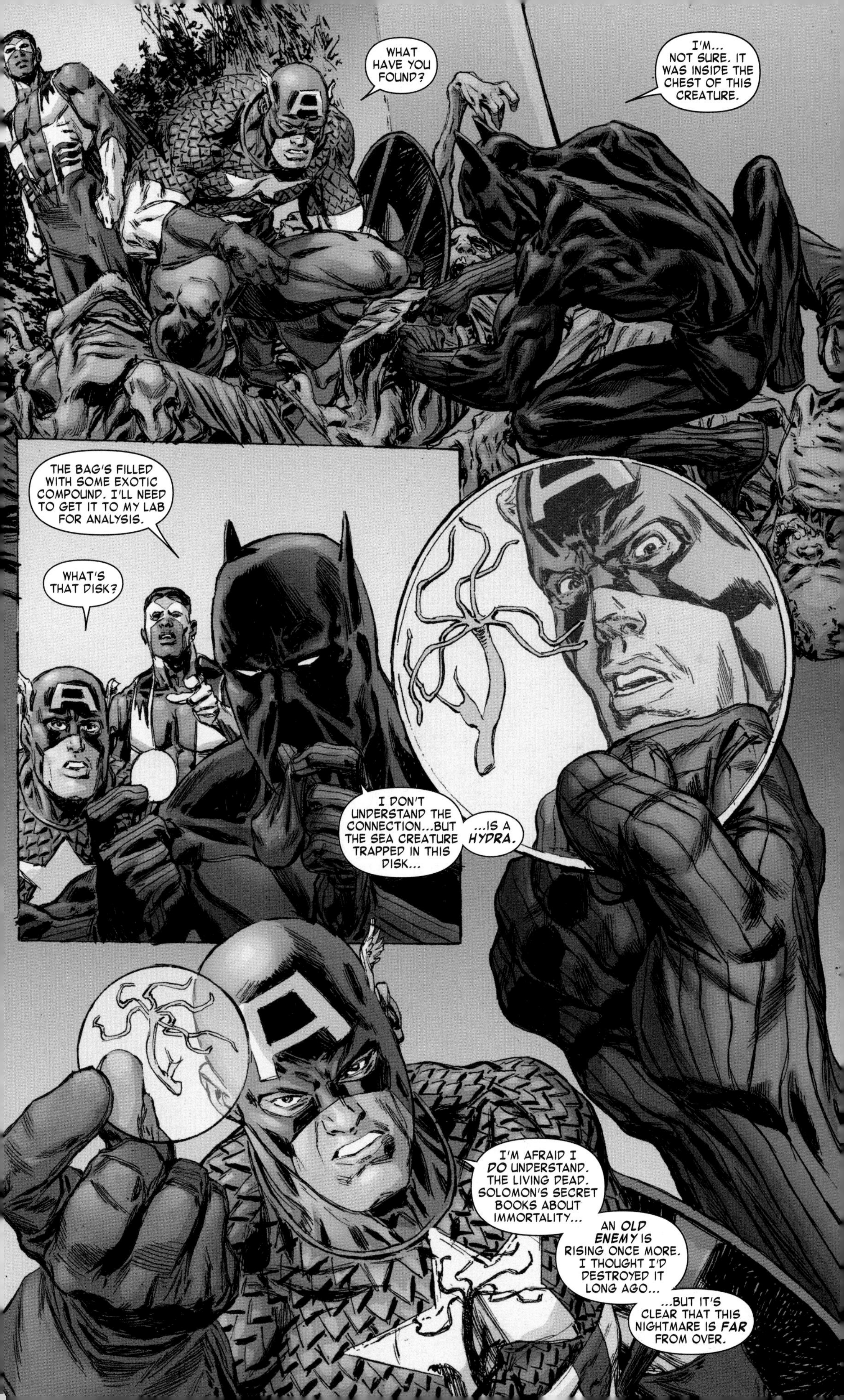
WHAT HAVE YOU FOUND?
I'M... NOT SURE. IT WAS INSIDE THE CHEST OF THIS CREATURE.
THE BAG'S FILLED WITH SOME EXOTIC COMPOUND. I'LL NEED TO GET IT TO MY LAB FOR ANALYSIS.
WHAT'S THAT DISK?
I DON'T UNDERSTAND THE CONNECTION...BUT THE SEA CREATURE TRAPPED IN THIS DISK...
...IS A HYDRA.
I'M AFRAID I DO UNDERSTAND. THE LIVING DEAD. SOLOMON'S SECRET BOOKS ABOUT IMMORTALITY...
AN OLD ENEMY IS RISING ONCE MORE. I THOUGHT I'D DESTROYED IT LONG AGO...
...BUT IT'S CLEAR THAT THIS NIGHTMARE IS FAR FROM OVER.

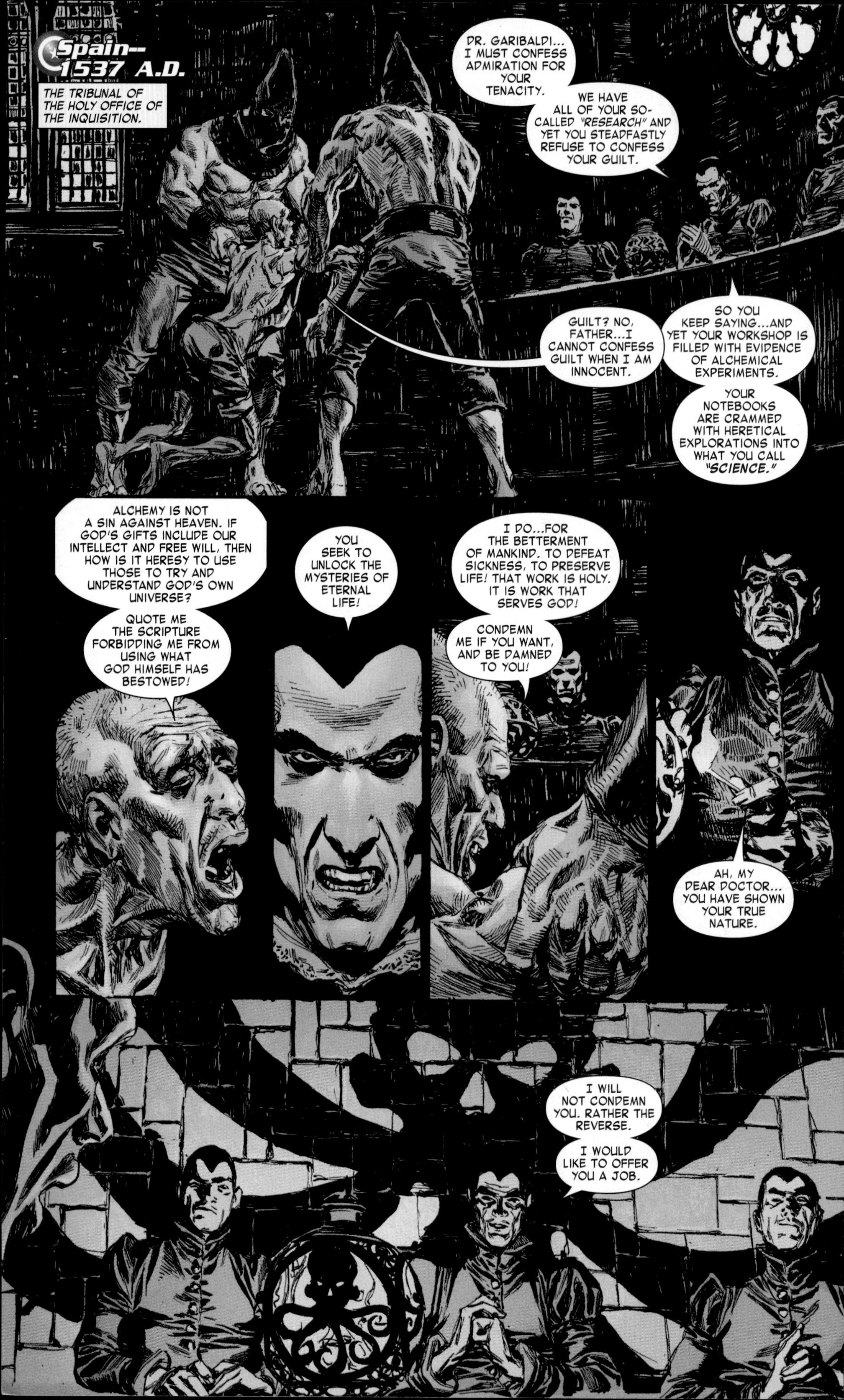
Spain-- 1537 A.D.
THE TRIBUNAL OF THE HOLY OFFICE OF THE INQUISITION.
DR. GARIBALDI... I MUST CONFESS ADMIRATION FOR YOUR TENACITY.
WE HAVE ALL OF YOUR SO-CALLED "RESEARCH" AND YET YOU STEADFASTLY REFUSE TO CONFESS YOUR GUILT.
GUILT? NO, FATHER...I CANNOT CONFESS GUILT WHEN I AM INNOCENT.
SO YOU KEEP SAYING...AND YET YOUR WORKSHOP IS FILLED WITH EVIDENCE OF ALCHEMICAL EXPERIMENTS.
YOUR NOTEBOOKS ARE CRAMMED WITH HERETICAL EXPLORATIONS INTO WHAT YOU CALL "SCIENCE."
ALCHEMY IS NOT A SIN AGAINST HEAVEN. IF GOD'S GIFTS INCLUDE OUR INTELLECT AND FREE WILL, THEN HOW IS IT HERESY TO USE THOSE TO TRY AND UNDERSTAND GOD'S OWN UNIVERSE?
QUOTE ME THE SCRIPTURE FORBIDDING ME FROM USING WHAT GOD HIMSELF HAS BESTOWED!
YOU SEEK TO UNLOCK THE MYSTERIES OF ETERNAL LIFE!
I DO...FOR THE BETTERMENT OF MANKIND. TO DEFEAT SICKNESS, TO PRESERVE LIFE! THAT WORK IS HOLY. IT IS WORK THAT SERVES GOD!
CONDEMN ME IF YOU WANT, AND BE DAMNED TO YOU!
AH, MY DEAR DOCTOR... YOU HAVE SHOWN YOUR TRUE NATURE.
I WILL NOT CONDEMN YOU. RATHER THE REVERSE.
I WOULD LIKE TO OFFER YOU A JOB.

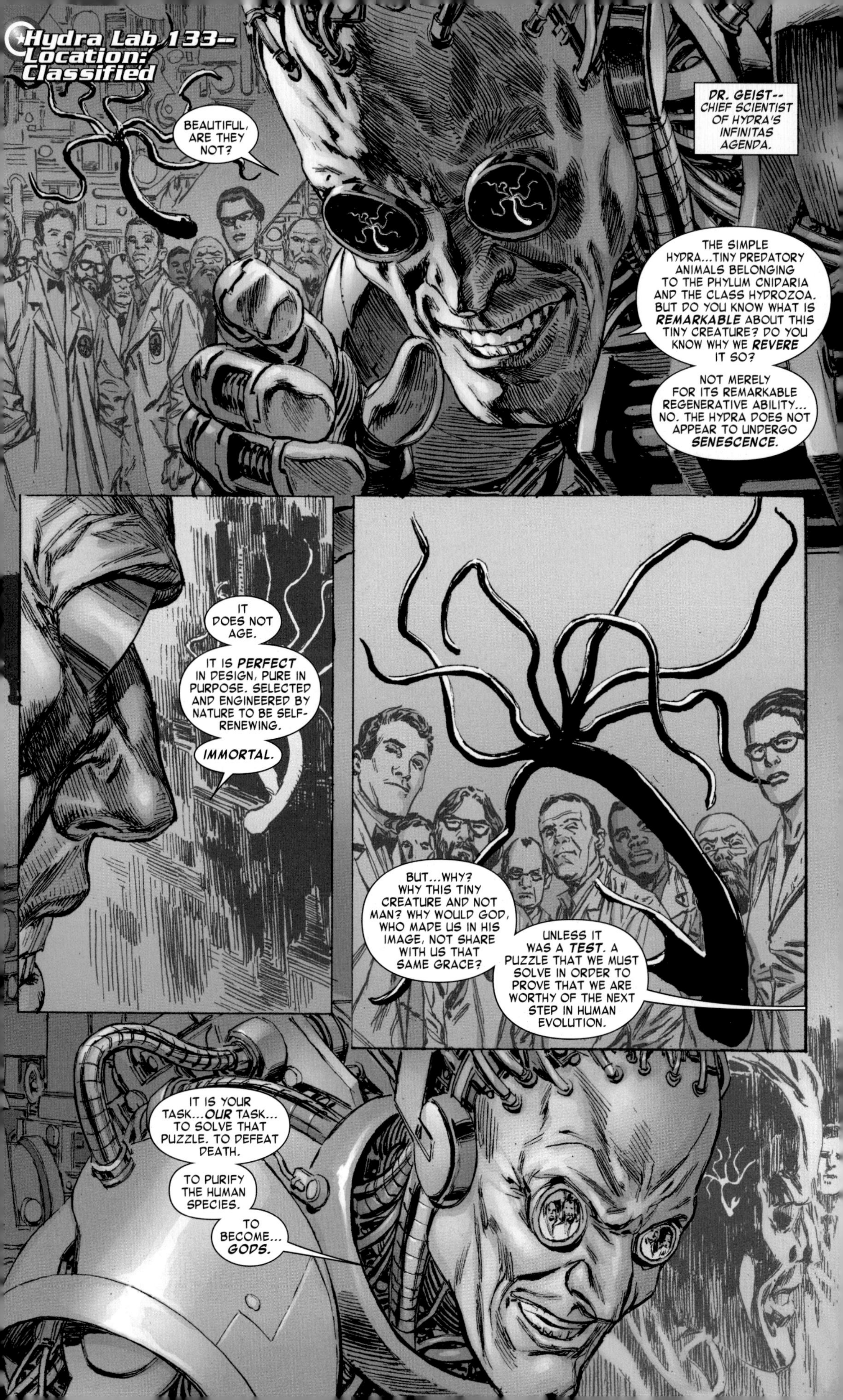
Hydra Lab 133-- Location: Classified
BEAUTIFUL, ARE THEY NOT?
DR. GEIST-- CHIEF SCIENTIST OF HYDRA'S INFINITAS AGENDA.
THE SIMPLE HYDRA...TINY PREDATORY ANIMALS BELONGING TO THE PHYLUM CNIDARIA AND THE CLASS HYDROZOA. BUT DO YOU KNOW WHAT IS REMARKABLE ABOUT THIS TINY CREATURE? DO YOU KNOW WHY WE REVERE IT SO?
NOT MERELY FOR ITS REMARKABLE REGENERATIVE ABILITY... NO. THE HYDRA DOES NOT APPEAR TO UNDERGO SENESCENCE.
IT DOES NOT AGE.
IT IS PERFECT IN DESIGN, PURE IN PURPOSE. SELECTED AND ENGINEERED BY NATURE TO BE SELF-RENEWING.
IMMORTAL.
BUT...WHY? WHY THIS TINY CREATURE AND NOT MAN? WHY WOULD GOD, WHO MADE US IN HIS IMAGE, NOT SHARE WITH US THAT SAME GRACE?
UNLESS IT WAS A TEST. A PUZZLE THAT WE MUST SOLVE IN ORDER TO PROVE THAT WE ARE WORTHY OF THE NEXT STEP IN HUMAN EVOLUTION.
IT IS YOUR TASK...OUR TASK... TO SOLVE THAT PUZZLE. TO DEFEAT DEATH.
TO PURIFY THE HUMAN SPECIES.
TO BECOME... GODS.

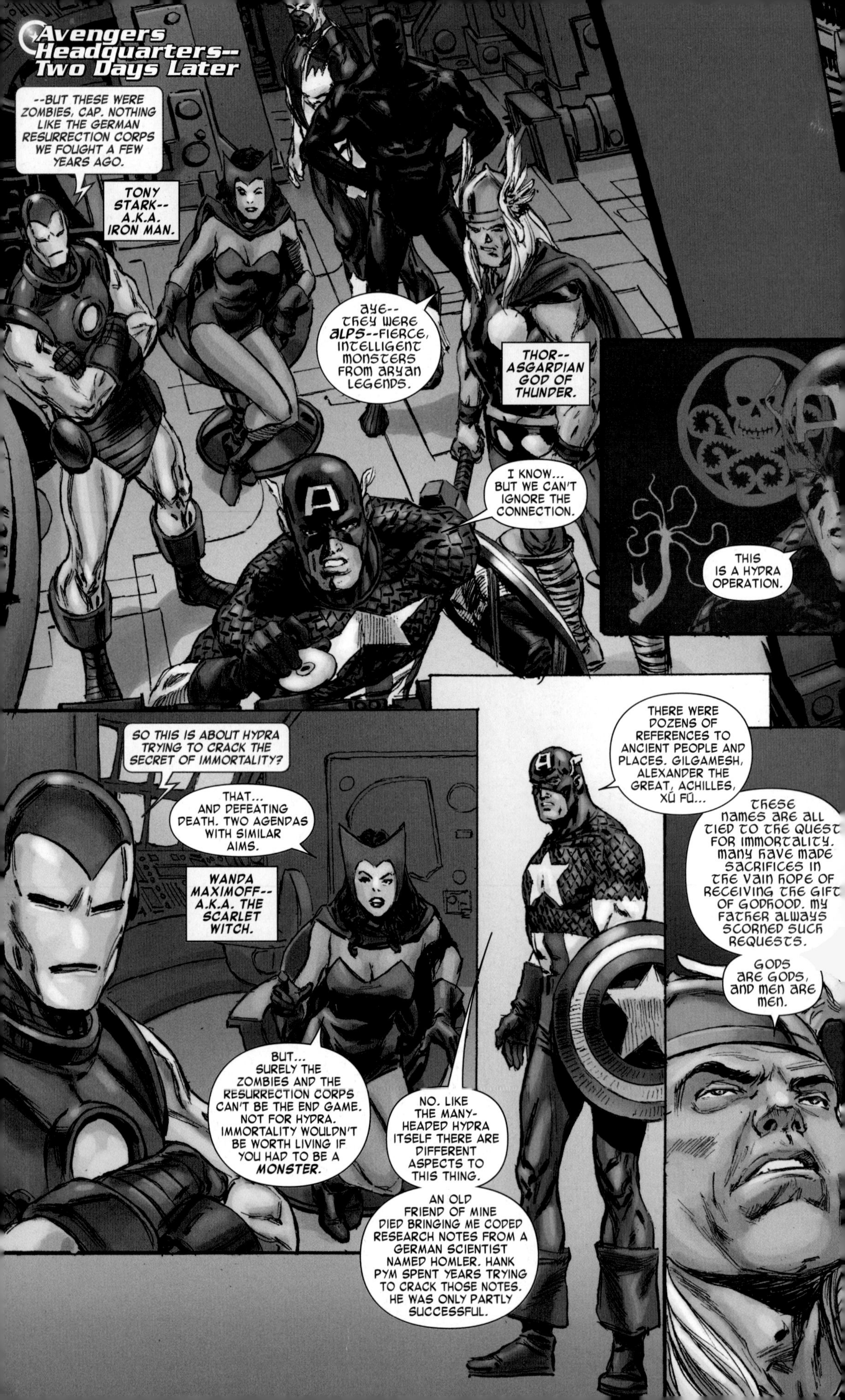
Avengers Headquarters-- Two Days Later
--BUT THESE WERE ZOMBIES, CAP. NOTHING LIKE THE GERMAN RESURRECTION CORPS WE FOUGHT A FEW YEARS AGO.
TONY STARK-- A.K.A. IRON MAN.
AYE-- THEY WERE ALPS--FIERCE, INTELLIGENT MONSTERS FROM ARYAN LEGENDS.
THOR-- ASGARDIAN GOD OF THUNDER.
I KNOW... BUT WE CAN'T IGNORE THE CONNECTION.
THIS IS A HYDRA OPERATION.
SO THIS IS ABOUT HYDRA TRYING TO CRACK THE SECRET OF IMMORTALITY?
THAT... AND DEFEATING DEATH. TWO AGENDAS WITH SIMILAR AIMS.
WANDA MAXIMOFF-- A.K.A. THE SCARLET WITCH.
THERE WERE DOZENS OF REFERENCES TO ANCIENT PEOPLE AND PLACES. GILGAMESH, ALEXANDER THE GREAT, ACHILLES, XÚ FÚ...
THESE NAMES ARE ALL TIED TO THE QUEST FOR IMMORTALITY. MANY HAVE MADE SACRIFICES IN THE VAIN HOPE OF RECEIVING THE GIFT OF GODHOOD. MY FATHER ALWAYS SCORNED SUCH REQUESTS.
GODS ARE GODS, AND MEN ARE MEN.
BUT... SURELY THE ZOMBIES AND THE RESURRECTION CORPS CAN'T BE THE END GAME. NOT FOR HYDRA. IMMORTALITY WOULDN'T BE WORTH LIVING IF YOU HAD TO BE A MONSTER.
NO. LIKE THE MANY-HEADED HYDRA ITSELF THERE ARE DIFFERENT ASPECTS TO THIS THING.
AN OLD FRIEND OF MINE DIED BRINGING ME CODED RESEARCH NOTES FROM A GERMAN SCIENTIST NAMED HOMLER. HANK PYM SPENT YEARS TRYING TO CRACK THOSE NOTES. HE WAS ONLY PARTLY SUCCESSFUL.

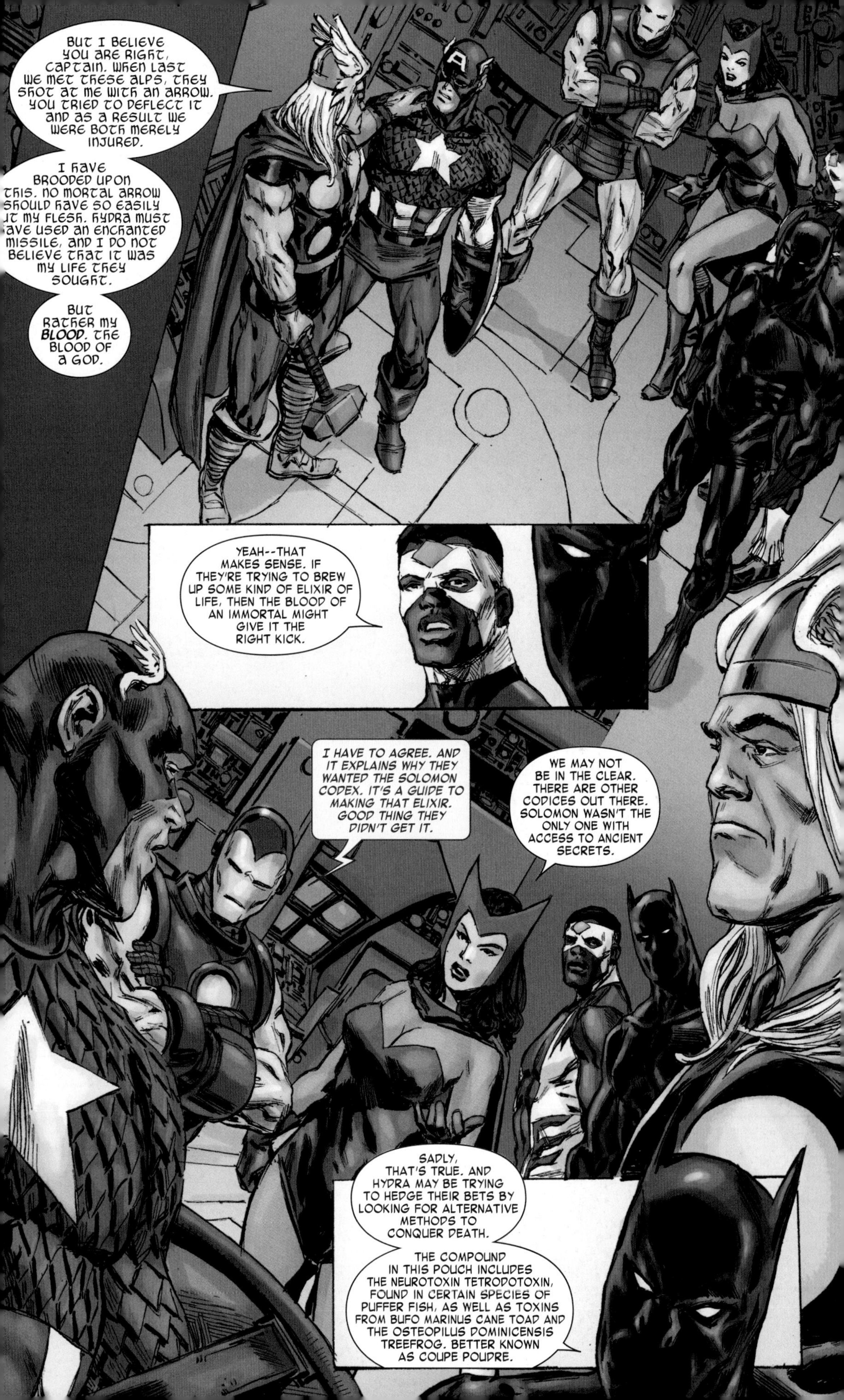
BUT I BELIEVE YOU ARE RIGHT, CAPTAIN. WHEN LAST WE MET THESE ALPS, THEY SHOT AT ME WITH AN ARROW. YOU TRIED TO DEFLECT IT AND AS A RESULT WE WERE BOTH MERELY INJURED.
I HAVE BROODED UPON THIS. NO MORTAL ARROW SHOULD HAVE SO EASILY IT MY FLESH. HYDRA MUST AVE USED AN ENCHANTED MISSILE, AND I DO NOT BELIEVE THAT IT WAS MY LIFE THEY SOUGHT.
BUT RATHER MY *BLOOD*. THE BLOOD OF A GOD.
YEAH--THAT MAKES SENSE. IF THEY'RE TRYING TO BREW UP SOME KIND OF ELIXIR OF LIFE, THEN THE BLOOD OF AN IMMORTAL MIGHT GIVE IT THE RIGHT KICK.
I HAVE TO AGREE. AND IT EXPLAINS WHY THEY WANTED THE SOLOMON CODEX. IT'S A GUIDE TO MAKING THAT ELIXIR. GOOD THING THEY DIDN'T GET IT.
WE MAY NOT BE IN THE CLEAR. THERE ARE OTHER CODICES OUT THERE. SOLOMON WASN'T THE ONLY ONE WITH ACCESS TO ANCIENT SECRETS.
SADLY, THAT'S TRUE. AND HYDRA MAY BE TRYING TO HEDGE THEIR BETS BY LOOKING FOR ALTERNATIVE METHODS TO CONQUER DEATH.
THE COMPOUND IN THIS POUCH INCLUDES THE NEUROTOXIN TETRODOTOXIN, FOUND IN CERTAIN SPECIES OF PUFFER FISH, AS WELL AS TOXINS FROM BUFO MARINUS CANE TOAD AND THE OSTEOPILUS DOMINICENSIS TREEFROG. BETTER KNOWN AS COUPE POUDRE.

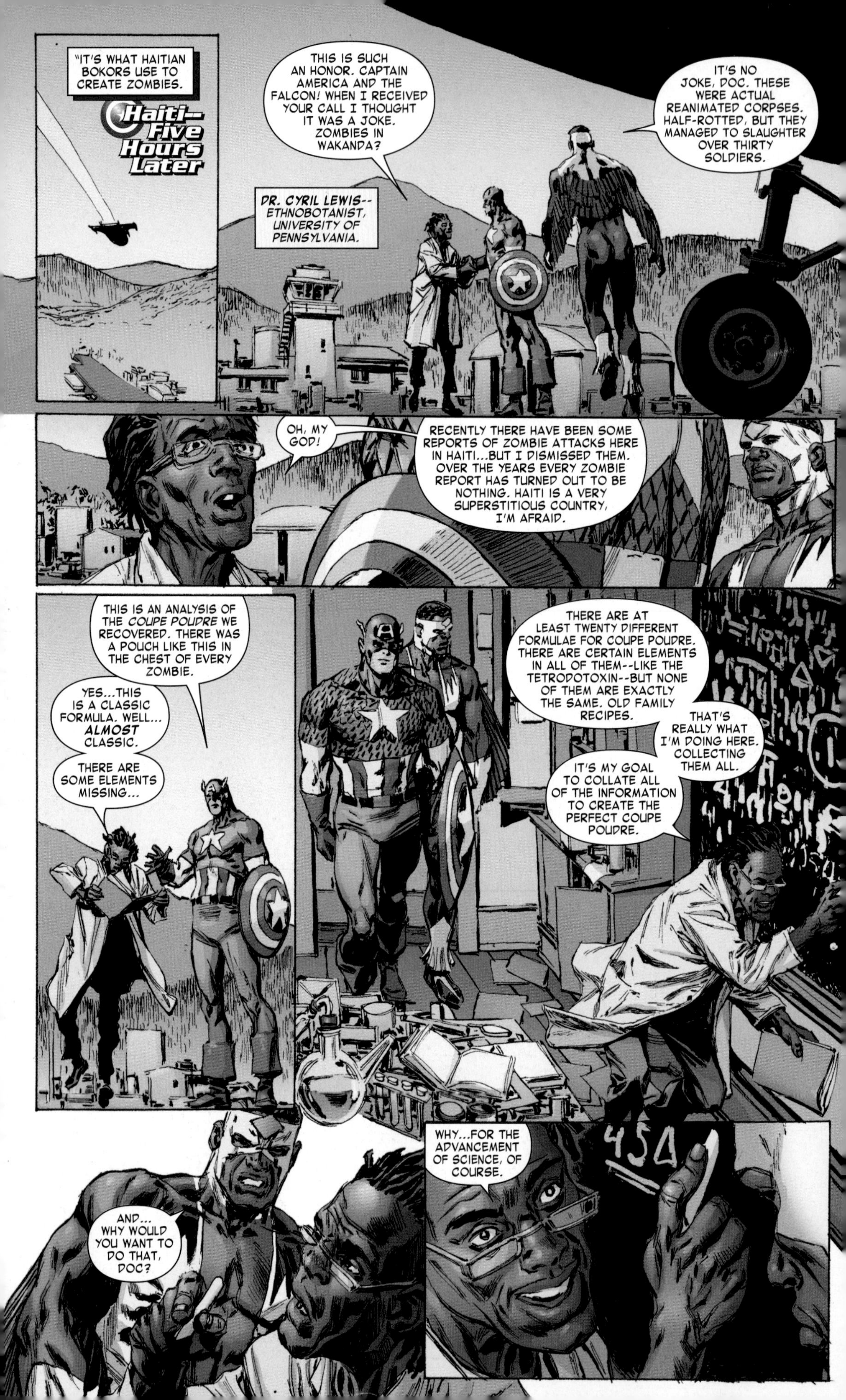

"IT'S WHAT HAITIAN BOKORS USE TO CREATE ZOMBIES.
Haiti-- Five Hours Later
THIS IS SUCH AN HONOR. CAPTAIN AMERICA AND THE FALCON! WHEN I RECEIVED YOUR CALL I THOUGHT IT WAS A JOKE. ZOMBIES IN WAKANDA?
DR. CYRIL LEWIS-- ETHNOBOTANIST, UNIVERSITY OF PENNSYLVANIA.
IT'S NO JOKE, DOC. THESE WERE ACTUAL REANIMATED CORPSES. HALF-ROTTED, BUT THEY MANAGED TO SLAUGHTER OVER THIRTY SOLDIERS.
OH, MY GOD!
RECENTLY THERE HAVE BEEN SOME REPORTS OF ZOMBIE ATTACKS HERE IN HAITI...BUT I DISMISSED THEM. OVER THE YEARS EVERY ZOMBIE REPORT HAS TURNED OUT TO BE NOTHING. HAITI IS A VERY SUPERSTITIOUS COUNTRY, I'M AFRAID.
THIS IS AN ANALYSIS OF THE *COUPE POUDRE* WE RECOVERED. THERE WAS A POUCH LIKE THIS IN THE CHEST OF EVERY ZOMBIE.
YES...THIS IS A CLASSIC FORMULA. WELL... **ALMOST** CLASSIC.
THERE ARE SOME ELEMENTS MISSING...
THERE ARE AT LEAST TWENTY DIFFERENT FORMULAE FOR COUPE POUDRE. THERE ARE CERTAIN ELEMENTS IN ALL OF THEM--LIKE THE TETRODOTOXIN--BUT NONE OF THEM ARE EXACTLY THE SAME. OLD FAMILY RECIPES.
THAT'S REALLY WHAT I'M DOING HERE. COLLECTING THEM ALL.
IT'S MY GOAL TO COLLATE ALL OF THE INFORMATION TO CREATE THE PERFECT COUPE POUDRE.
AND... WHY WOULD YOU WANT TO DO THAT, DOC?
WHY...FOR THE ADVANCEMENT OF SCIENCE, OF COURSE.

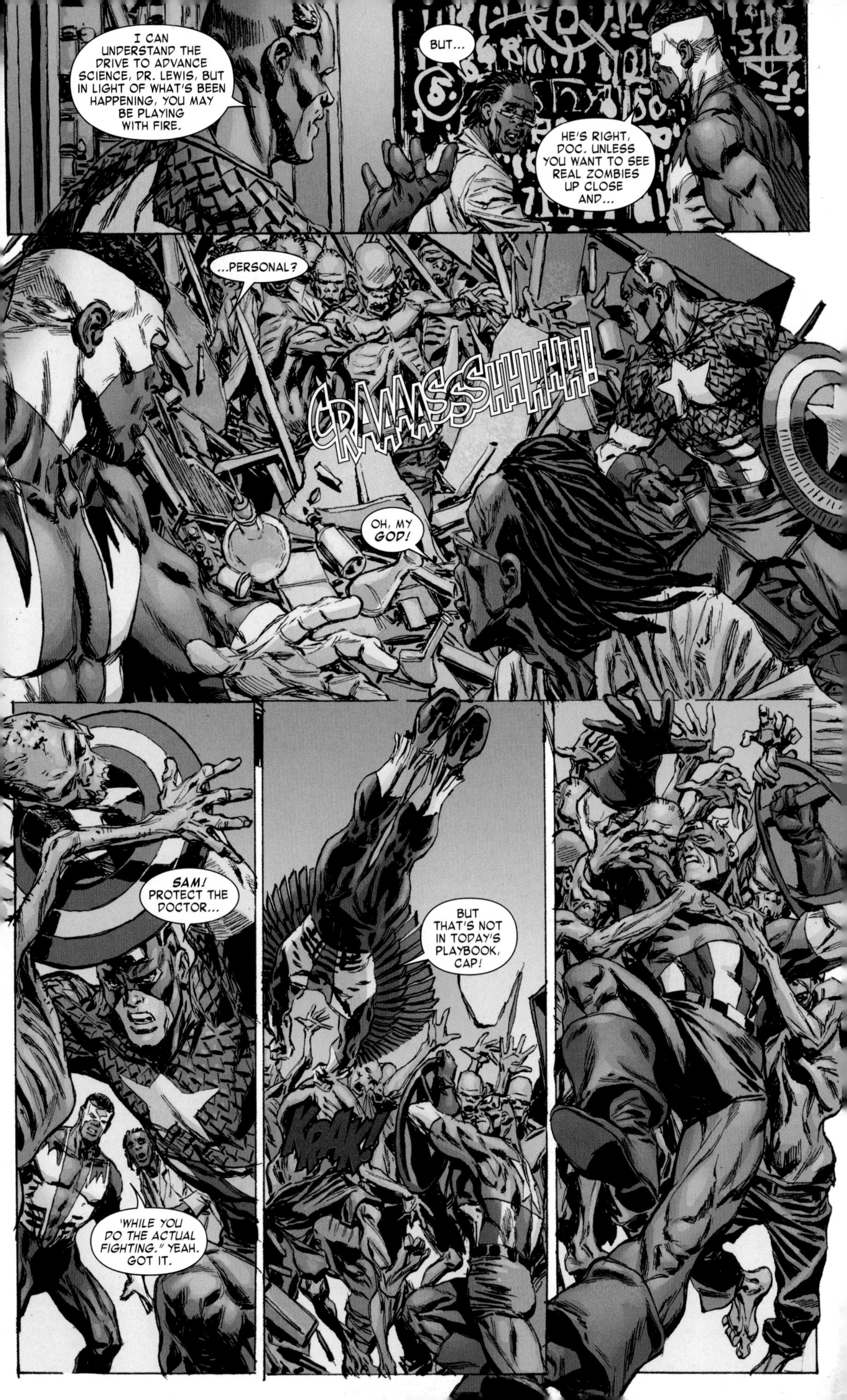

I CAN UNDERSTAND THE DRIVE TO ADVANCE SCIENCE, DR. LEWIS, BUT IN LIGHT OF WHAT'S BEEN HAPPENING, YOU MAY BE PLAYING WITH FIRE.
BUT...
HE'S RIGHT, DOC. UNLESS YOU WANT TO SEE REAL ZOMBIES UP CLOSE AND...
...PERSONAL?
CRAAAASSSHHHHHHH!
OH, MY GOD!
SAM! PROTECT THE DOCTOR...
"WHILE YOU DO THE ACTUAL FIGHTING." YEAH. GOT IT.
BUT THAT'S NOT IN TODAY'S PLAYBOOK, CAP!
KRAK!

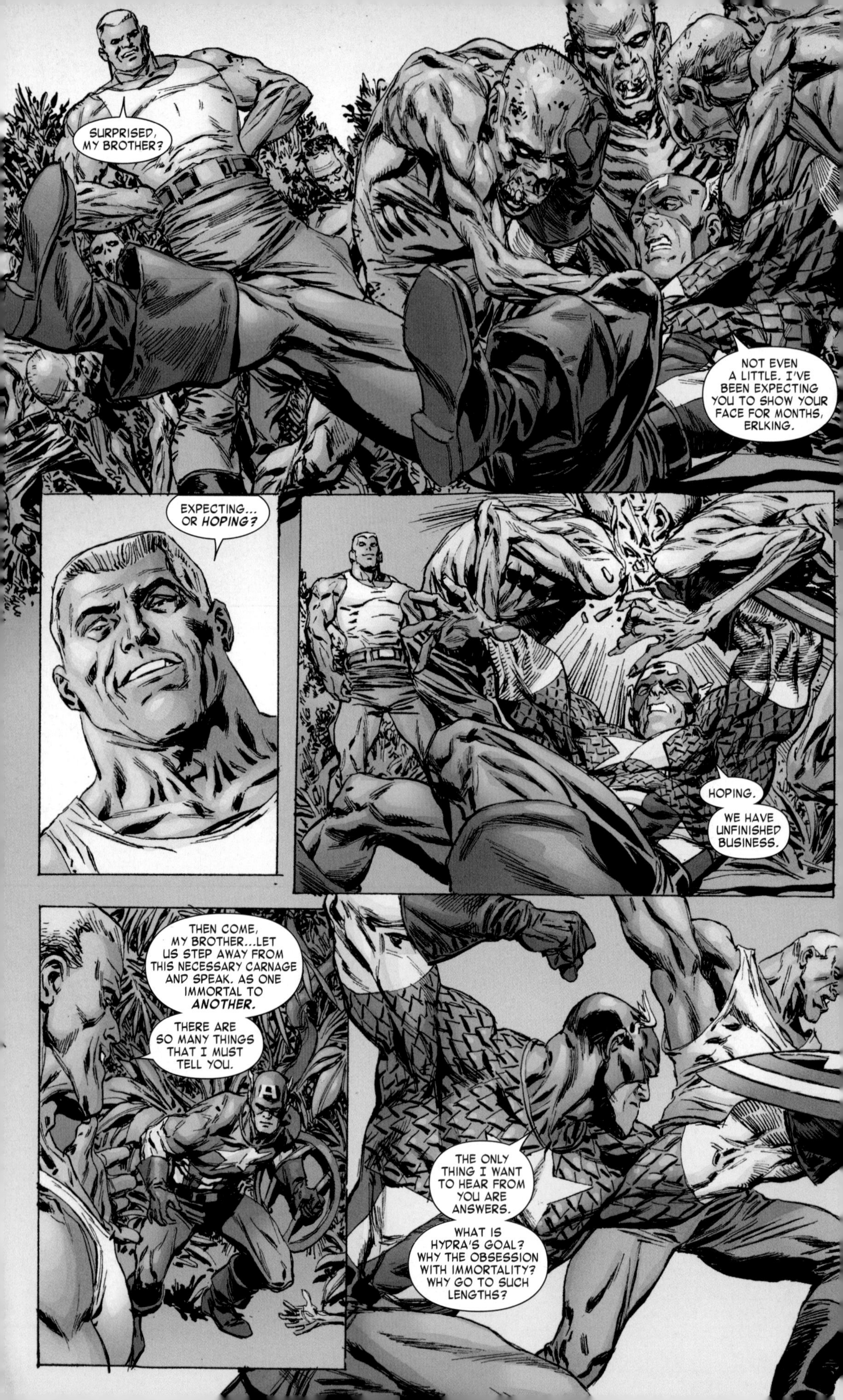
SURPRISED, MY BROTHER?
NOT EVEN A LITTLE. I'VE BEEN EXPECTING YOU TO SHOW YOUR FACE FOR MONTHS, ERLKING.
EXPECTING... OR *HOPING?*
HOPING.
WE HAVE UNFINISHED BUSINESS.
THEN COME, MY BROTHER...LET US STEP AWAY FROM THIS NECESSARY CARNAGE AND SPEAK. AS ONE IMMORTAL TO **ANOTHER.**
THERE ARE SO MANY THINGS THAT I MUST TELL YOU.
THE ONLY THING I WANT TO HEAR FROM YOU ARE ANSWERS.
WHAT IS HYDRA'S GOAL? WHY THE OBSESSION WITH IMMORTALITY? WHY GO TO SUCH LENGTHS?

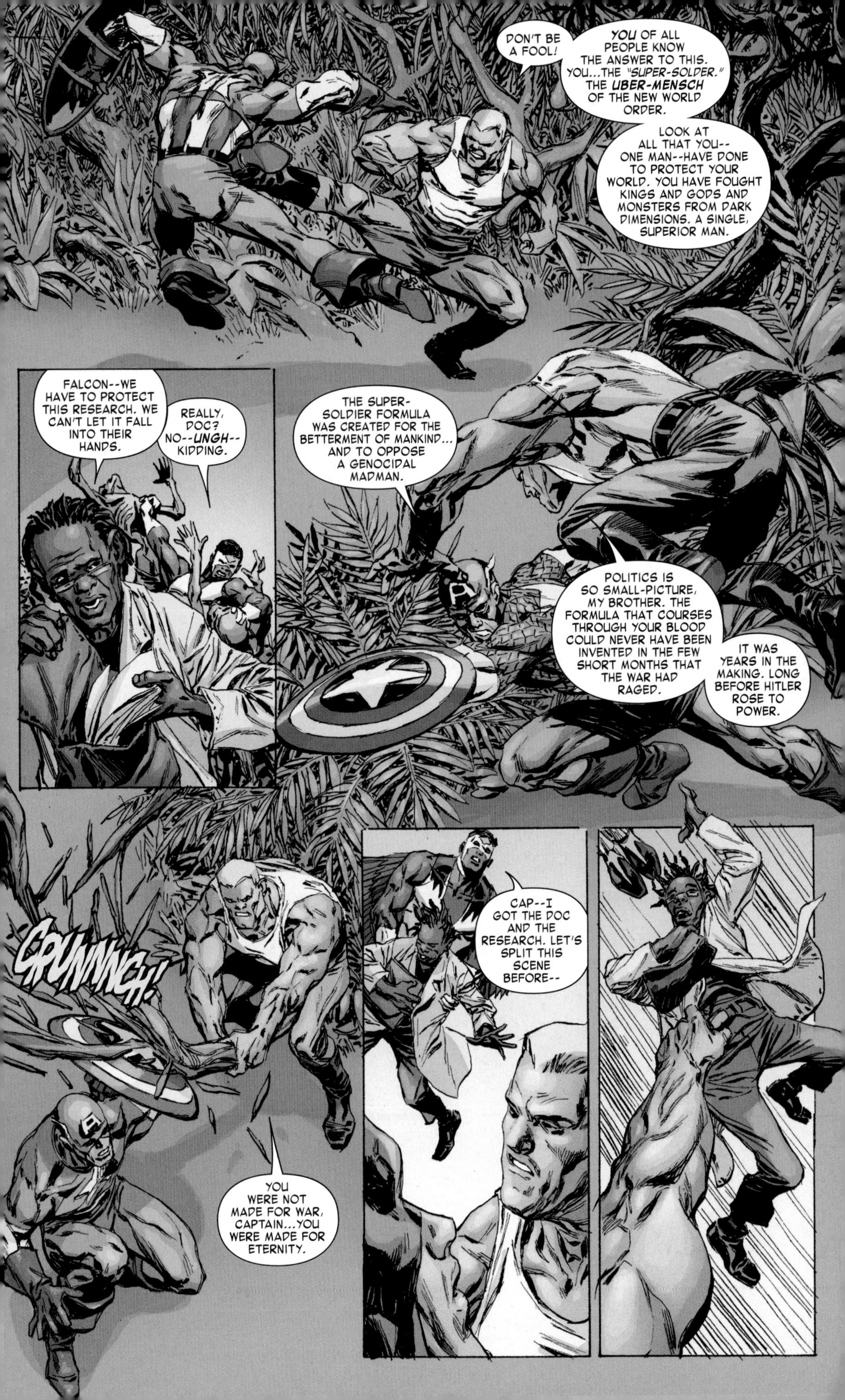
DON'T BE A FOOL!
YOU OF ALL PEOPLE KNOW THE ANSWER TO THIS. YOU...THE "SUPER-SOLDER." THE UBER-MENSCH OF THE NEW WORLD ORDER.
LOOK AT ALL THAT YOU--ONE MAN--HAVE DONE TO PROTECT YOUR WORLD. YOU HAVE FOUGHT KINGS AND GODS AND MONSTERS FROM DARK DIMENSIONS. A SINGLE, SUPERIOR MAN.
FALCON--WE HAVE TO PROTECT THIS RESEARCH. WE CAN'T LET IT FALL INTO THEIR HANDS.
REALLY, DOC? NO--UNGH--KIDDING.
THE SUPER-SOLDIER FORMULA WAS CREATED FOR THE BETTERMENT OF MANKIND... AND TO OPPOSE A GENOCIDAL MADMAN.
POLITICS IS SO SMALL-PICTURE, MY BROTHER. THE FORMULA THAT COURSES THROUGH YOUR BLOOD COULD NEVER HAVE BEEN INVENTED IN THE FEW SHORT MONTHS THAT THE WAR HAD RAGED.
IT WAS YEARS IN THE MAKING. LONG BEFORE HITLER ROSE TO POWER.
GRUNNNCH!
YOU WERE NOT MADE FOR WAR, CAPTAIN...YOU WERE MADE FOR ETERNITY.
CAP--I GOT THE DOC AND THE RESEARCH. LET'S SPLIT THIS SCENE BEFORE--

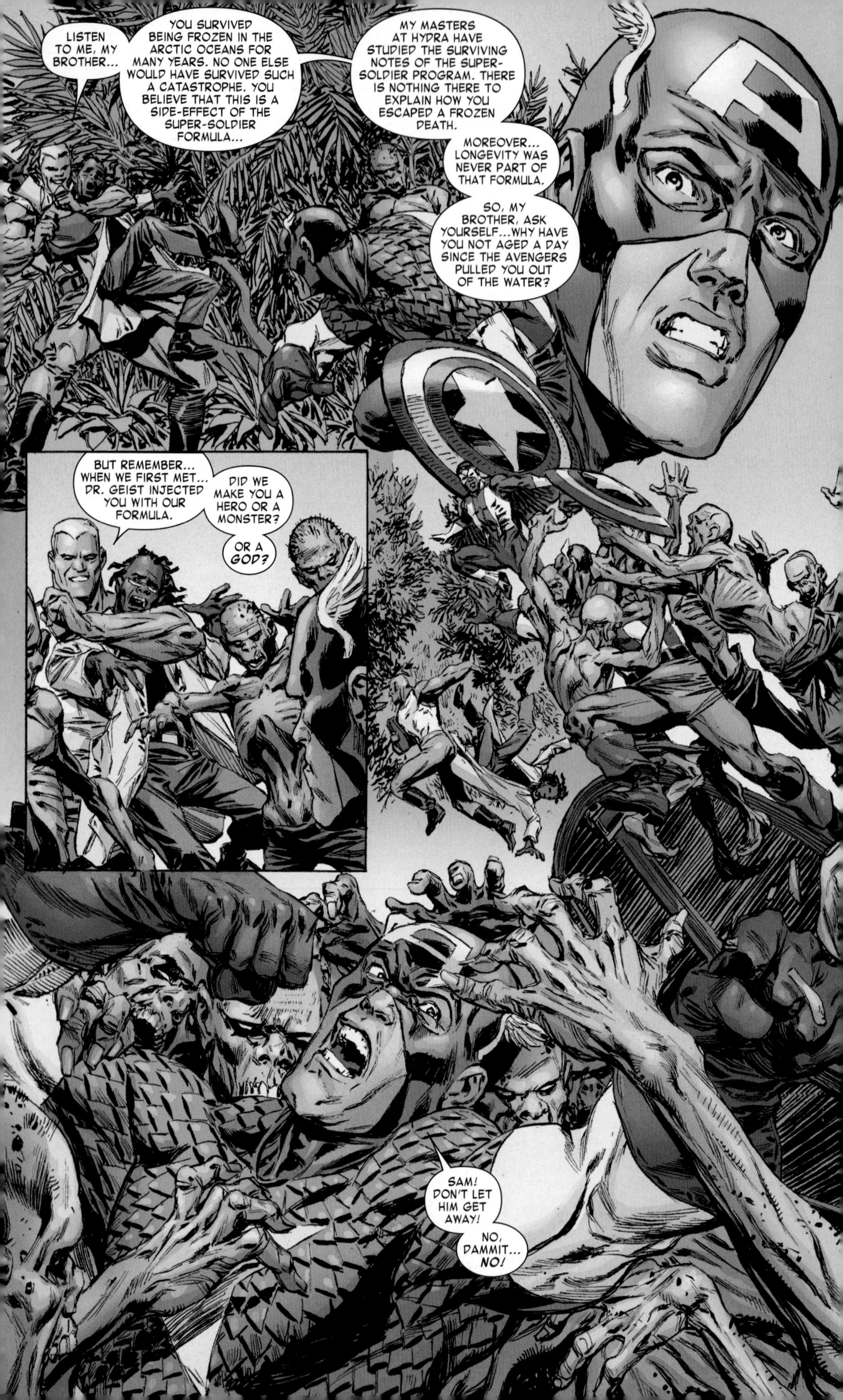
LISTEN TO ME, MY BROTHER...
YOU SURVIVED BEING FROZEN IN THE ARCTIC OCEANS FOR MANY YEARS. NO ONE ELSE WOULD HAVE SURVIVED SUCH A CATASTROPHE. YOU BELIEVE THAT THIS IS A SIDE-EFFECT OF THE SUPER-SOLDIER FORMULA...
MY MASTERS AT HYDRA HAVE STUDIED THE SURVIVING NOTES OF THE SUPER-SOLDIER PROGRAM. THERE IS NOTHING THERE TO EXPLAIN HOW YOU ESCAPED A FROZEN DEATH.
MOREOVER... LONGEVITY WAS NEVER PART OF THAT FORMULA.
SO, MY BROTHER, ASK YOURSELF...WHY HAVE YOU NOT AGED A DAY SINCE THE AVENGERS PULLED YOU OUT OF THE WATER?
BUT REMEMBER... WHEN WE FIRST MET... DR. GEIST INJECTED YOU WITH OUR FORMULA.
DID WE MAKE YOU A HERO OR A MONSTER?
OR A GOD?
SAM! DON'T LET HIM GET AWAY!
NO, DAMMIT... NO!

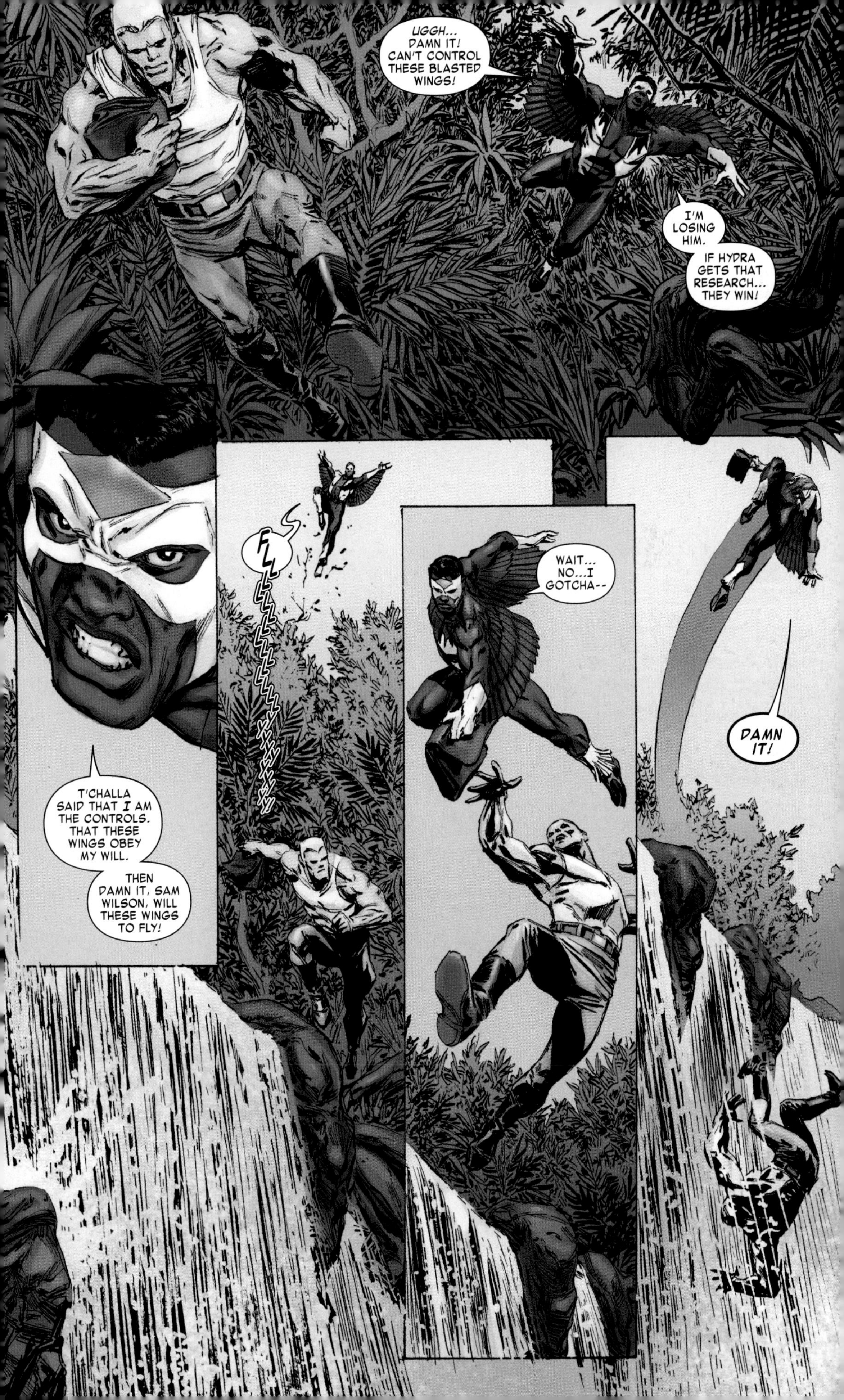
UGGH... DAMN IT! CAN'T CONTROL THESE BLASTED WINGS!
I'M LOSING HIM.
IF HYDRA GETS THAT RESEARCH... THEY WIN!
T'CHALLA SAID THAT I AM THE CONTROLS. THAT THESE WINGS OBEY MY WILL.
THEN DAMN IT, SAM WILSON, WILL THESE WINGS TO FLY!
WAIT... NO...I GOTCHA--
DAMN IT!

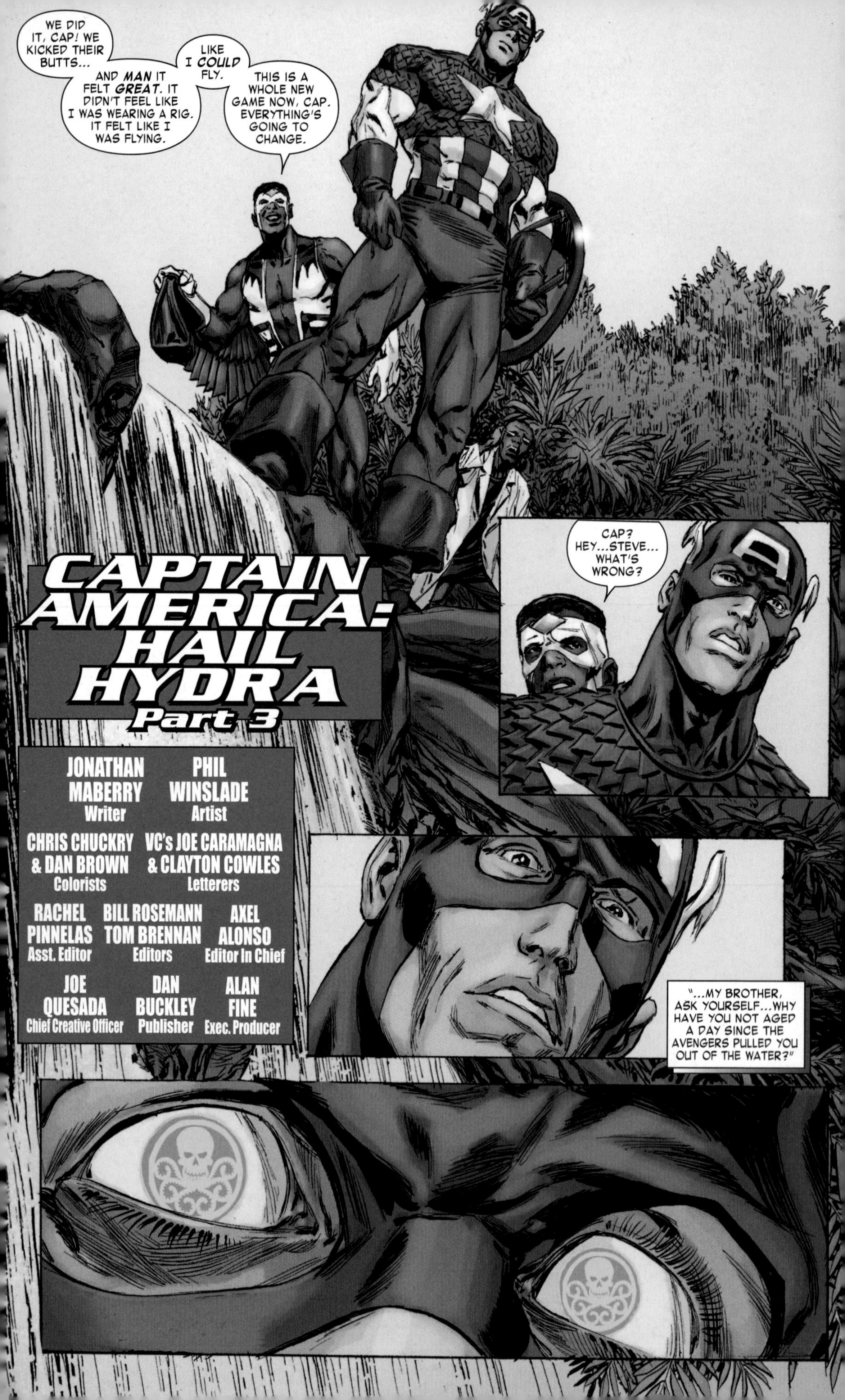
WE DID IT, CAP! WE KICKED THEIR BUTTS...
AND MAN IT FELT GREAT. IT DIDN'T FEEL LIKE I WAS WEARING A RIG. IT FELT LIKE I WAS FLYING.
LIKE I COULD FLY.
THIS IS A WHOLE NEW GAME NOW, CAP. EVERYTHING'S GOING TO CHANGE.
CAPTAIN AMERICA: HAIL HYDRA
Part 3
JONATHAN MABERRY Writer
PHIL WINSLADE Artist
CHRIS CHUCKRY & DAN BROWN Colorists
VC's JOE CARAMAGNA & CLAYTON COWLES Letterers
RACHEL PINNELAS Asst. Editor
BILL ROSEMANN TOM BRENNAN Editors
AXEL ALONSO Editor In Chief
JOE QUESADA Chief Creative Officer
DAN BUCKLEY Publisher
ALAN FINE Exec. Producer
CAP? HEY...STEVE... WHAT'S WRONG?
"...MY BROTHER, ASK YOURSELF...WHY HAVE YOU NOT AGED A DAY SINCE THE AVENGERS PULLED YOU OUT OF THE WATER?"

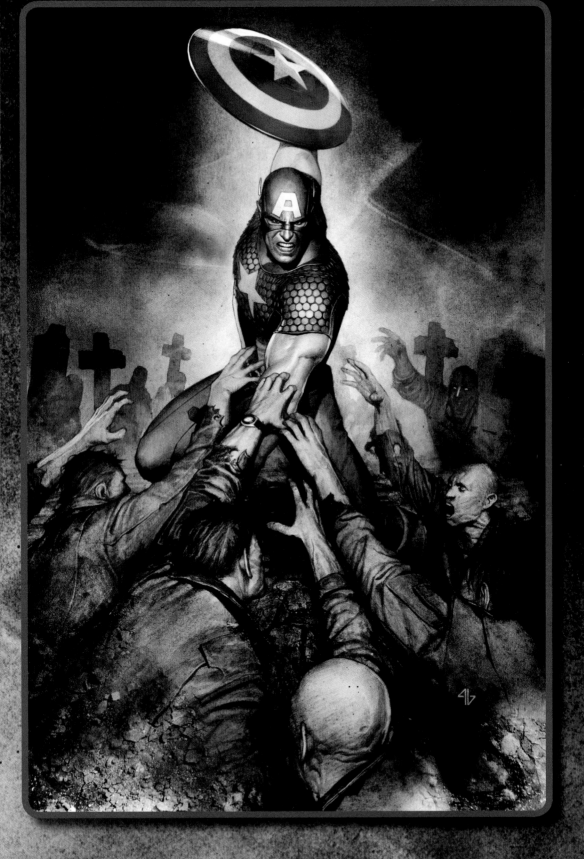

FOUR

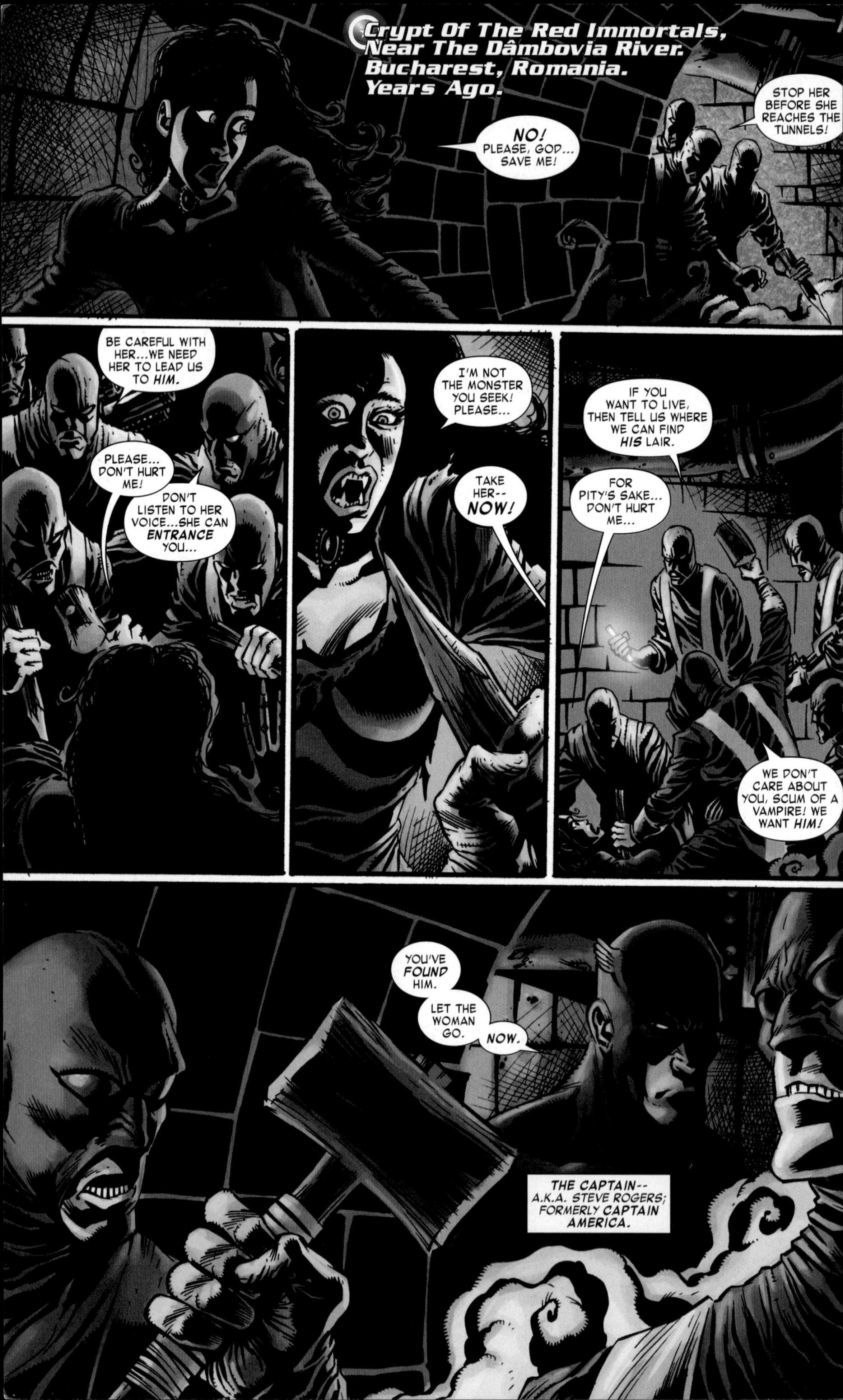
Crypt Of The Red Immortals, Near The Dâmbovia River. Bucharest, Romania. Years Ago.
NO! PLEASE, GOD... SAVE ME!
STOP HER BEFORE SHE REACHES THE TUNNELS!
BE CAREFUL WITH HER...WE NEED HER TO LEAD US TO HIM.
PLEASE... DON'T HURT ME!
DON'T LISTEN TO HER VOICE...SHE CAN ENTRANCE YOU...
I'M NOT THE MONSTER YOU SEEK! PLEASE...
TAKE HER-- NOW!
IF YOU WANT TO LIVE, THEN TELL US WHERE WE CAN FIND HIS LAIR.
FOR PITY'S SAKE... DON'T HURT ME...
WE DON'T CARE ABOUT YOU, SCUM OF A VAMPIRE! WE WANT HIM!
YOU'VE FOUND HIM.
LET THE WOMAN GO.
NOW.
THE CAPTAIN-- A.K.A. STEVE ROGERS; FORMERLY CAPTAIN AMERICA.

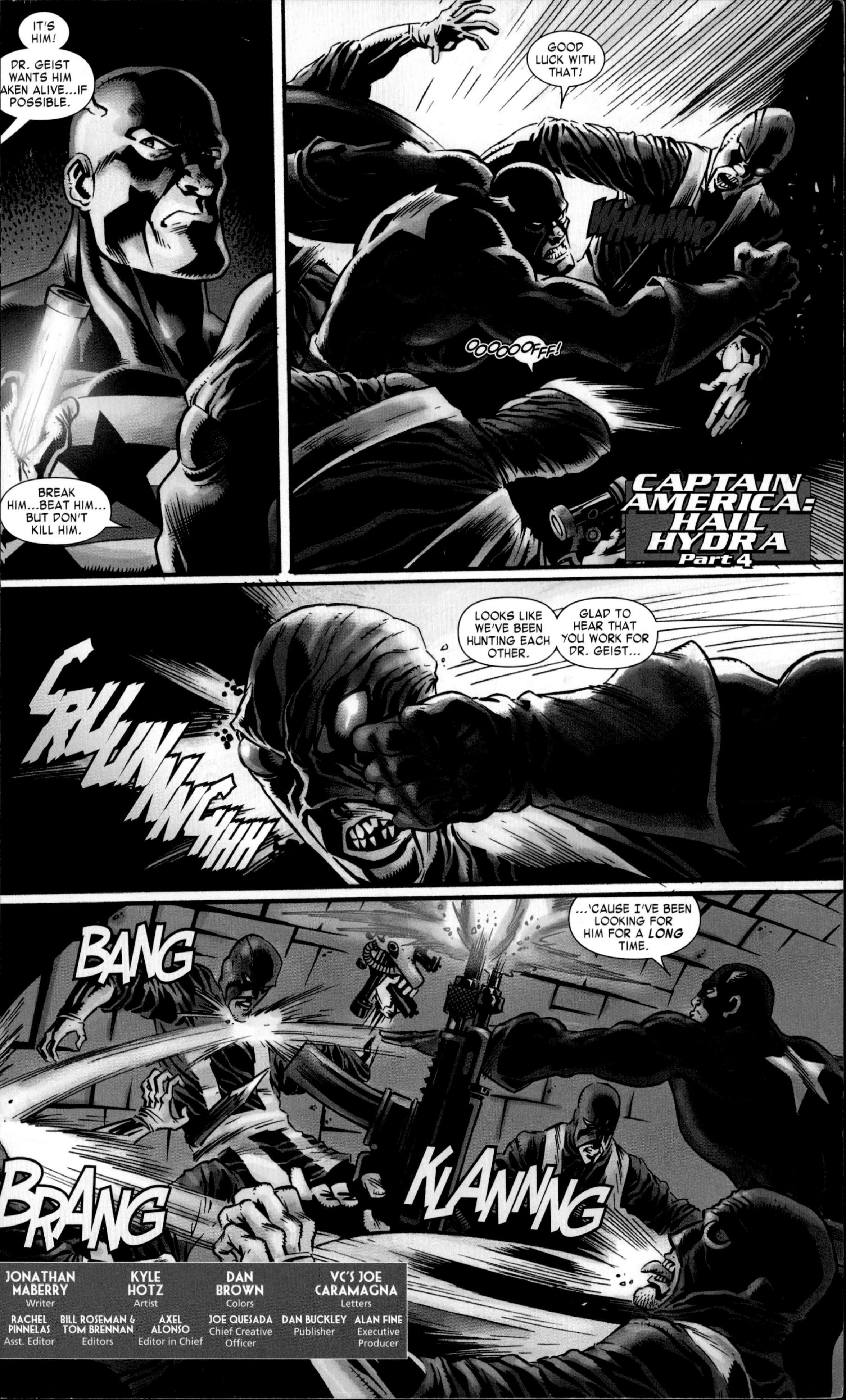
IT'S HIM!
DR. GEIST WANTS HIM TAKEN ALIVE...IF POSSIBLE.
BREAK HIM...BEAT HIM... BUT DON'T KILL HIM.
GOOD LUCK WITH THAT!
WHUMMMP
OOOOOOFFF!
CAPTAIN AMERICA: HAIL HYDRA
Part 4
LOOKS LIKE WE'VE BEEN HUNTING EACH OTHER.
GLAD TO HEAR THAT YOU WORK FOR DR. GEIST...
GRUUNNNGHHH
...'CAUSE I'VE BEEN LOOKING FOR HIM FOR A LONG TIME.
BANG
BRANG
KLANNNG
JONATHAN MABERRY Writer
KYLE HOTZ Artist
DAN BROWN Colors
VC'S JOE CARAMAGNA Letters
RACHEL PINNELAS Asst. Editor
BILL ROSEMAN & TOM BRENNAN Editors
AXEL ALONSO Editor in Chief
JOE QUESADA Chief Creative Officer
DAN BUCKLEY Publisher
ALAN FINE Executive Producer

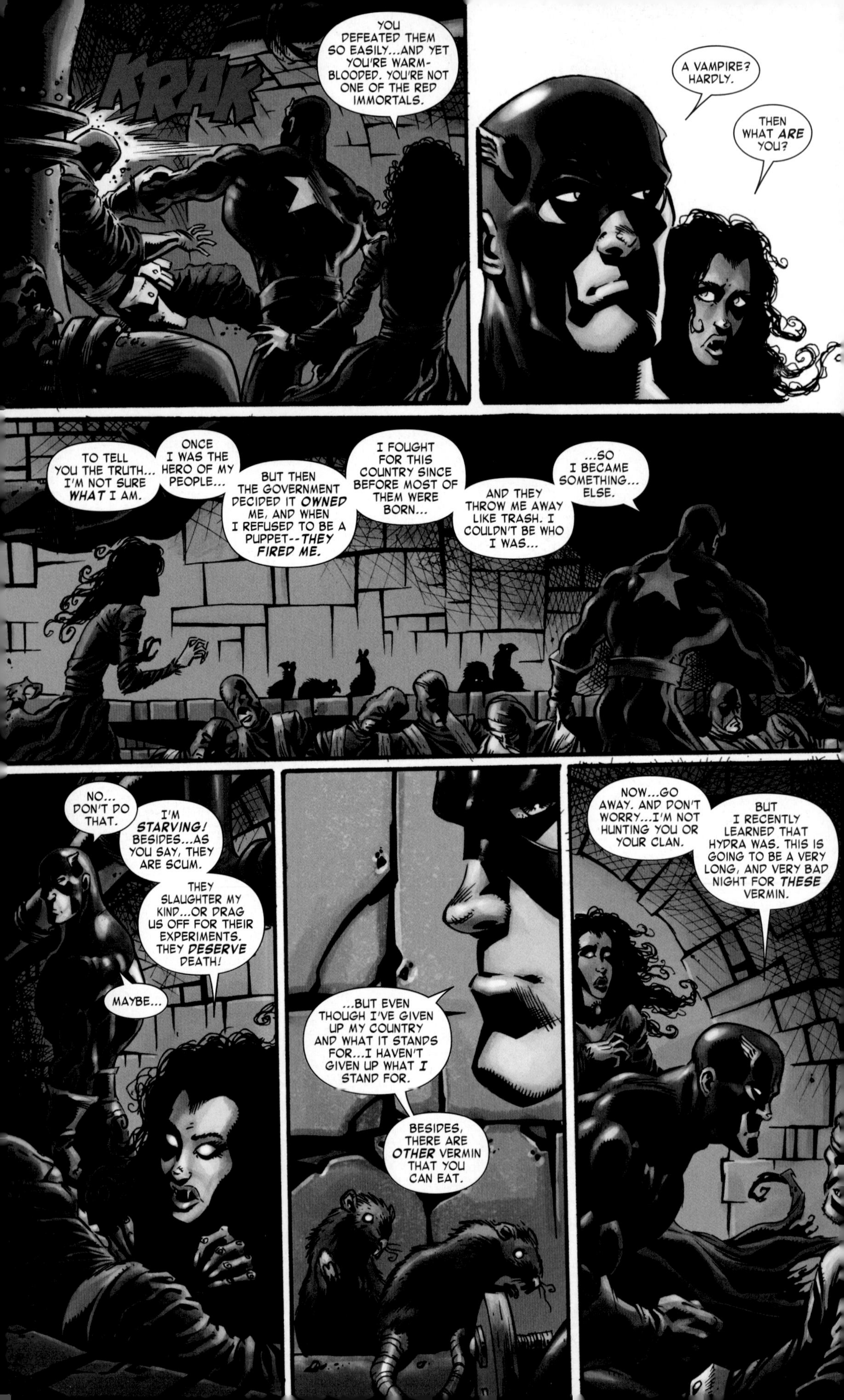
KRAK
YOU DEFEATED THEM SO EASILY...AND YET YOU'RE WARM-BLOODED. YOU'RE NOT ONE OF THE RED IMMORTALS.
A VAMPIRE? HARDLY.
THEN WHAT **ARE** YOU?
TO TELL YOU THE TRUTH... I'M NOT SURE **WHAT** I AM.
ONCE I WAS THE HERO OF MY PEOPLE...
BUT THEN THE GOVERNMENT DECIDED IT **OWNED** ME, AND WHEN I REFUSED TO BE A PUPPET--**THEY FIRED ME.**
I FOUGHT FOR THIS COUNTRY SINCE BEFORE MOST OF THEM WERE BORN...
AND THEY THROW ME AWAY LIKE TRASH. I COULDN'T BE WHO I WAS...
...SO I BECAME SOMETHING... ELSE.
NO... DON'T DO THAT.
I'M **STARVING!** BESIDES...AS YOU SAY, THEY ARE SCUM.
THEY SLAUGHTER MY KIND...OR DRAG US OFF FOR THEIR EXPERIMENTS. THEY **DESERVE** DEATH!
MAYBE...
...BUT EVEN THOUGH I'VE GIVEN UP MY COUNTRY AND WHAT IT STANDS FOR...I HAVEN'T GIVEN UP WHAT **I** STAND FOR.
BESIDES, THERE ARE **OTHER** VERMIN THAT YOU CAN EAT.
NOW...GO AWAY. AND DON'T WORRY...I'M NOT HUNTING YOU OR YOUR CLAN.
BUT I RECENTLY LEARNED THAT HYDRA WAS. THIS IS GOING TO BE A VERY LONG, AND VERY BAD NIGHT FOR **THESE** VERMIN.

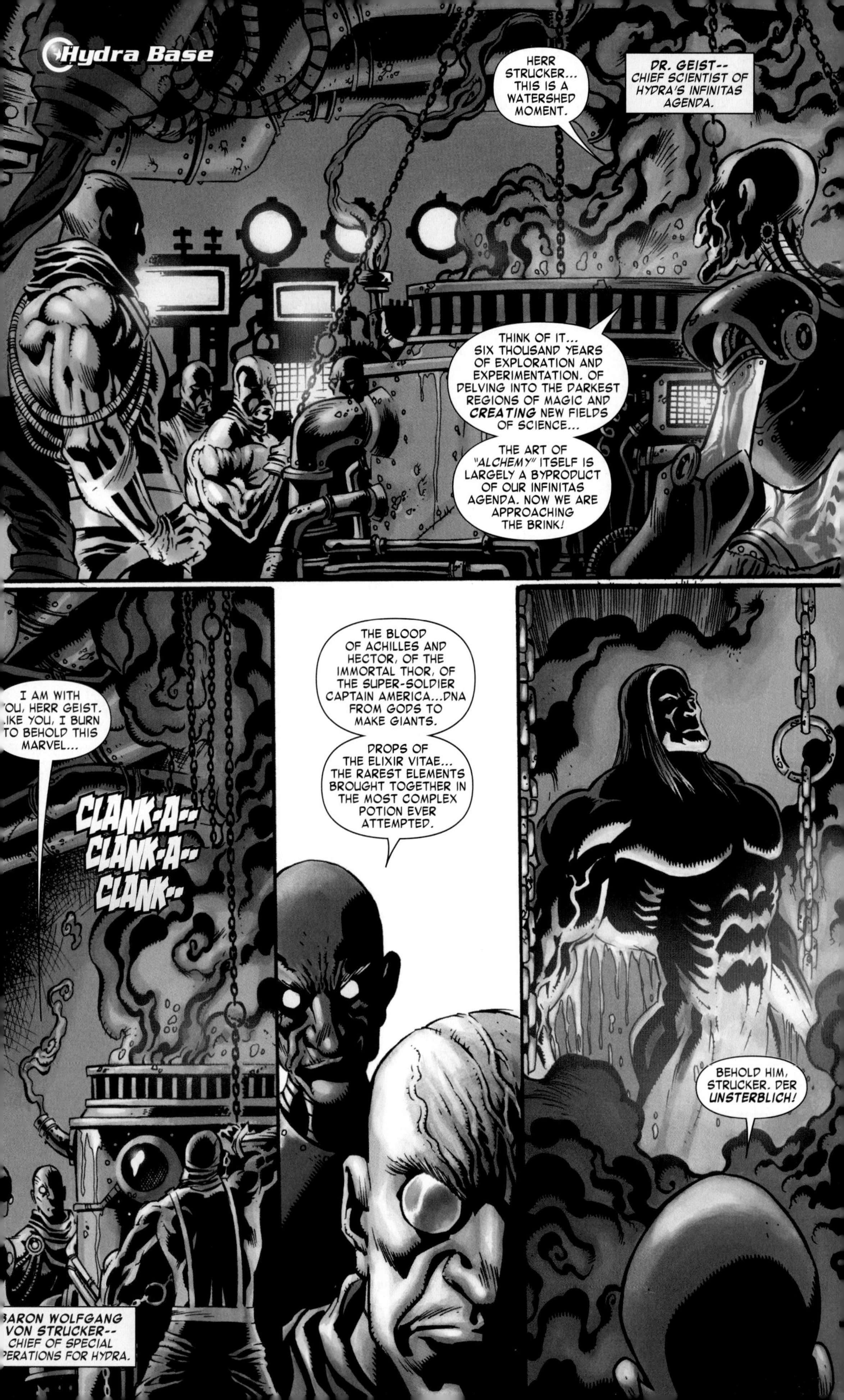
Hydra Base
HERR STRUCKER... THIS IS A WATERSHED MOMENT.
DR. GEIST-- CHIEF SCIENTIST OF HYDRA'S INFINITAS AGENDA.
THINK OF IT... SIX THOUSAND YEARS OF EXPLORATION AND EXPERIMENTATION. OF DELVING INTO THE DARKEST REGIONS OF MAGIC AND CREATING NEW FIELDS OF SCIENCE...
THE ART OF "ALCHEMY" ITSELF IS LARGELY A BYPRODUCT OF OUR INFINITAS AGENDA. NOW WE ARE APPROACHING THE BRINK!
I AM WITH YOU, HERR GEIST. LIKE YOU, I BURN TO BEHOLD THIS MARVEL...
CLANK-A-- CLANK-A-- CLANK--
BARON WOLFGANG VON STRUCKER-- CHIEF OF SPECIAL OPERATIONS FOR HYDRA.
THE BLOOD OF ACHILLES AND HECTOR, OF THE IMMORTAL THOR, OF THE SUPER-SOLDIER CAPTAIN AMERICA...DNA FROM GODS TO MAKE GIANTS.
DROPS OF THE ELIXIR VITAE... THE RAREST ELEMENTS BROUGHT TOGETHER IN THE MOST COMPLEX POTION EVER ATTEMPTED.
BEHOLD HIM, STRUCKER. DER UNSTERBLICH!

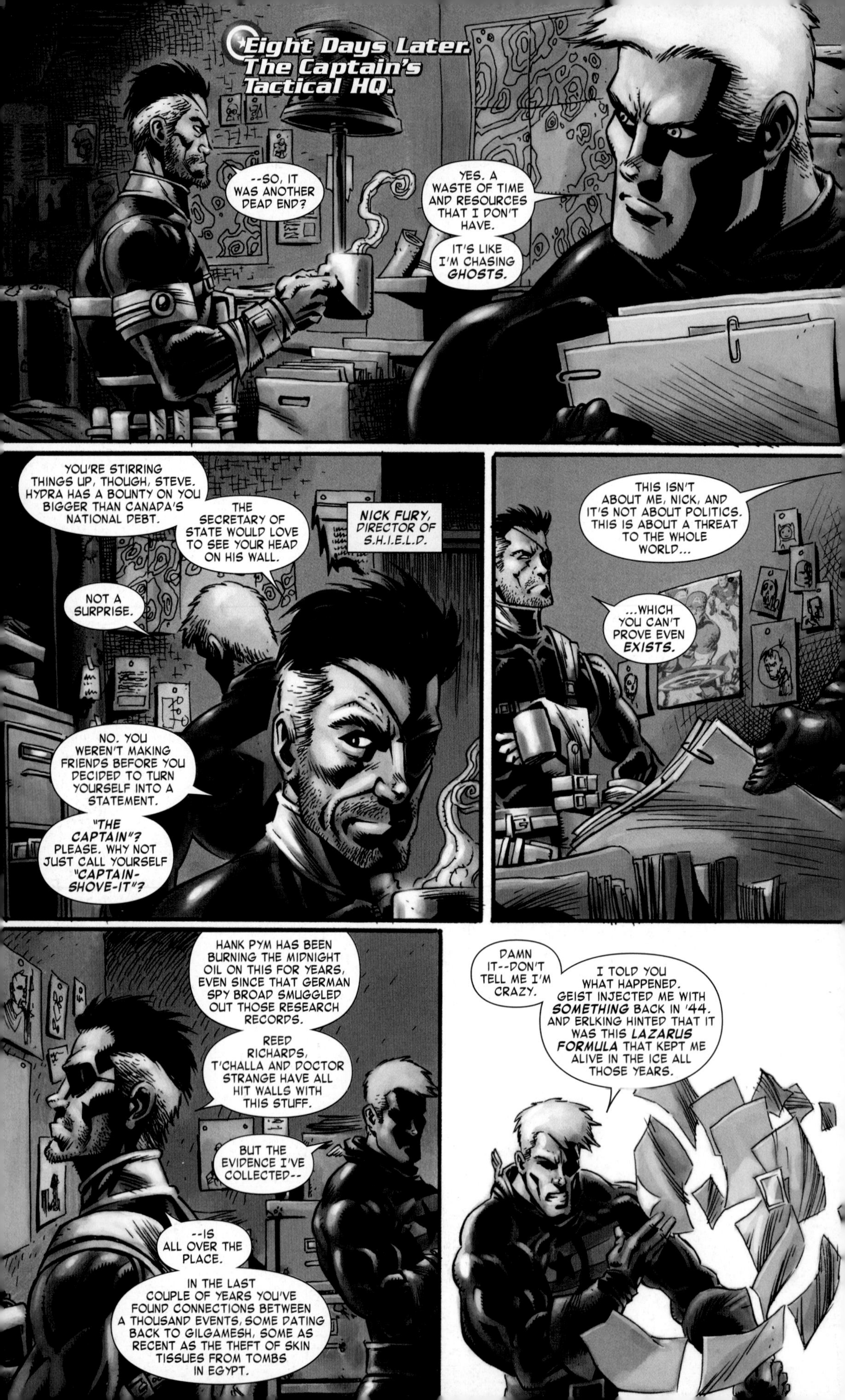
Eight Days Later. The Captain's Tactical HQ.
--SO, IT WAS ANOTHER DEAD END?
YES. A WASTE OF TIME AND RESOURCES THAT I DON'T HAVE.
IT'S LIKE I'M CHASING GHOSTS.
YOU'RE STIRRING THINGS UP, THOUGH, STEVE. HYDRA HAS A BOUNTY ON YOU BIGGER THAN CANADA'S NATIONAL DEBT.
THE SECRETARY OF STATE WOULD LOVE TO SEE YOUR HEAD ON HIS WALL.
NICK FURY, DIRECTOR OF S.H.I.E.L.D.
NOT A SURPRISE.
NO. YOU WEREN'T MAKING FRIENDS BEFORE YOU DECIDED TO TURN YOURSELF INTO A STATEMENT.
"THE CAPTAIN"? PLEASE. WHY NOT JUST CALL YOURSELF "CAPTAIN-SHOVE-IT"?
THIS ISN'T ABOUT ME, NICK, AND IT'S NOT ABOUT POLITICS. THIS IS ABOUT A THREAT TO THE WHOLE WORLD...
...WHICH YOU CAN'T PROVE EVEN EXISTS.
HANK PYM HAS BEEN BURNING THE MIDNIGHT OIL ON THIS FOR YEARS, EVEN SINCE THAT GERMAN SPY BROAD SMUGGLED OUT THOSE RESEARCH RECORDS.
REED RICHARDS, T'CHALLA AND DOCTOR STRANGE HAVE ALL HIT WALLS WITH THIS STUFF.
BUT THE EVIDENCE I'VE COLLECTED--
--IS ALL OVER THE PLACE.
IN THE LAST COUPLE OF YEARS YOU'VE FOUND CONNECTIONS BETWEEN A THOUSAND EVENTS, SOME DATING BACK TO GILGAMESH, SOME AS RECENT AS THE THEFT OF SKIN TISSUES FROM TOMBS IN EGYPT.
DAMN IT--DON'T TELL ME I'M CRAZY.
I TOLD YOU WHAT HAPPENED. GEIST INJECTED ME WITH SOMETHING BACK IN '44. AND ERLKING HINTED THAT IT WAS THIS LAZARUS FORMULA THAT KEPT ME ALIVE IN THE ICE ALL THOSE YEARS.

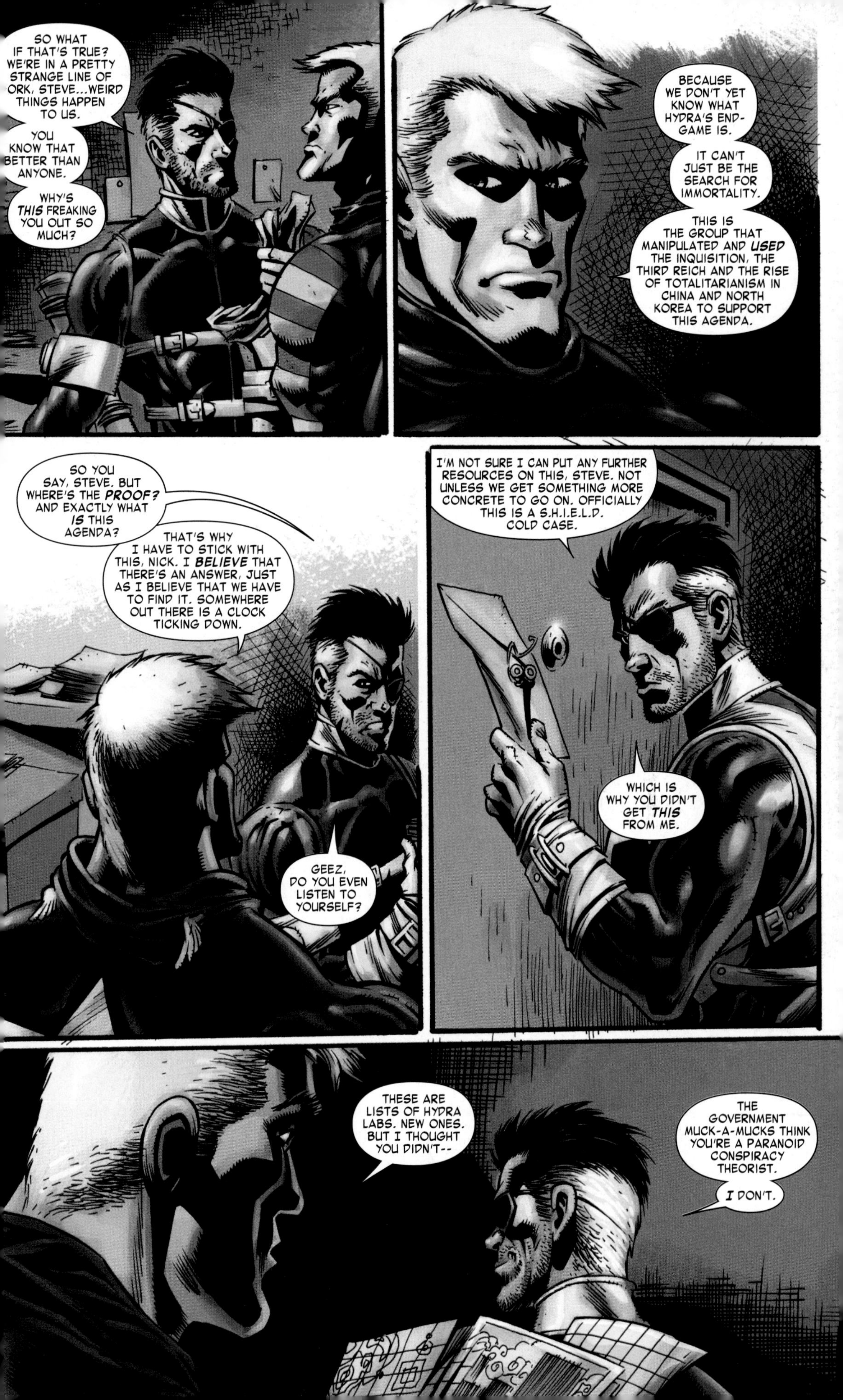

SO WHAT IF THAT'S TRUE? WE'RE IN A PRETTY STRANGE LINE OF ORK, STEVE...WEIRD THINGS HAPPEN TO US.
YOU KNOW THAT BETTER THAN ANYONE.
WHY'S THIS FREAKING YOU OUT SO MUCH?
BECAUSE WE DON'T YET KNOW WHAT HYDRA'S END-GAME IS.
IT CAN'T JUST BE THE SEARCH FOR IMMORTALITY.
THIS IS THE GROUP THAT MANIPULATED AND USED THE INQUISITION, THE THIRD REICH AND THE RISE OF TOTALITARIANISM IN CHINA AND NORTH KOREA TO SUPPORT THIS AGENDA.
SO YOU SAY, STEVE. BUT WHERE'S THE PROOF? AND EXACTLY WHAT IS THIS AGENDA?
THAT'S WHY I HAVE TO STICK WITH THIS, NICK. I BELIEVE THAT THERE'S AN ANSWER, JUST AS I BELIEVE THAT WE HAVE TO FIND IT. SOMEWHERE OUT THERE IS A CLOCK TICKING DOWN.
GEEZ, DO YOU EVEN LISTEN TO YOURSELF?
I'M NOT SURE I CAN PUT ANY FURTHER RESOURCES ON THIS, STEVE. NOT UNLESS WE GET SOMETHING MORE CONCRETE TO GO ON. OFFICIALLY THIS IS A S.H.I.E.L.D. COLD CASE.
WHICH IS WHY YOU DIDN'T GET THIS FROM ME.
THESE ARE LISTS OF HYDRA LABS. NEW ONES. BUT I THOUGHT YOU DIDN'T--
THE GOVERNMENT MUCK-A-MUCKS THINK YOU'RE A PARANOID CONSPIRACY THEORIST.
I DON'T.

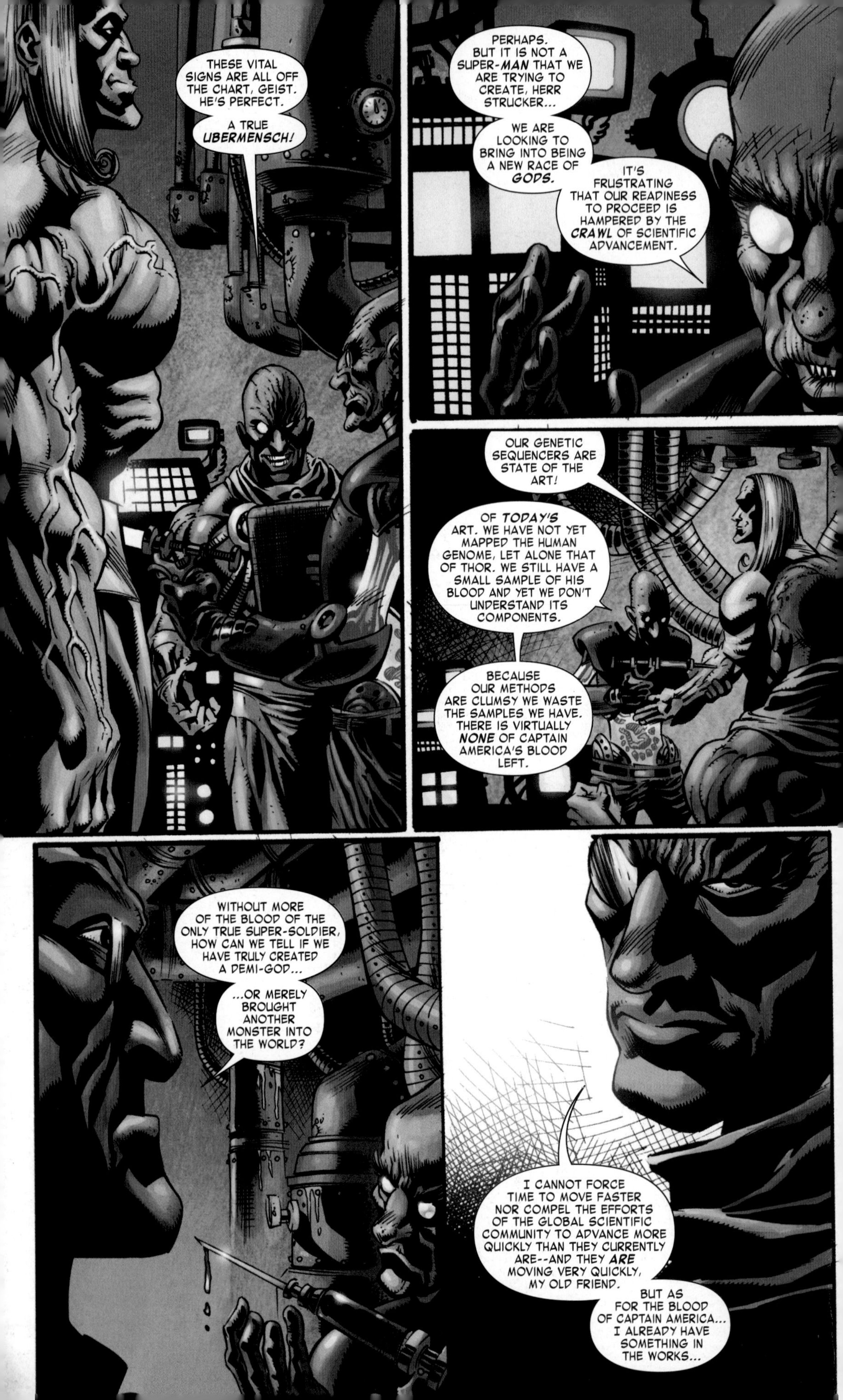
THESE VITAL SIGNS ARE ALL OFF THE CHART, GEIST. HE'S PERFECT.
A TRUE UBERMENSCH!
PERHAPS. BUT IT IS NOT A SUPER-MAN THAT WE ARE TRYING TO CREATE, HERR STRUCKER...
WE ARE LOOKING TO BRING INTO BEING A NEW RACE OF GODS.
IT'S FRUSTRATING THAT OUR READINESS TO PROCEED IS HAMPERED BY THE CRAWL OF SCIENTIFIC ADVANCEMENT.
OUR GENETIC SEQUENCERS ARE STATE OF THE ART!
OF TODAY'S ART. WE HAVE NOT YET MAPPED THE HUMAN GENOME, LET ALONE THAT OF THOR. WE STILL HAVE A SMALL SAMPLE OF HIS BLOOD AND YET WE DON'T UNDERSTAND ITS COMPONENTS.
BECAUSE OUR METHODS ARE CLUMSY WE WASTE THE SAMPLES WE HAVE. THERE IS VIRTUALLY NONE OF CAPTAIN AMERICA'S BLOOD LEFT.
WITHOUT MORE OF THE BLOOD OF THE ONLY TRUE SUPER-SOLDIER, HOW CAN WE TELL IF WE HAVE TRULY CREATED A DEMI-GOD...
...OR MERELY BROUGHT ANOTHER MONSTER INTO THE WORLD?
I CANNOT FORCE TIME TO MOVE FASTER NOR COMPEL THE EFFORTS OF THE GLOBAL SCIENTIFIC COMMUNITY TO ADVANCE MORE QUICKLY THAN THEY CURRENTLY ARE--AND THEY ARE MOVING VERY QUICKLY, MY OLD FRIEND.
BUT AS FOR THE BLOOD OF CAPTAIN AMERICA... I ALREADY HAVE SOMETHING IN THE WORKS...

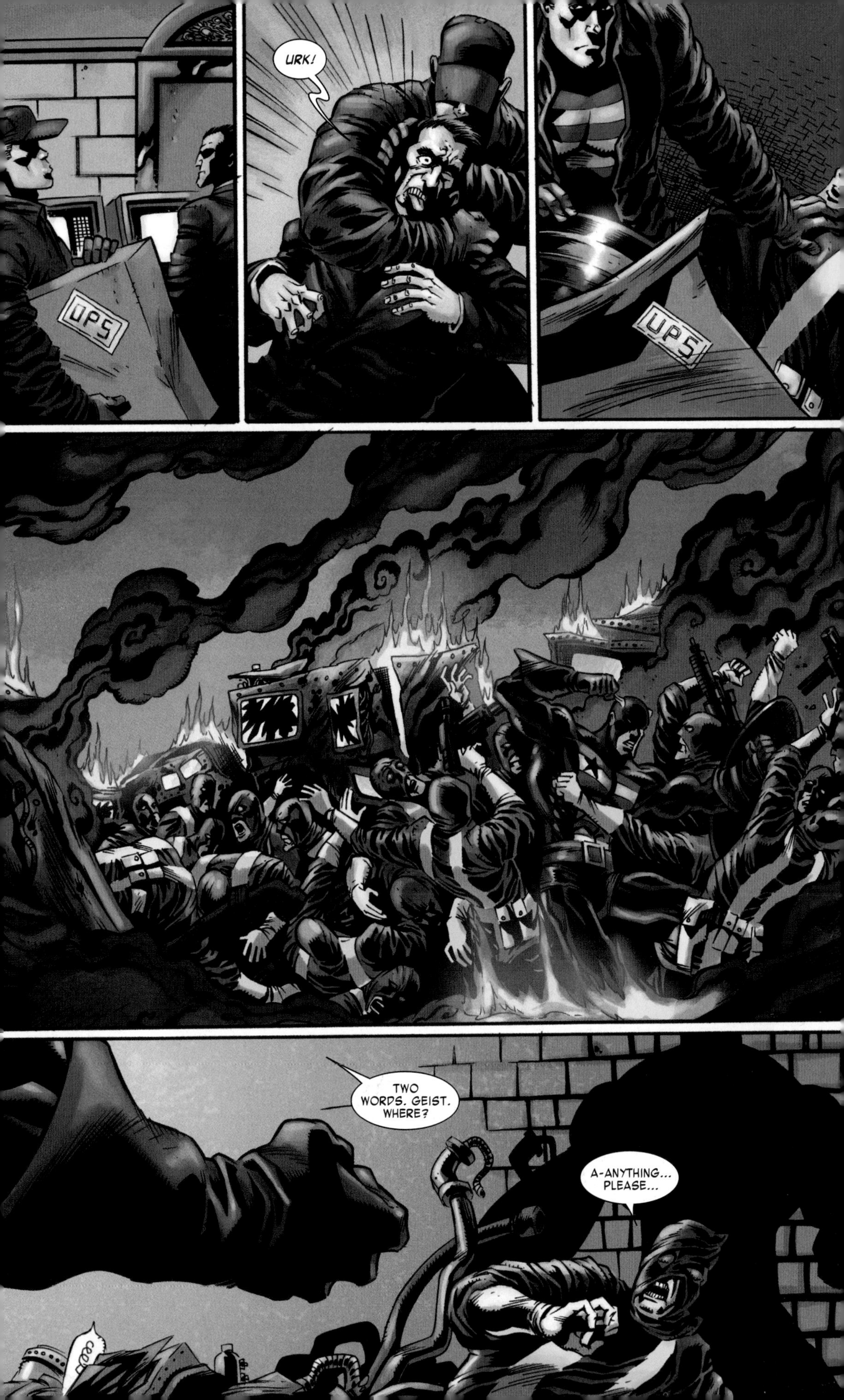
URK!
TWO WORDS. GEIST. WHERE?
A-ANYTHING... PLEASE...

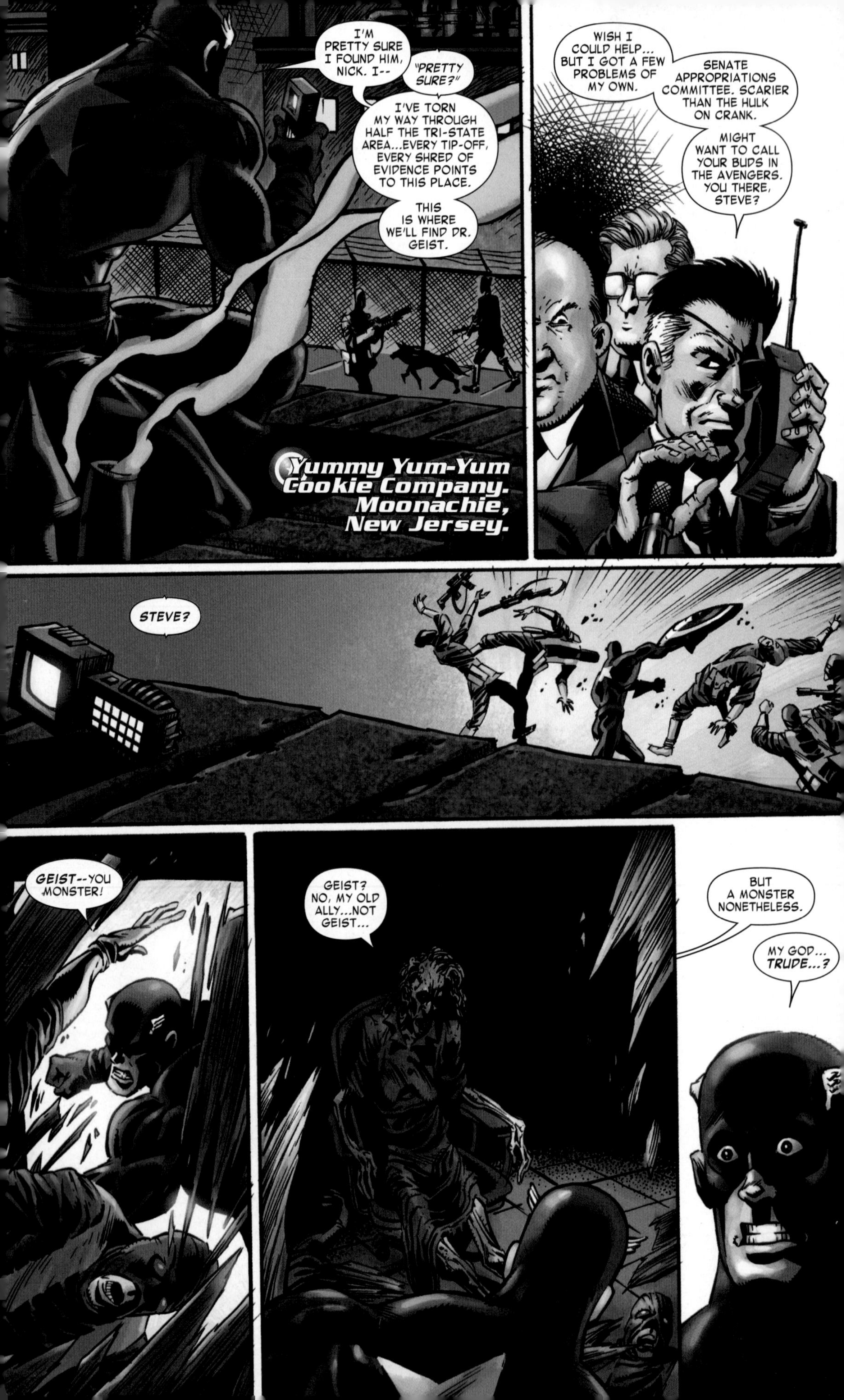

Yummy Yum-Yum Cookie Company. Moonachie, New Jersey.
I'M PRETTY SURE I FOUND HIM, NICK. I--
"PRETTY SURE?"
I'VE TORN MY WAY THROUGH HALF THE TRI-STATE AREA...EVERY TIP-OFF, EVERY SHRED OF EVIDENCE POINTS TO THIS PLACE.
THIS IS WHERE WE'LL FIND DR. GEIST.
WISH I COULD HELP... BUT I GOT A FEW PROBLEMS OF MY OWN.
SENATE APPROPRIATIONS COMMITTEE. SCARIER THAN THE HULK ON CRANK.
MIGHT WANT TO CALL YOUR BUDS IN THE AVENGERS. YOU THERE, STEVE?
STEVE?
GEIST--YOU MONSTER!
GEIST? NO, MY OLD ALLY...NOT GEIST...
BUT A MONSTER NONETHELESS.
MY GOD... TRUDE...?

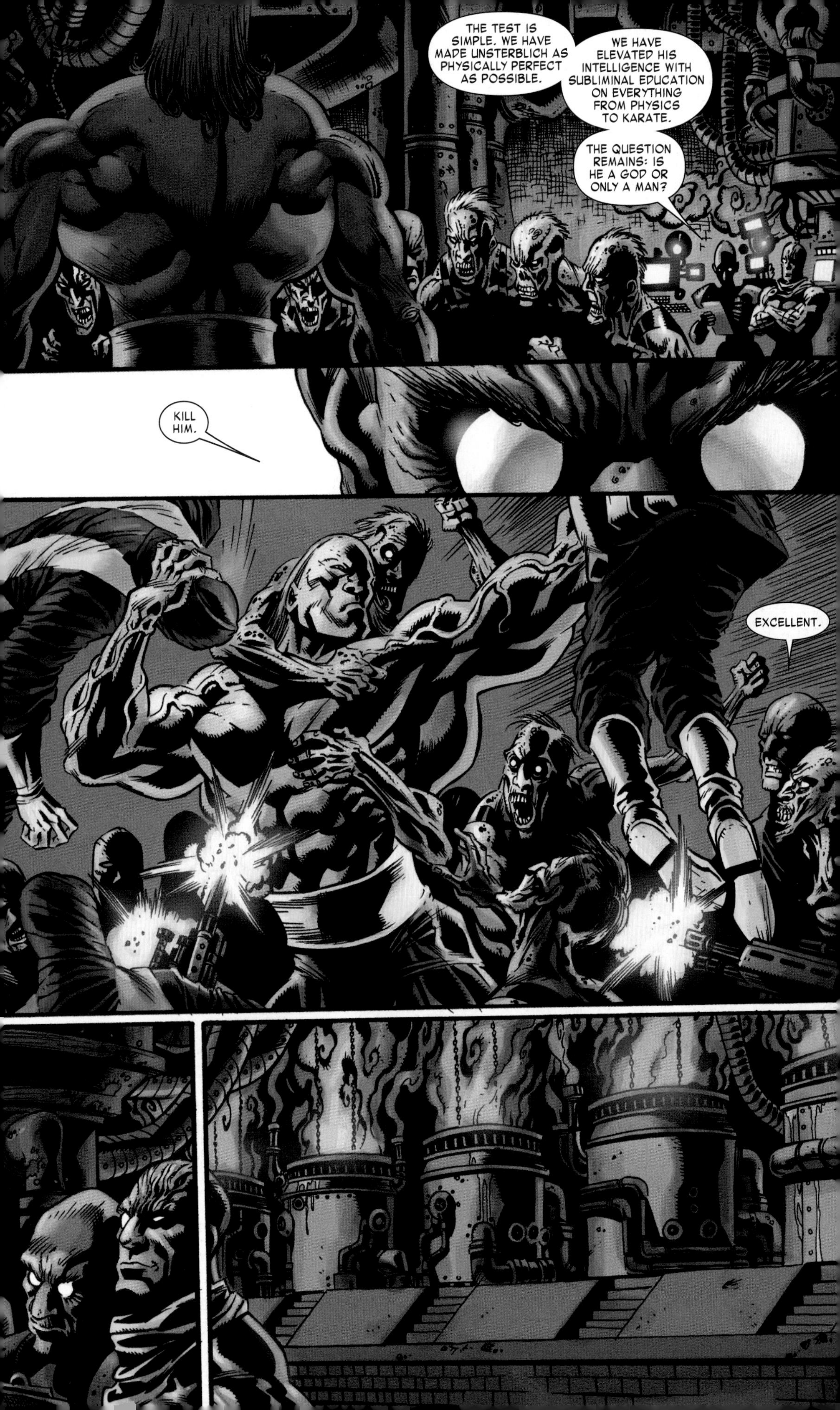
THE TEST IS SIMPLE. WE HAVE MADE UNSTERBLICH AS PHYSICALLY PERFECT AS POSSIBLE.
WE HAVE ELEVATED HIS INTELLIGENCE WITH SUBLIMINAL EDUCATION ON EVERYTHING FROM PHYSICS TO KARATE.
THE QUESTION REMAINS: IS HE A GOD OR ONLY A MAN?
KILL HIM.
EXCELLENT.

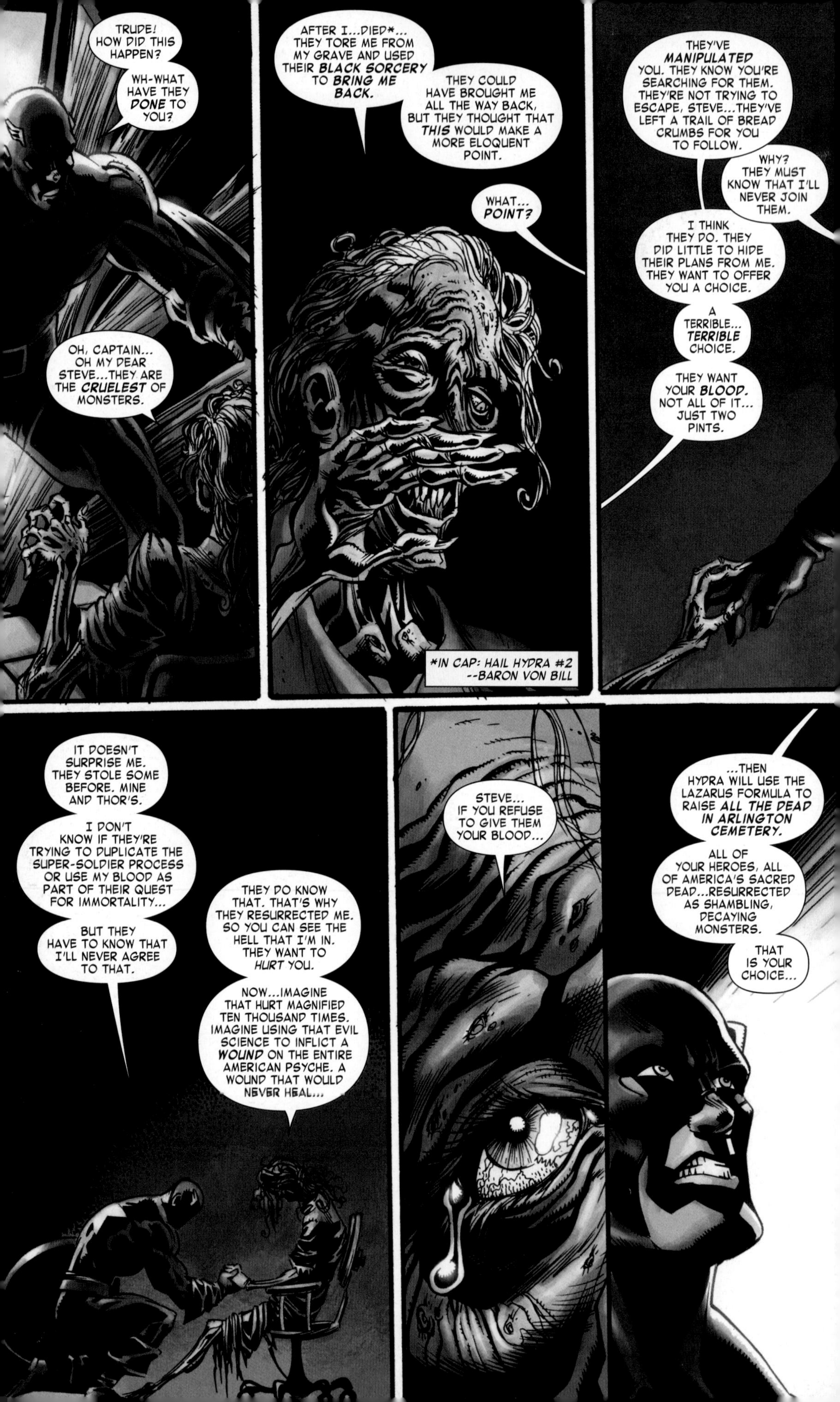
TRUDE! HOW DID THIS HAPPEN?
WH-WHAT HAVE THEY DONE TO YOU?
OH, CAPTAIN... OH MY DEAR STEVE...THEY ARE THE CRUELEST OF MONSTERS.
AFTER I...DIED*... THEY TORE ME FROM MY GRAVE AND USED THEIR BLACK SORCERY TO BRING ME BACK.
THEY COULD HAVE BROUGHT ME ALL THE WAY BACK, BUT THEY THOUGHT THAT THIS WOULD MAKE A MORE ELOQUENT POINT.
WHAT... POINT?
*IN CAP: HAIL HYDRA #2 --BARON VON BILL
THEY'VE MANIPULATED YOU. THEY KNOW YOU'RE SEARCHING FOR THEM. THEY'RE NOT TRYING TO ESCAPE, STEVE...THEY'VE LEFT A TRAIL OF BREAD CRUMBS FOR YOU TO FOLLOW.
WHY? THEY MUST KNOW THAT I'LL NEVER JOIN THEM.
I THINK THEY DO. THEY DID LITTLE TO HIDE THEIR PLANS FROM ME. THEY WANT TO OFFER YOU A CHOICE.
A TERRIBLE... TERRIBLE CHOICE.
THEY WANT YOUR BLOOD. NOT ALL OF IT... JUST TWO PINTS.
IT DOESN'T SURPRISE ME. THEY STOLE SOME BEFORE. MINE AND THOR'S.
I DON'T KNOW IF THEY'RE TRYING TO DUPLICATE THE SUPER-SOLDIER PROCESS OR USE MY BLOOD AS PART OF THEIR QUEST FOR IMMORTALITY...
BUT THEY HAVE TO KNOW THAT I'LL NEVER AGREE TO THAT.
THEY DO KNOW THAT. THAT'S WHY THEY RESURRECTED ME. SO YOU CAN SEE THE HELL THAT I'M IN. THEY WANT TO HURT YOU.
NOW...IMAGINE THAT HURT MAGNIFIED TEN THOUSAND TIMES. IMAGINE USING THAT EVIL SCIENCE TO INFLICT A WOUND ON THE ENTIRE AMERICAN PSYCHE. A WOUND THAT WOULD NEVER HEAL...
STEVE... IF YOU REFUSE TO GIVE THEM YOUR BLOOD...
...THEN HYDRA WILL USE THE LAZARUS FORMULA TO RAISE ALL THE DEAD IN ARLINGTON CEMETERY.
ALL OF YOUR HEROES, ALL OF AMERICA'S SACRED DEAD...RESURRECTED AS SHAMBLING, DECAYING MONSTERS.
THAT IS YOUR CHOICE...

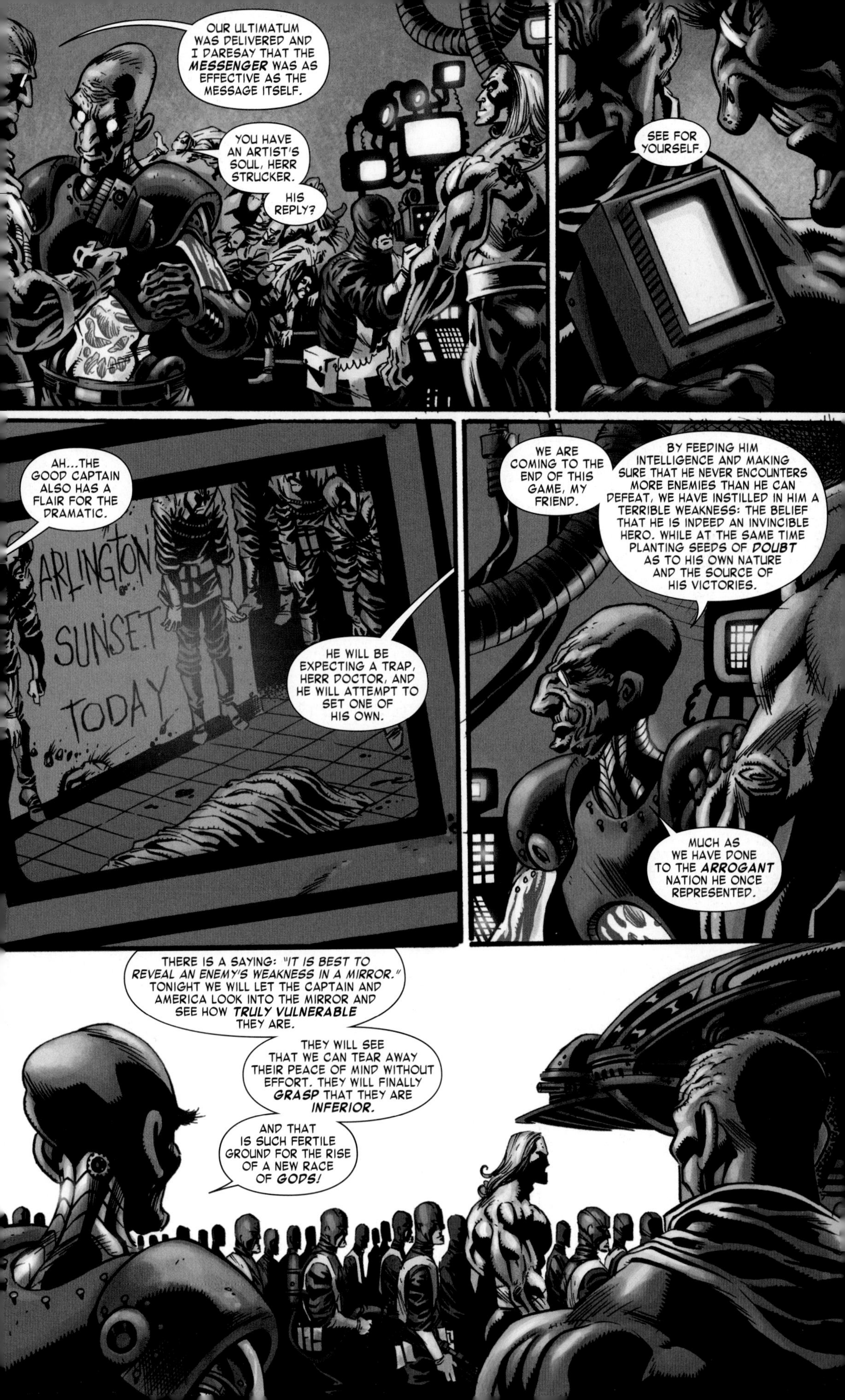
OUR ULTIMATUM WAS DELIVERED AND I DARESAY THAT THE MESSENGER WAS AS EFFECTIVE AS THE MESSAGE ITSELF.
YOU HAVE AN ARTIST'S SOUL, HERR STRUCKER.
HIS REPLY?
SEE FOR YOURSELF.
AH...THE GOOD CAPTAIN ALSO HAS A FLAIR FOR THE DRAMATIC.
ARLINGTON SUNSET TODAY
HE WILL BE EXPECTING A TRAP, HERR DOCTOR, AND HE WILL ATTEMPT TO SET ONE OF HIS OWN.
WE ARE COMING TO THE END OF THIS GAME, MY FRIEND.
BY FEEDING HIM INTELLIGENCE AND MAKING SURE THAT HE NEVER ENCOUNTERS MORE ENEMIES THAN HE CAN DEFEAT, WE HAVE INSTILLED IN HIM A TERRIBLE WEAKNESS: THE BELIEF THAT HE IS INDEED AN INVINCIBLE HERO. WHILE AT THE SAME TIME PLANTING SEEDS OF DOUBT AS TO HIS OWN NATURE AND THE SOURCE OF HIS VICTORIES.
MUCH AS WE HAVE DONE TO THE ARROGANT NATION HE ONCE REPRESENTED.
THERE IS A SAYING: "IT IS BEST TO REVEAL AN ENEMY'S WEAKNESS IN A MIRROR." TONIGHT WE WILL LET THE CAPTAIN AND AMERICA LOOK INTO THE MIRROR AND SEE HOW TRULY VULNERABLE THEY ARE.
THEY WILL SEE THAT WE CAN TEAR AWAY THEIR PEACE OF MIND WITHOUT EFFORT. THEY WILL FINALLY GRASP THAT THEY ARE INFERIOR.
AND THAT IS SUCH FERTILE GROUND FOR THE RISE OF A NEW RACE OF GODS!

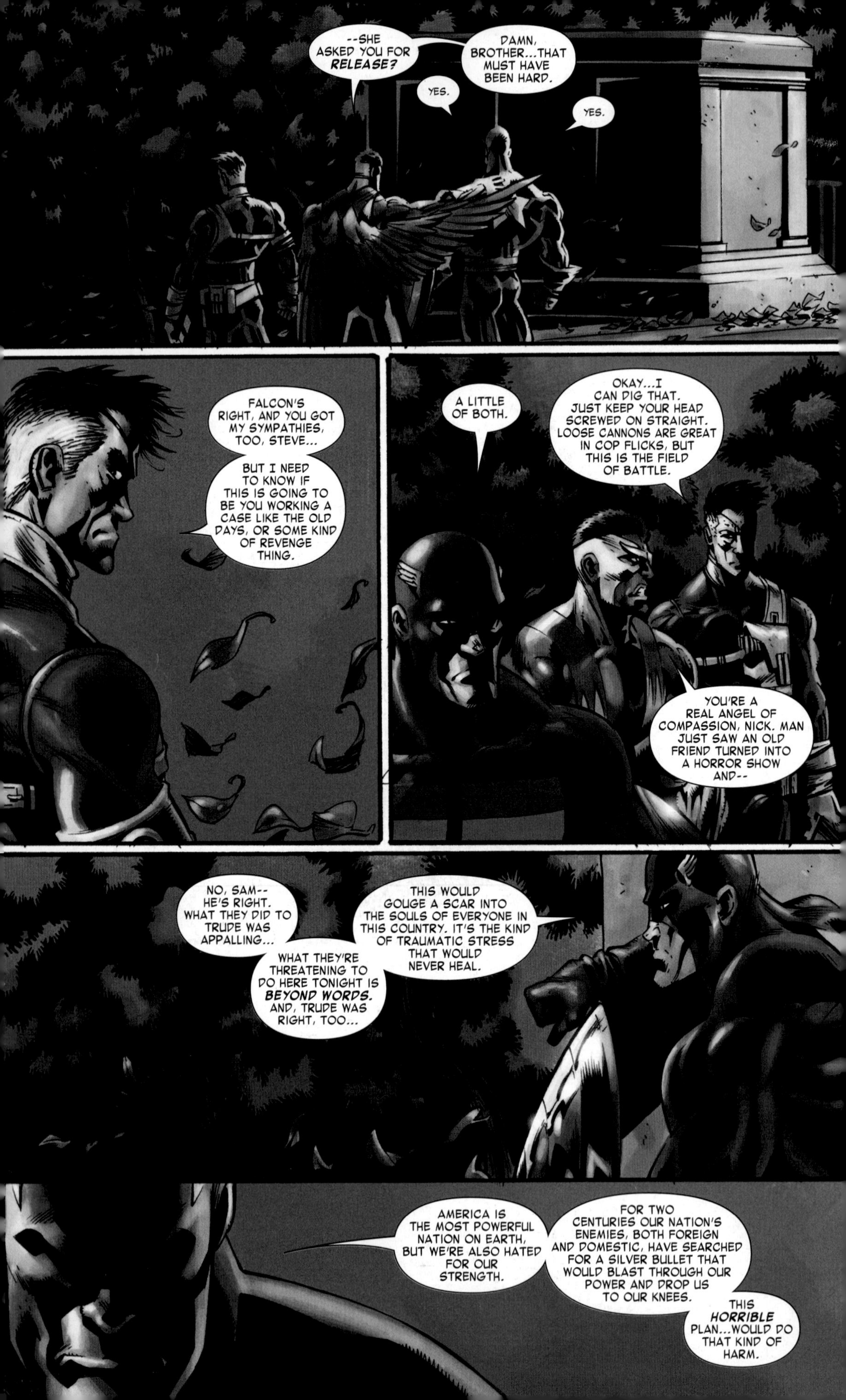
--SHE ASKED YOU FOR *RELEASE?*
YES.
DAMN, BROTHER...THAT MUST HAVE BEEN HARD.
YES.
FALCON'S RIGHT, AND YOU GOT MY SYMPATHIES, TOO, STEVE...
BUT I NEED TO KNOW IF THIS IS GOING TO BE YOU WORKING A CASE LIKE THE OLD DAYS, OR SOME KIND OF REVENGE THING.
A LITTLE OF BOTH.
OKAY...I CAN DIG THAT. JUST KEEP YOUR HEAD SCREWED ON STRAIGHT. LOOSE CANNONS ARE GREAT IN COP FLICKS, BUT THIS IS THE FIELD OF BATTLE.
YOU'RE A REAL ANGEL OF COMPASSION, NICK. MAN JUST SAW AN OLD FRIEND TURNED INTO A HORROR SHOW AND--
NO, SAM-- HE'S RIGHT. WHAT THEY DID TO TRUDE WAS APPALLING...
WHAT THEY'RE THREATENING TO DO HERE TONIGHT IS *BEYOND WORDS.* AND, TRUDE WAS RIGHT, TOO...
THIS WOULD GOUGE A SCAR INTO THE SOULS OF EVERYONE IN THIS COUNTRY. IT'S THE KIND OF TRAUMATIC STRESS THAT WOULD NEVER HEAL.
AMERICA IS THE MOST POWERFUL NATION ON EARTH, BUT WE'RE ALSO HATED FOR OUR STRENGTH.
FOR TWO CENTURIES OUR NATION'S ENEMIES, BOTH FOREIGN AND DOMESTIC, HAVE SEARCHED FOR A SILVER BULLET THAT WOULD BLAST THROUGH OUR POWER AND DROP US TO OUR KNEES.
THIS *HORRIBLE* PLAN...WOULD DO THAT KIND OF HARM.

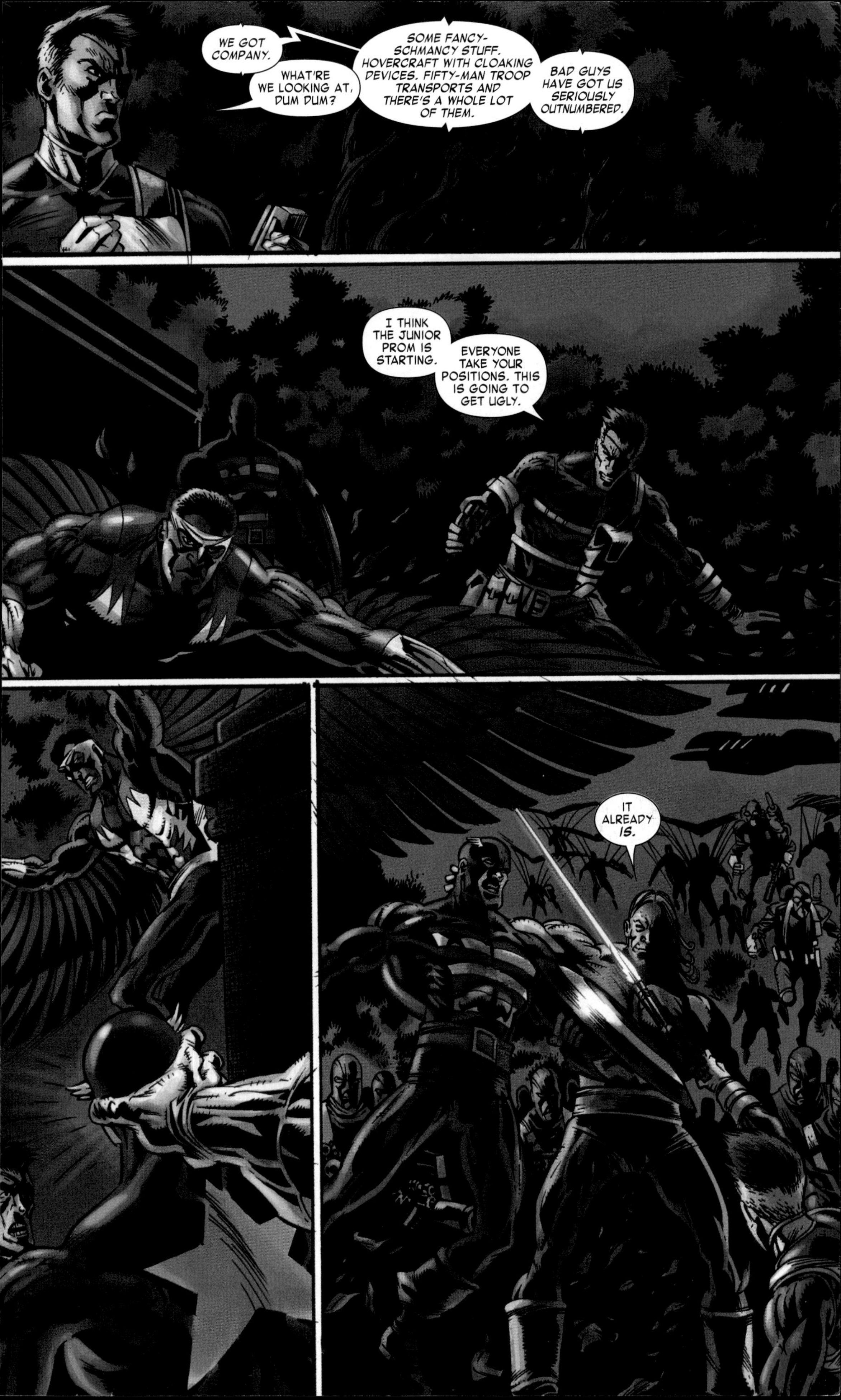
WE GOT COMPANY.
WHAT'RE WE LOOKING AT, DUM DUM?
SOME FANCY-SCHMANCY STUFF. HOVERCRAFT WITH CLOAKING DEVICES. FIFTY-MAN TROOP TRANSPORTS AND THERE'S A WHOLE LOT OF THEM.
BAD GUYS HAVE GOT US SERIOUSLY OUTNUMBERED.
I THINK THE JUNIOR PROM IS STARTING.
EVERYONE TAKE YOUR POSITIONS. THIS IS GOING TO GET UGLY.
IT ALREADY IS.

ALL PERSONNEL! HOSTILES ARE ON DECK. TAKE *IMMEDIATE* COUNTER-MEASURES!

ZZZZZZZT

ZZZZZZZ-ZZ-ZZZZZZZT

TAKE 'EM DOWN HARD!

HHHHH-HOOOOOOOO

UNNGH... I SUPPOSE... YOU'RE THE... UNGHH...LATEST GENERATION OF... SUPER-SOLDIER...

KRRRAAACCCK

NEWS FLASH...AT THE END OF THE DAY, YOU'RE JUST ANOTHER...

...PAWN?

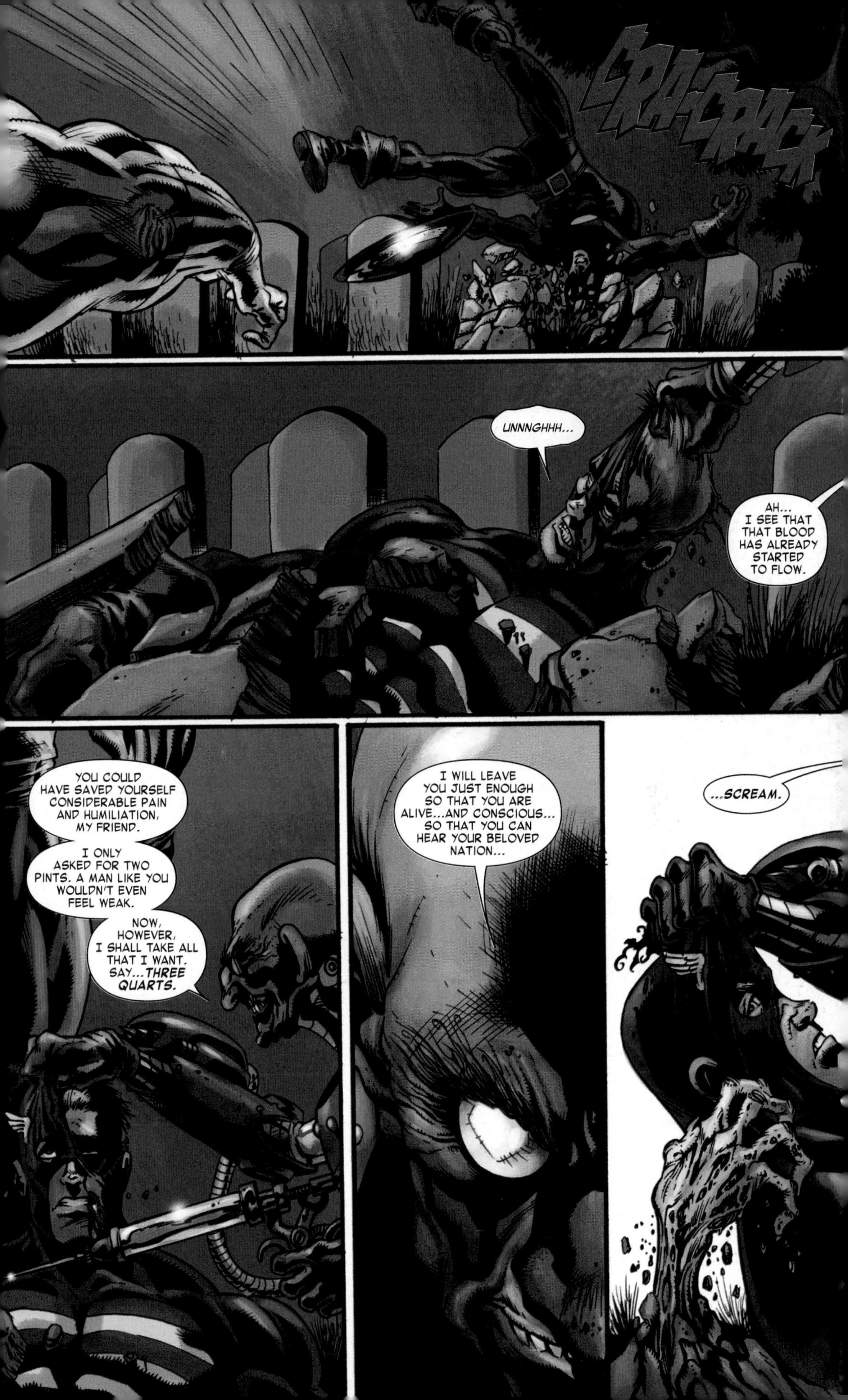
CRAK-CRACK
UNNNGHHH...
AH... I SEE THAT THAT BLOOD HAS ALREADY STARTED TO FLOW.
YOU COULD HAVE SAVED YOURSELF CONSIDERABLE PAIN AND HUMILIATION, MY FRIEND.
I ONLY ASKED FOR TWO PINTS. A MAN LIKE YOU WOULDN'T EVEN FEEL WEAK.
NOW, HOWEVER, I SHALL TAKE ALL THAT I WANT. SAY...THREE QUARTS.
I WILL LEAVE YOU JUST ENOUGH SO THAT YOU ARE ALIVE...AND CONSCIOUS... SO THAT YOU CAN HEAR YOUR BELOVED NATION...
...SCREAM.

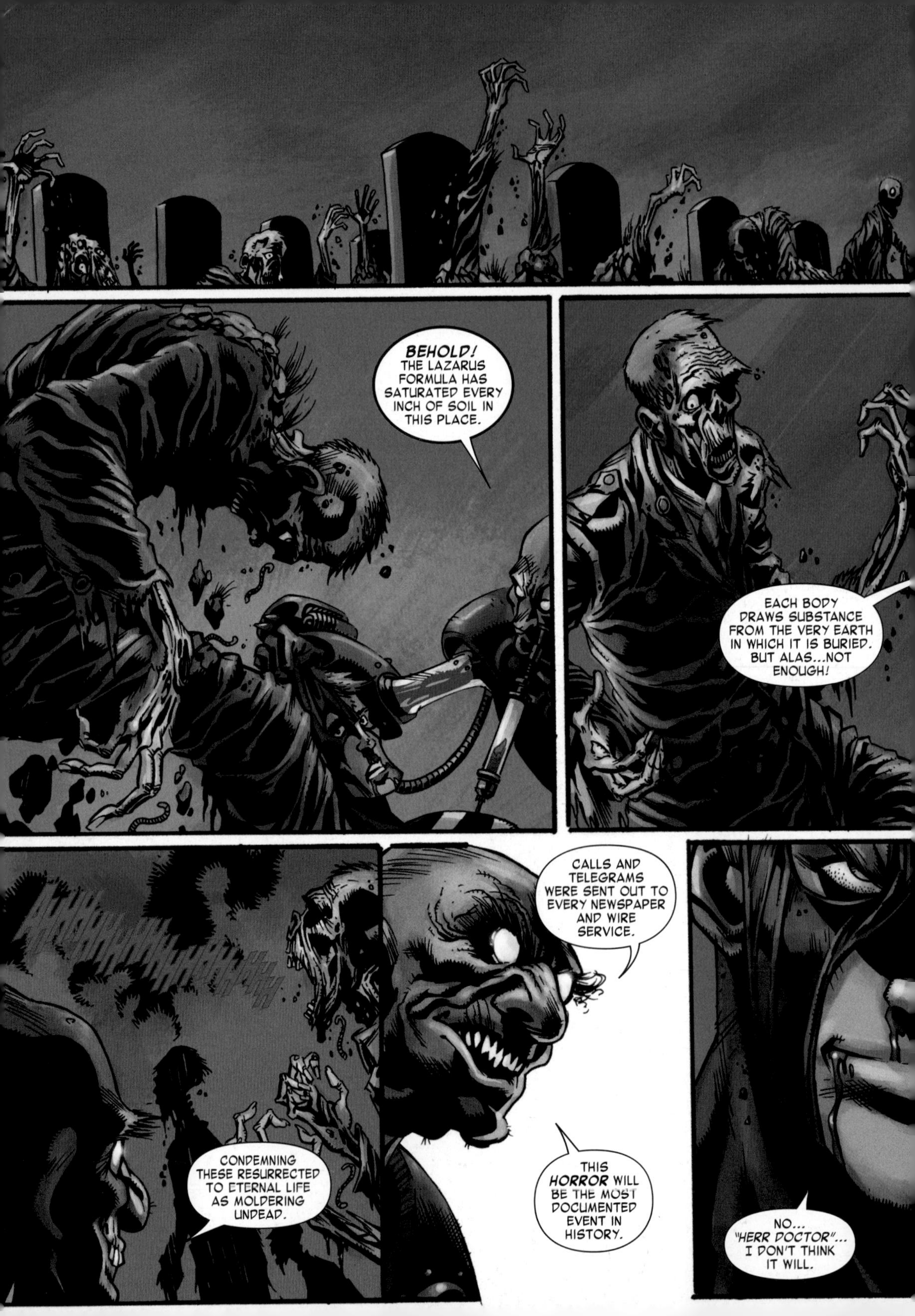
BEHOLD! THE LAZARUS FORMULA HAS SATURATED EVERY INCH OF SOIL IN THIS PLACE.
EACH BODY DRAWS SUBSTANCE FROM THE VERY EARTH IN WHICH IT IS BURIED. BUT ALAS...NOT ENOUGH!
CONDEMNING THESE RESURRECTED TO ETERNAL LIFE AS MOLDERING UNDEAD.
CALLS AND TELEGRAMS WERE SENT OUT TO EVERY NEWSPAPER AND WIRE SERVICE.
THIS HORROR WILL BE THE MOST DOCUMENTED EVENT IN HISTORY.
NO... "HERR DOCTOR"... I DON'T THINK IT WILL.

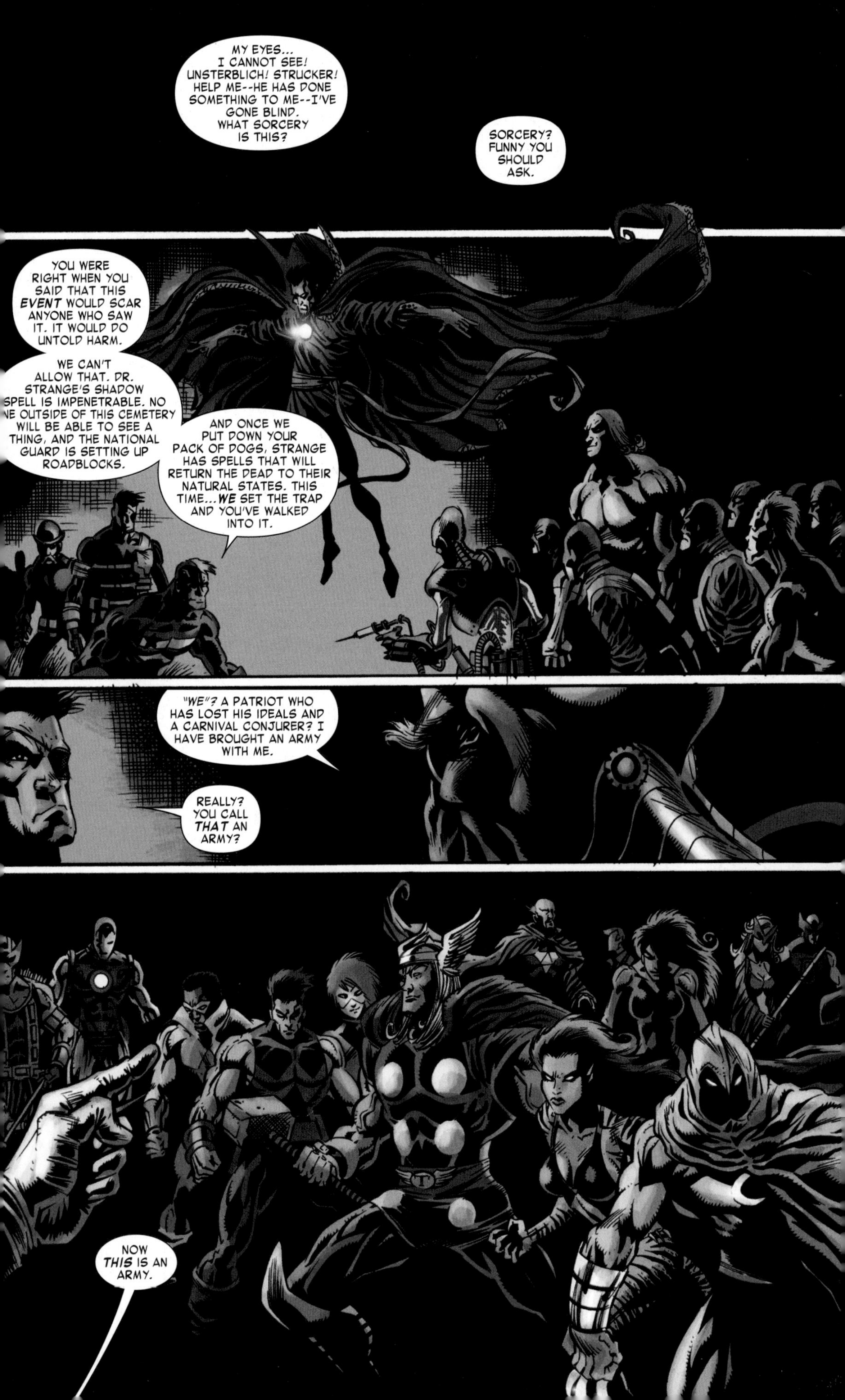

MY EYES... I CANNOT SEE! UNSTERBLICH! STRUCKER! HELP ME--HE HAS DONE SOMETHING TO ME--I'VE GONE BLIND. WHAT SORCERY IS THIS?
SORCERY? FUNNY YOU SHOULD ASK.
YOU WERE RIGHT WHEN YOU SAID THAT THIS EVENT WOULD SCAR ANYONE WHO SAW IT. IT WOULD DO UNTOLD HARM.
WE CAN'T ALLOW THAT. DR. STRANGE'S SHADOW SPELL IS IMPENETRABLE. NO NE OUTSIDE OF THIS CEMETERY WILL BE ABLE TO SEE A THING, AND THE NATIONAL GUARD IS SETTING UP ROADBLOCKS.
AND ONCE WE PUT DOWN YOUR PACK OF DOGS, STRANGE HAS SPELLS THAT WILL RETURN THE DEAD TO THEIR NATURAL STATES. THIS TIME... WE SET THE TRAP AND YOU'VE WALKED INTO IT.
"WE"? A PATRIOT WHO HAS LOST HIS IDEALS AND A CARNIVAL CONJURER? I HAVE BROUGHT AN ARMY WITH ME.
REALLY? YOU CALL THAT AN ARMY?
NOW THIS IS AN ARMY.

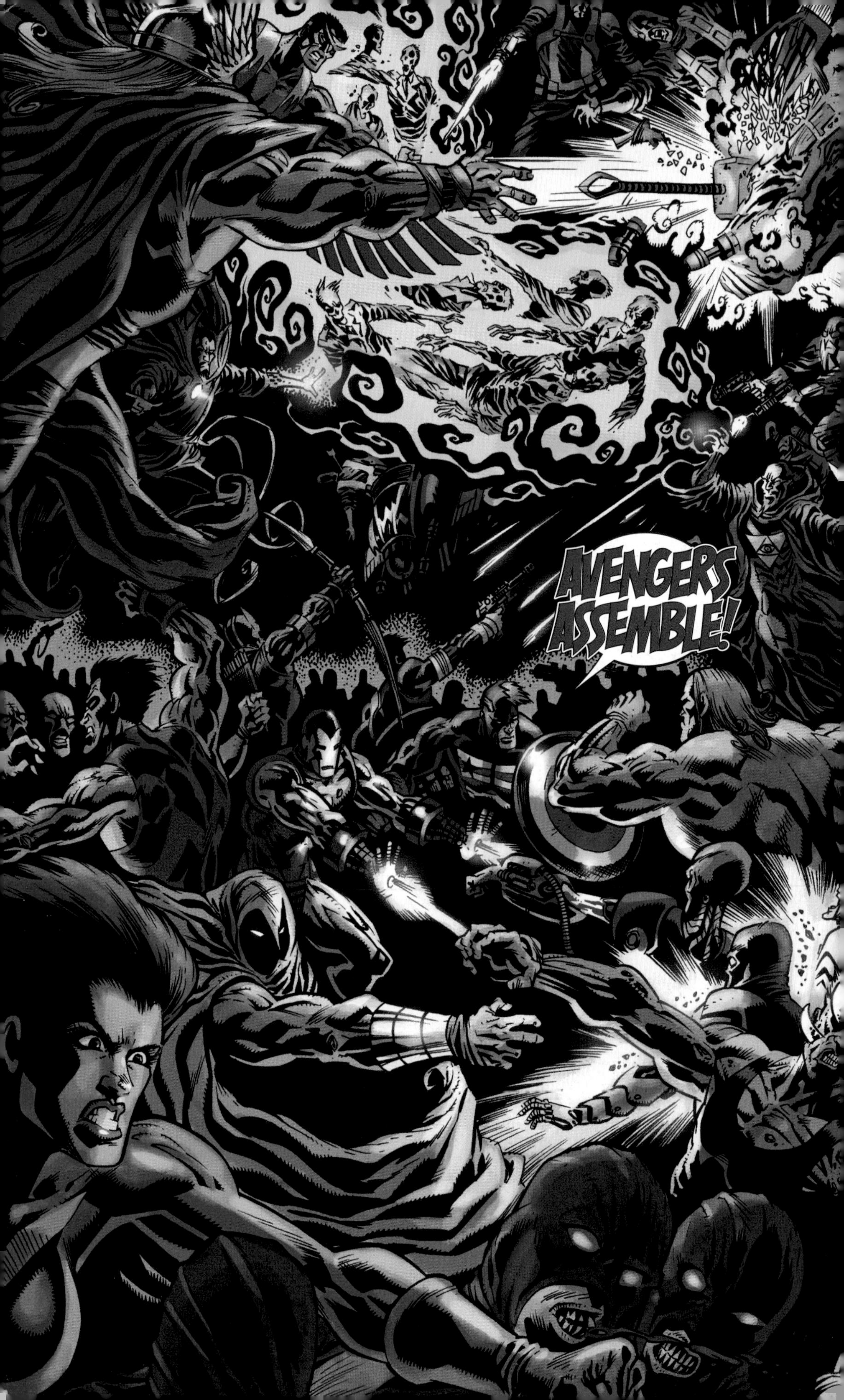
AVENGERS ASSEMBLE!

DO YOUR **WORST!** KILL US ALL IF YOU THINK IT WILL HELP...BUT IT WON'T STOP THE LAZARUS PROJECT.

ONE DAY SOON A RACE OF NEW GODS WILL WALK THE EARTH AND RATTLE THE PILLARS OF HEAVEN...AND THERE'S NOTHING YOU CAN DO TO STOP IT!

UNNNNNNNHHH

IF THESE BE YOUR GODS, MORTAL, THEN HYDRA HAS WASTED MILLENNIA ON A FOOL'S ERRAND.

AH, HE WAS A DISAPPOINTMENT. VERY STRONG, VERY PRETTY...STUPID AS A ROCK. A WORK IN PROGRESS...AND THAT WORK CONTINUES.

NOT FOR YOU IT DOESN'T. I'VE WAITED FOR A LOT OF YEARS FOR THIS, HERR DOCTOR, BUT IN THE NAME OF THE UNITED STATES OF AMERICA, I ARREST YOU FOR CRIMES AGAINST HUMANITY.

EUGENICS, ETHNIC GENOCIDE, MASS MURDER... DESECRATION...

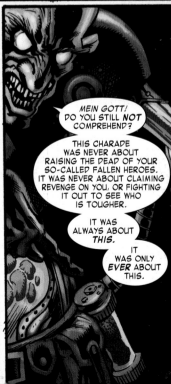

MEIN GOTT! DO YOU STILL **NOT** COMPREHEND?

THIS CHARADE WAS NEVER ABOUT RAISING THE DEAD OF YOUR SO-CALLED FALLEN HEROES. IT WAS NEVER ABOUT CLAIMING REVENGE ON YOU, OR FIGHTING IT OUT TO SEE WHO IS TOUGHER.

IT WAS ALWAYS ABOUT **THIS.**

IT WAS ONLY **EVER** ABOUT THIS.

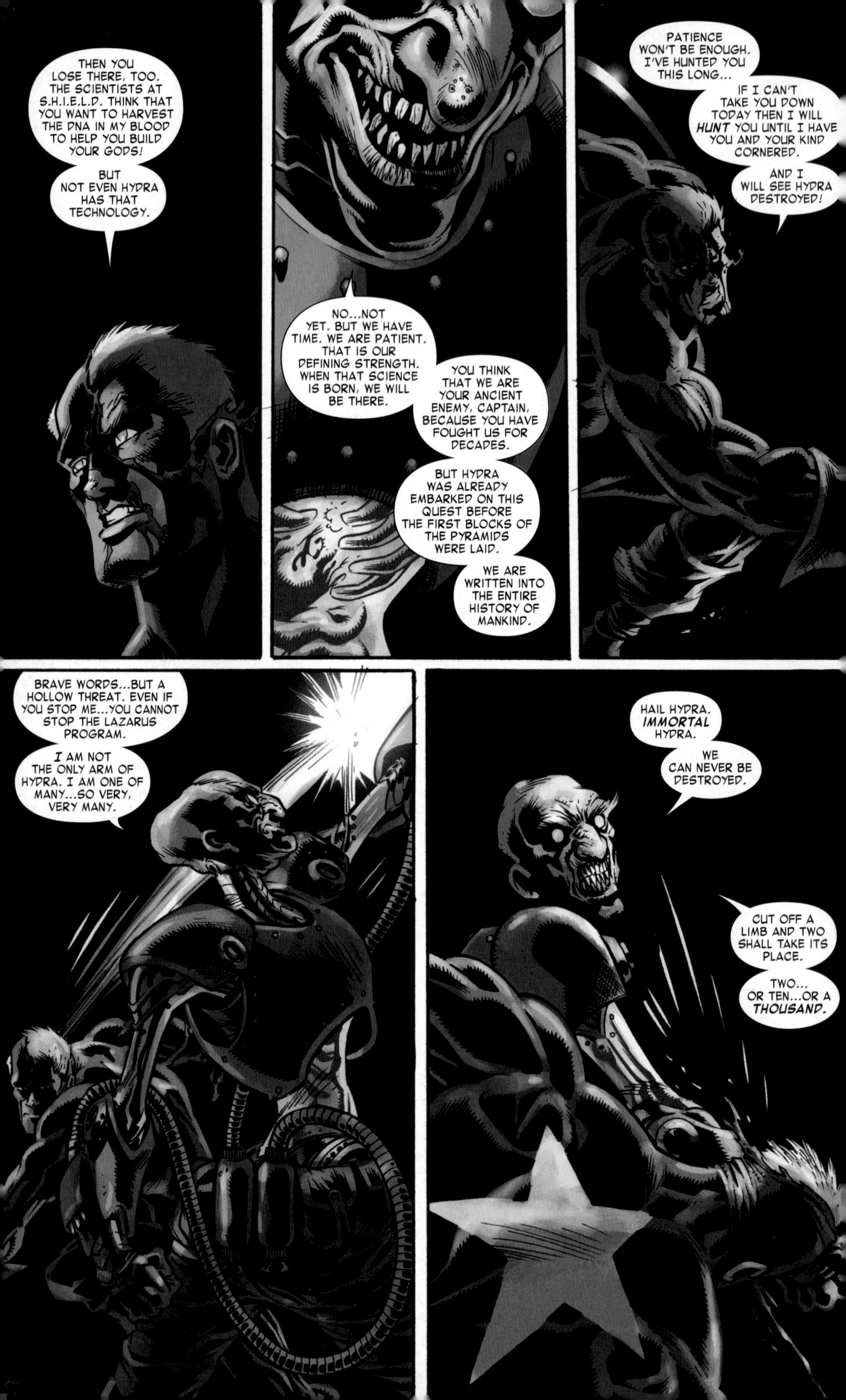
THEN YOU LOSE THERE, TOO. THE SCIENTISTS AT S.H.I.E.L.D. THINK THAT YOU WANT TO HARVEST THE DNA IN MY BLOOD TO HELP YOU BUILD YOUR GODS!
BUT NOT EVEN HYDRA HAS THAT TECHNOLOGY.
NO...NOT YET. BUT WE HAVE TIME. WE ARE PATIENT. THAT IS OUR DEFINING STRENGTH. WHEN THAT SCIENCE IS BORN, WE WILL BE THERE.
YOU THINK THAT WE ARE YOUR ANCIENT ENEMY, CAPTAIN, BECAUSE YOU HAVE FOUGHT US FOR DECADES.
BUT HYDRA WAS ALREADY EMBARKED ON THIS QUEST BEFORE THE FIRST BLOCKS OF THE PYRAMIDS WERE LAID.
WE ARE WRITTEN INTO THE ENTIRE HISTORY OF MANKIND.
PATIENCE WON'T BE ENOUGH. I'VE HUNTED YOU THIS LONG...
IF I CAN'T TAKE YOU DOWN TODAY THEN I WILL *HUNT* YOU UNTIL I HAVE YOU AND YOUR KIND CORNERED.
AND I WILL SEE HYDRA DESTROYED!
BRAVE WORDS...BUT A HOLLOW THREAT. EVEN IF YOU STOP ME...YOU CANNOT STOP THE LAZARUS PROGRAM.
I AM NOT THE ONLY ARM OF HYDRA. I AM ONE OF MANY...SO VERY, VERY MANY.
HAIL HYDRA. *IMMORTAL* HYDRA.
WE CAN NEVER BE DESTROYED.
CUT OFF A LIMB AND TWO SHALL TAKE ITS PLACE.
TWO... OR TEN...OR A *THOUSAND.*

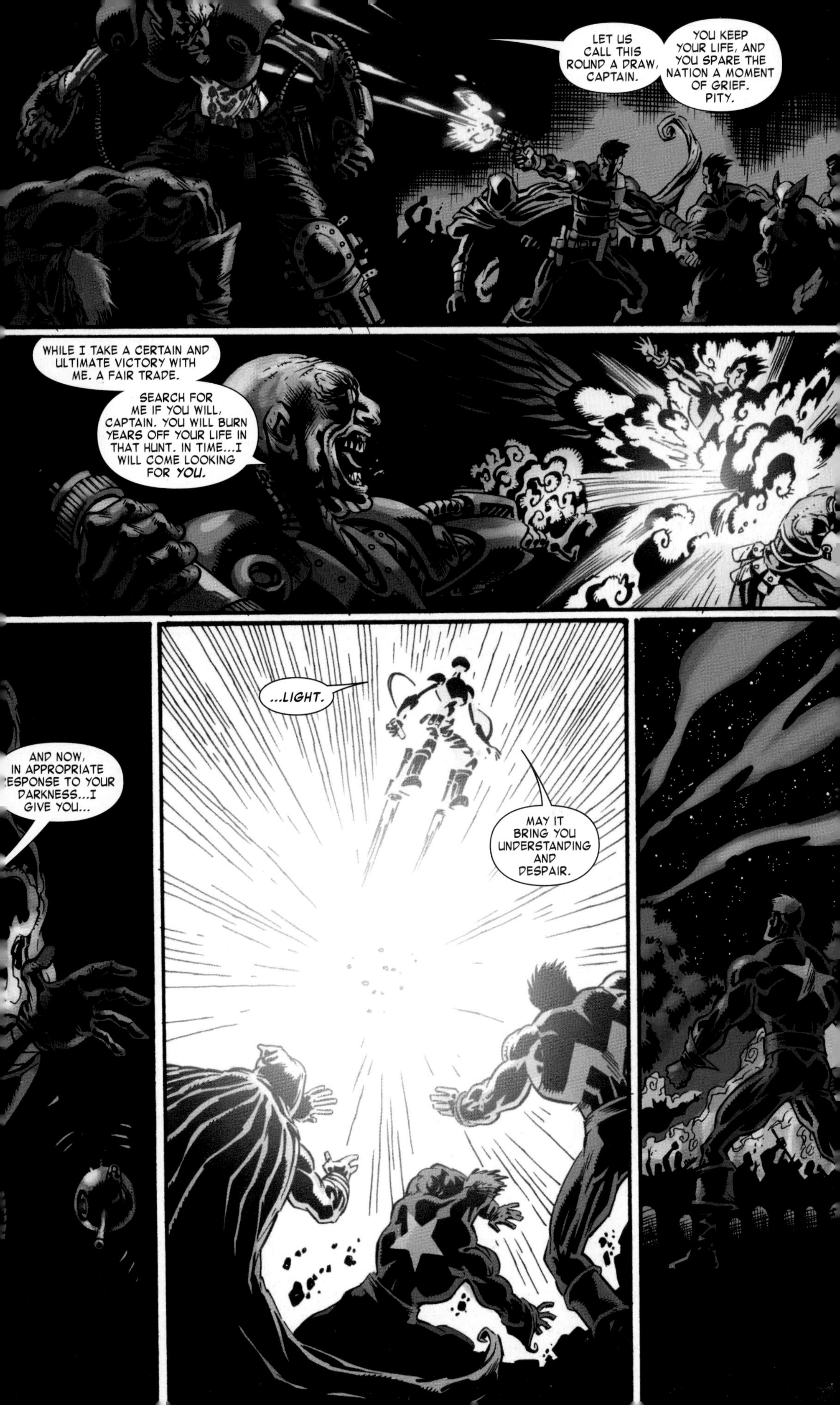
LET US CALL THIS ROUND A DRAW, CAPTAIN.
YOU KEEP YOUR LIFE, AND YOU SPARE THE NATION A MOMENT OF GRIEF. PITY.
WHILE I TAKE A CERTAIN AND ULTIMATE VICTORY WITH ME. A FAIR TRADE.
SEARCH FOR ME IF YOU WILL, CAPTAIN. YOU WILL BURN YEARS OFF YOUR LIFE IN THAT HUNT. IN TIME...I WILL COME LOOKING FOR *YOU.*
AND NOW, IN APPROPRIATE ESPONSE TO YOUR DARKNESS...I GIVE YOU...
...LIGHT.
MAY IT BRING YOU UNDERSTANDING AND DESPAIR.

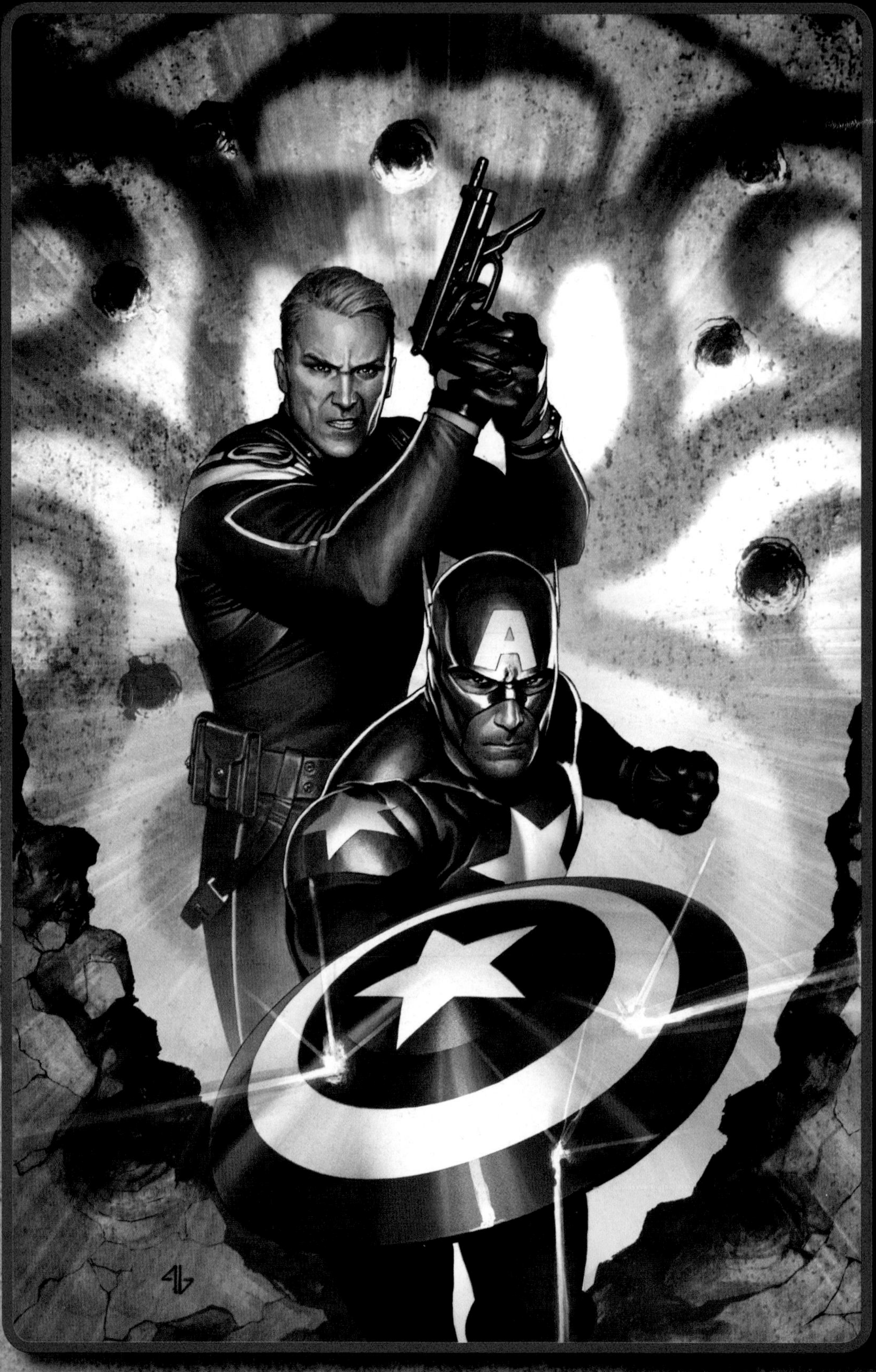

FIVE

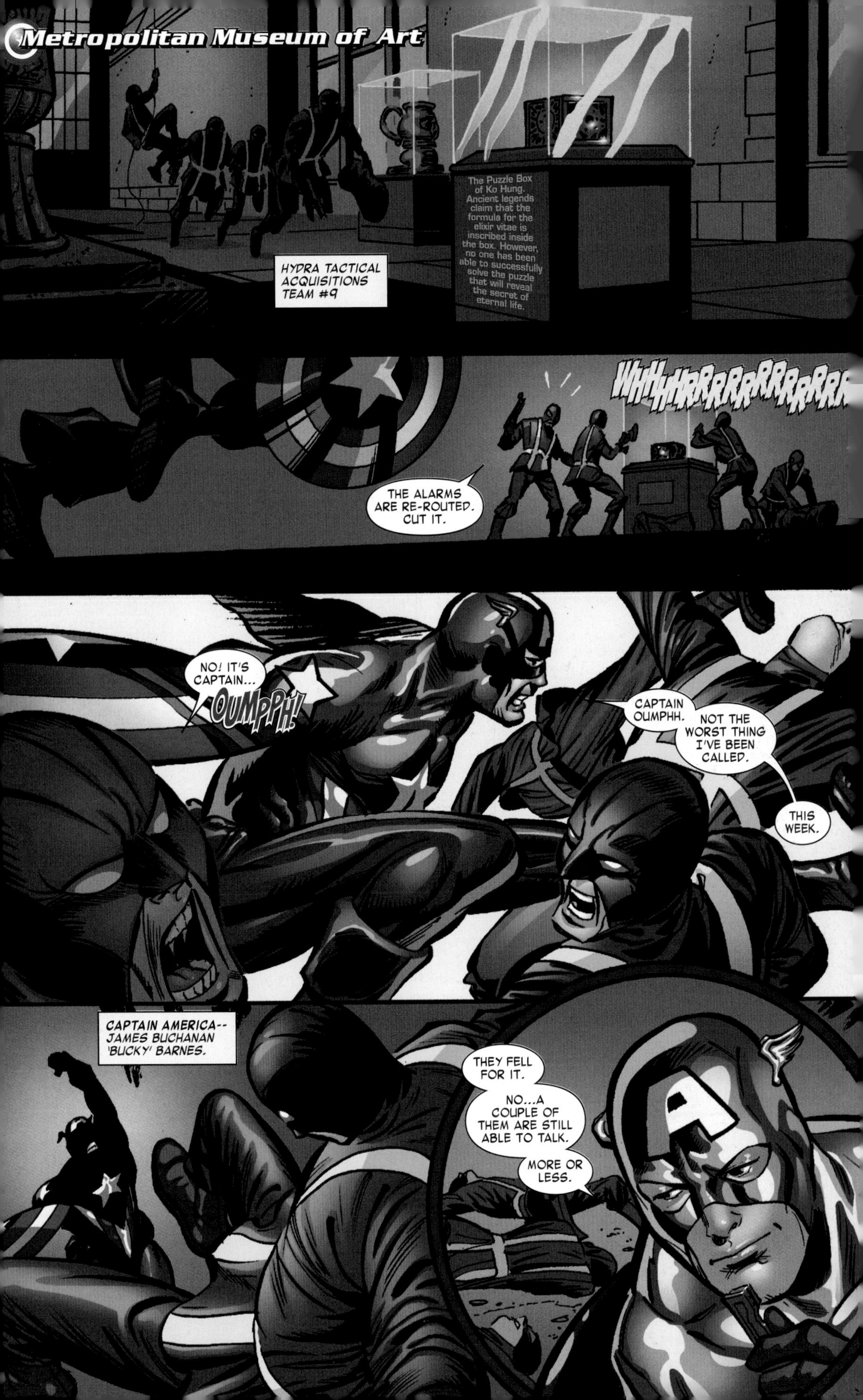
Metropolitan Museum of Art
The Puzzle Box of Ko Hung. Ancient legends claim that the formula for the elixir vitae is inscribed inside the box. However, no one has been able to successfully solve the puzzle that will reveal the secret of eternal life.
HYDRA TACTICAL ACQUISITIONS TEAM #9
WHHHHRRRRRRRRRRRR
THE ALARMS ARE RE-ROUTED. CUT IT.
NO! IT'S CAPTAIN...
OUMPPH!
CAPTAIN OUMPHH.
NOT THE WORST THING I'VE BEEN CALLED.
THIS WEEK.
CAPTAIN AMERICA-- JAMES BUCHANAN 'BUCKY' BARNES.
THEY FELL FOR IT.
NO...A COUPLE OF THEM ARE STILL ABLE TO TALK.
MORE OR LESS.

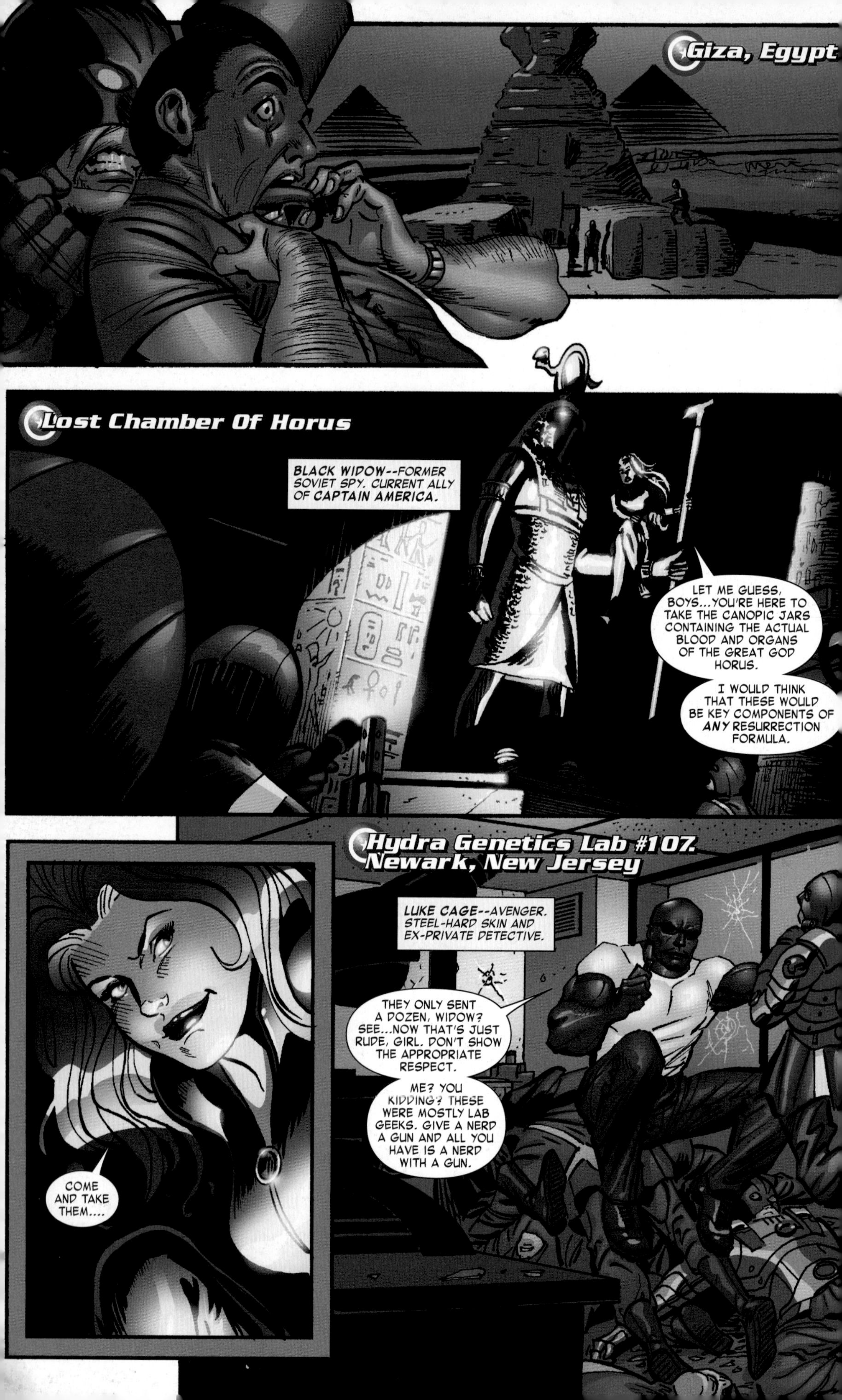
Giza, Egypt
Lost Chamber Of Horus
BLACK WIDOW--FORMER SOVIET SPY. CURRENT ALLY OF CAPTAIN AMERICA.
LET ME GUESS, BOYS...YOU'RE HERE TO TAKE THE CANOPIC JARS CONTAINING THE ACTUAL BLOOD AND ORGANS OF THE GREAT GOD HORUS.
I WOULD THINK THAT THESE WOULD BE KEY COMPONENTS OF ANY RESURRECTION FORMULA.
COME AND TAKE THEM....
Hydra Genetics Lab #107. Newark, New Jersey
LUKE CAGE--AVENGER. STEEL-HARD SKIN AND EX-PRIVATE DETECTIVE.
THEY ONLY SENT A DOZEN, WIDOW? SEE...NOW THAT'S JUST RUDE, GIRL. DON'T SHOW THE APPROPRIATE RESPECT.
ME? YOU KIDDING? THESE WERE MOSTLY LAB GEEKS. GIVE A NERD A GUN AND ALL YOU HAVE IS A NERD WITH A GUN.

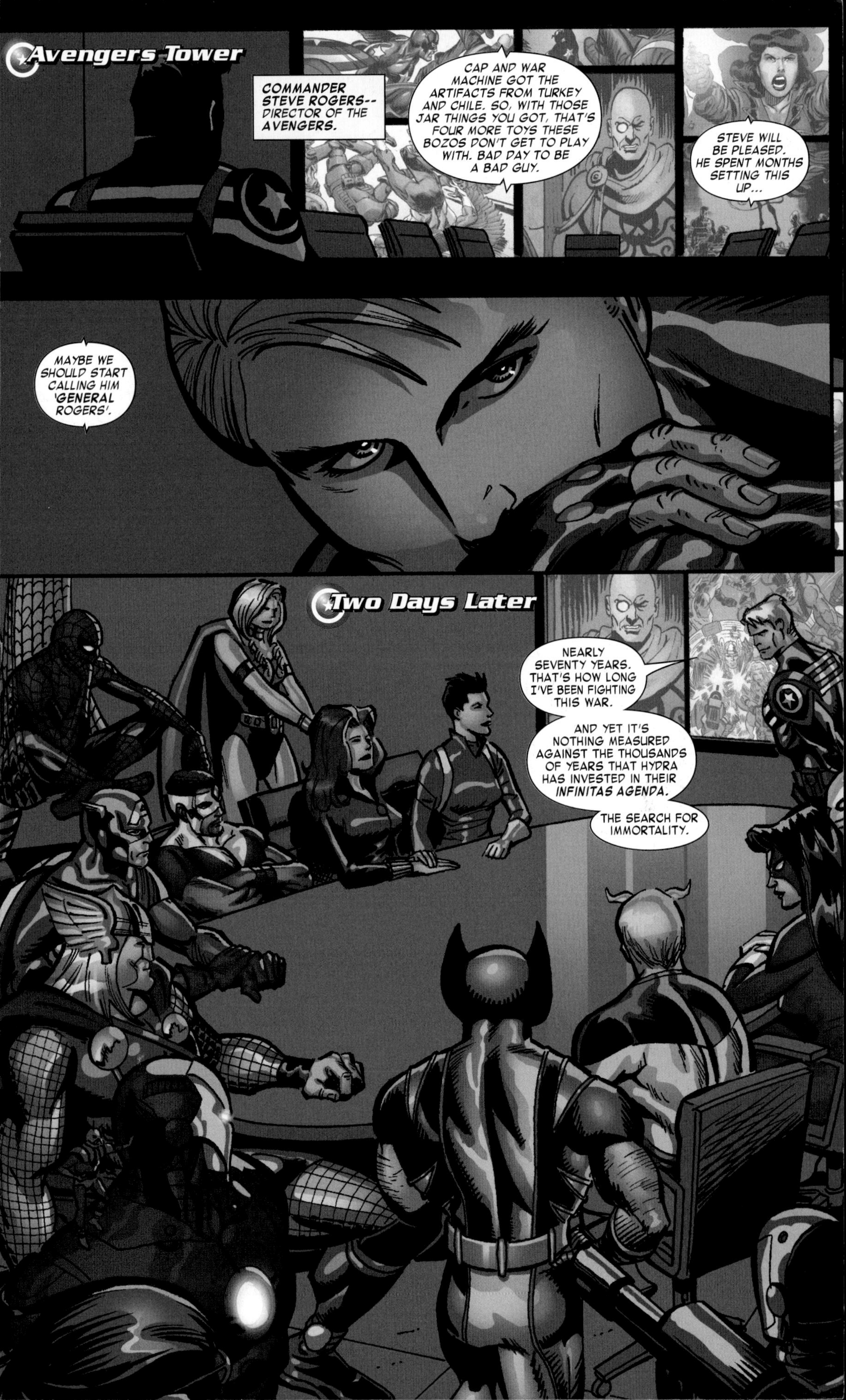
Avengers Tower
COMMANDER STEVE ROGERS-- DIRECTOR OF THE AVENGERS.
CAP AND WAR MACHINE GOT THE ARTIFACTS FROM TURKEY AND CHILE. SO, WITH THOSE JAR THINGS YOU GOT, THAT'S FOUR MORE TOYS THESE BOZOS DON'T GET TO PLAY WITH. BAD DAY TO BE A BAD GUY.
STEVE WILL BE PLEASED. HE SPENT MONTHS SETTING THIS UP...
MAYBE WE SHOULD START CALLING HIM 'GENERAL ROGERS'.
Two Days Later
NEARLY SEVENTY YEARS. THAT'S HOW LONG I'VE BEEN FIGHTING THIS WAR.
AND YET IT'S NOTHING MEASURED AGAINST THE THOUSANDS OF YEARS THAT HYDRA HAS INVESTED IN THEIR INFINITAS AGENDA.
THE SEARCH FOR IMMORTALITY.

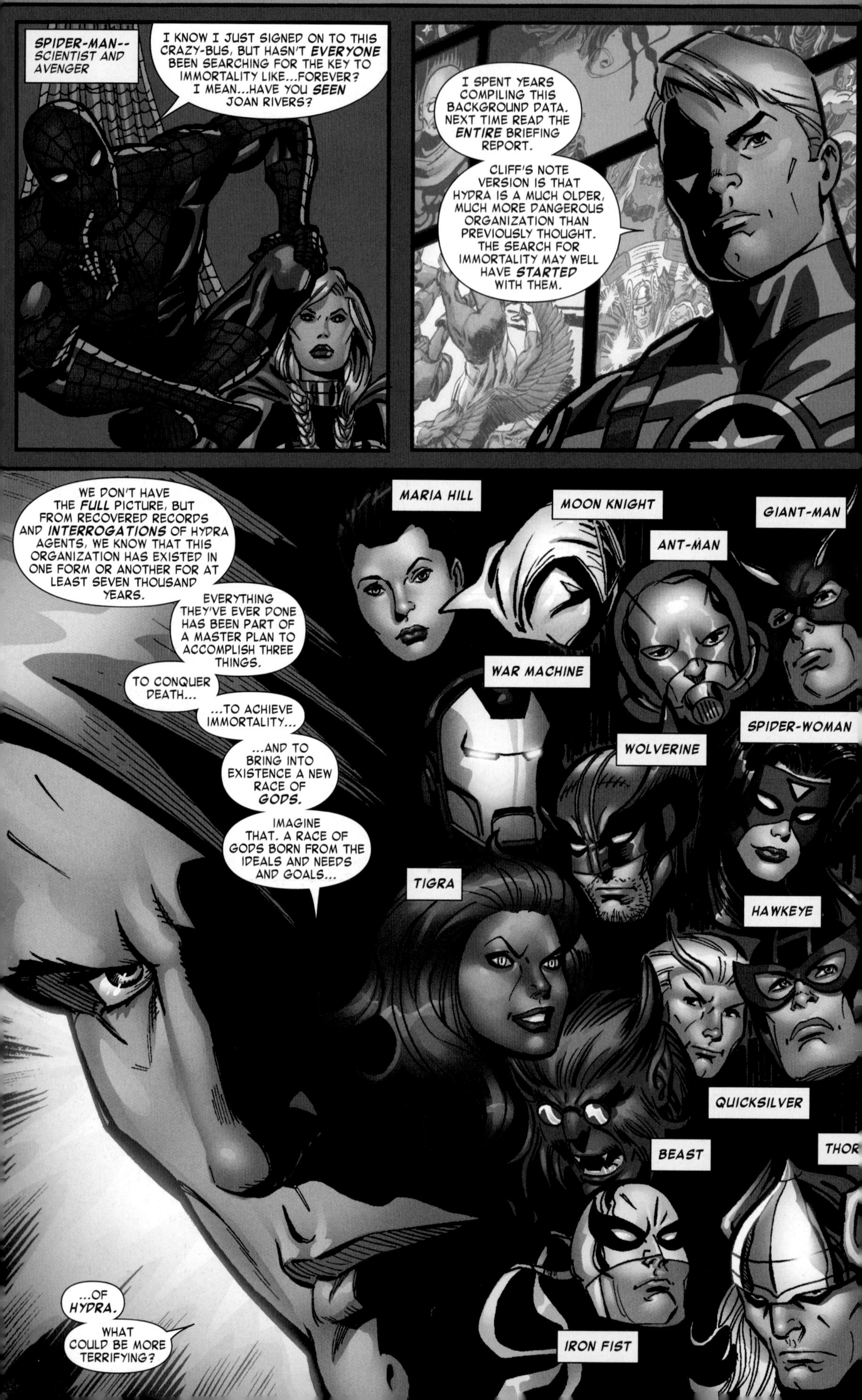

SPIDER-MAN-- SCIENTIST AND AVENGER
I KNOW I JUST SIGNED ON TO THIS CRAZY-BUS, BUT HASN'T EVERYONE BEEN SEARCHING FOR THE KEY TO IMMORTALITY LIKE...FOREVER? I MEAN...HAVE YOU SEEN JOAN RIVERS?
I SPENT YEARS COMPILING THIS BACKGROUND DATA. NEXT TIME READ THE ENTIRE BRIEFING REPORT.
CLIFF'S NOTE VERSION IS THAT HYDRA IS A MUCH OLDER, MUCH MORE DANGEROUS ORGANIZATION THAN PREVIOUSLY THOUGHT. THE SEARCH FOR IMMORTALITY MAY WELL HAVE STARTED WITH THEM.
WE DON'T HAVE THE FULL PICTURE, BUT FROM RECOVERED RECORDS AND INTERROGATIONS OF HYDRA AGENTS, WE KNOW THAT THIS ORGANIZATION HAS EXISTED IN ONE FORM OR ANOTHER FOR AT LEAST SEVEN THOUSAND YEARS.
EVERYTHING THEY'VE EVER DONE HAS BEEN PART OF A MASTER PLAN TO ACCOMPLISH THREE THINGS.
TO CONQUER DEATH...
...TO ACHIEVE IMMORTALITY...
...AND TO BRING INTO EXISTENCE A NEW RACE OF GODS.
IMAGINE THAT. A RACE OF GODS BORN FROM THE IDEALS AND NEEDS AND GOALS...
...OF HYDRA.
WHAT COULD BE MORE TERRIFYING?
MARIA HILL
MOON KNIGHT
GIANT-MAN
ANT-MAN
WAR MACHINE
SPIDER-WOMAN
WOLVERINE
TIGRA
HAWKEYE
QUICKSILVER
BEAST
THOR
IRON FIST

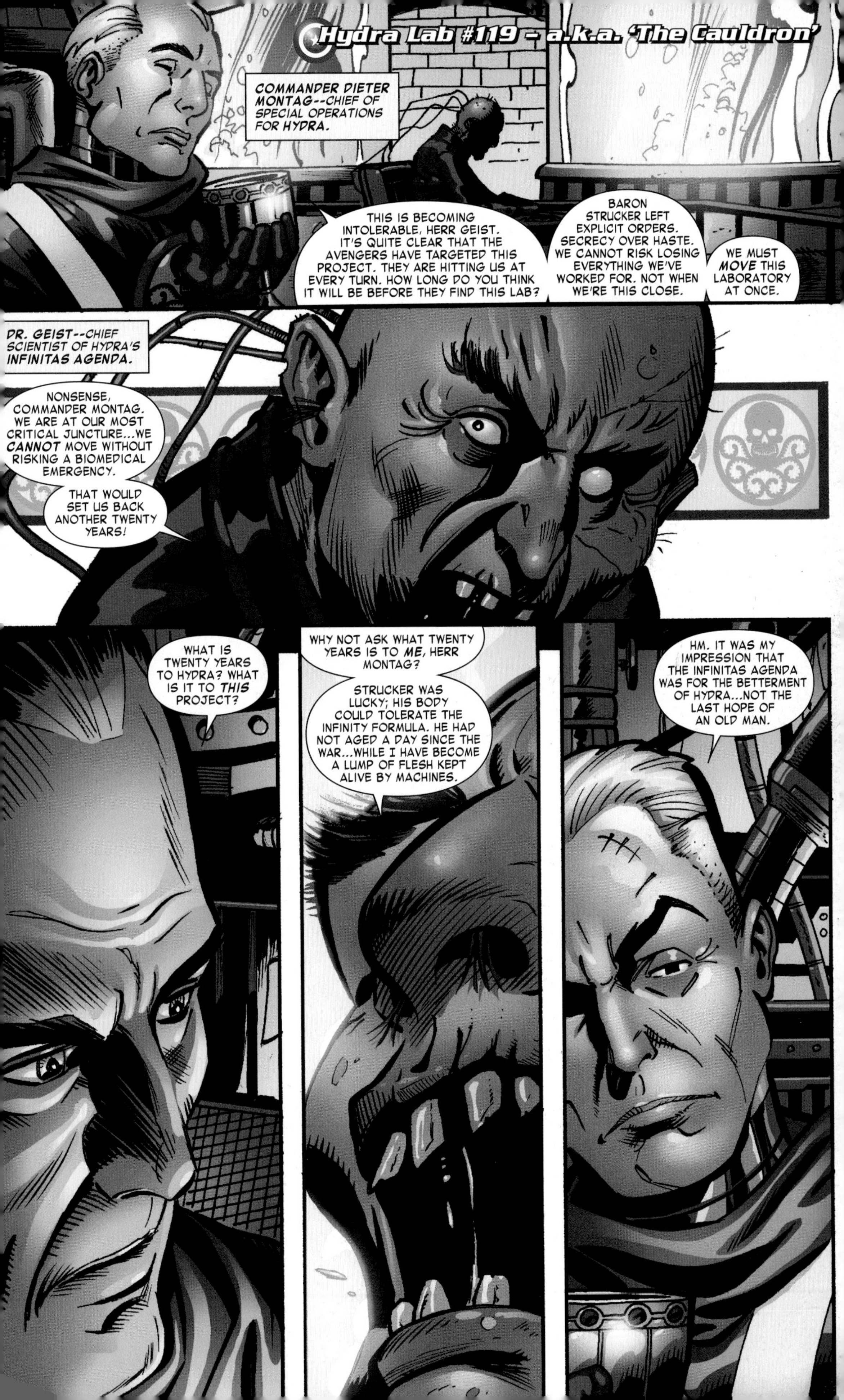
Hydra Lab #119 – a.k.a. 'The Cauldron'
COMMANDER DIETER MONTAG--CHIEF OF SPECIAL OPERATIONS FOR HYDRA.
THIS IS BECOMING INTOLERABLE, HERR GEIST. IT'S QUITE CLEAR THAT THE AVENGERS HAVE TARGETED THIS PROJECT. THEY ARE HITTING US AT EVERY TURN. HOW LONG DO YOU THINK IT WILL BE BEFORE THEY FIND THIS LAB?
BARON STRUCKER LEFT EXPLICIT ORDERS. SECRECY OVER HASTE. WE CANNOT RISK LOSING EVERYTHING WE'VE WORKED FOR. NOT WHEN WE'RE THIS CLOSE.
WE MUST MOVE THIS LABORATORY AT ONCE.
DR. GEIST--CHIEF SCIENTIST OF HYDRA'S INFINITAS AGENDA.
NONSENSE, COMMANDER MONTAG. WE ARE AT OUR MOST CRITICAL JUNCTURE...WE CANNOT MOVE WITHOUT RISKING A BIOMEDICAL EMERGENCY.
THAT WOULD SET US BACK ANOTHER TWENTY YEARS!
WHAT IS TWENTY YEARS TO HYDRA? WHAT IS IT TO THIS PROJECT?
WHY NOT ASK WHAT TWENTY YEARS IS TO ME, HERR MONTAG?
STRUCKER WAS LUCKY; HIS BODY COULD TOLERATE THE INFINITY FORMULA. HE HAD NOT AGED A DAY SINCE THE WAR...WHILE I HAVE BECOME A LUMP OF FLESH KEPT ALIVE BY MACHINES.
HM. IT WAS MY IMPRESSION THAT THE INFINITAS AGENDA WAS FOR THE BETTERMENT OF HYDRA...NOT THE LAST HOPE OF AN OLD MAN.

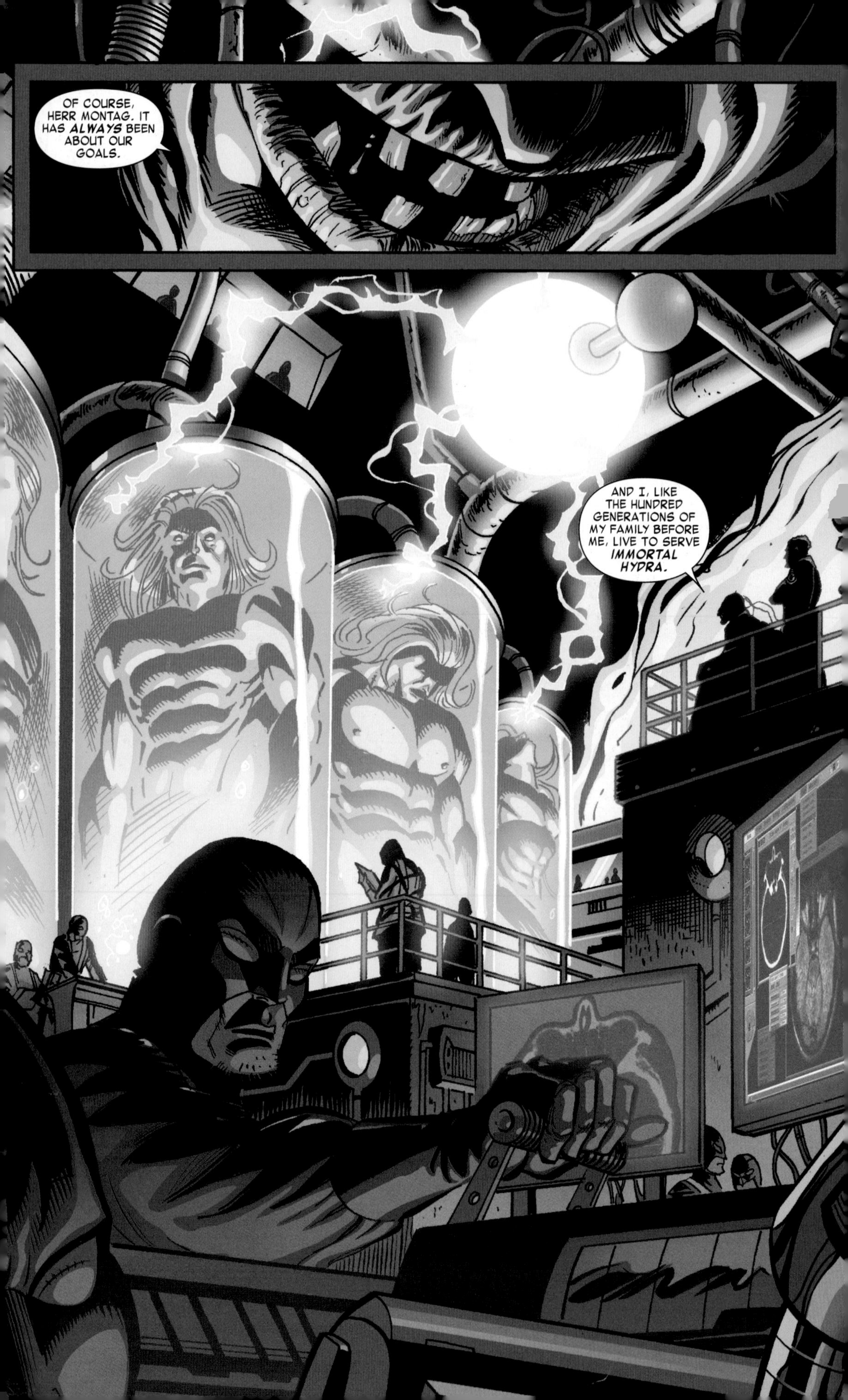
OF COURSE, HERR MONTAG. IT HAS ALWAYS BEEN ABOUT OUR GOALS.
AND I, LIKE THE HUNDRED GENERATIONS OF MY FAMILY BEFORE ME, LIVE TO SERVE IMMORTAL HYDRA.

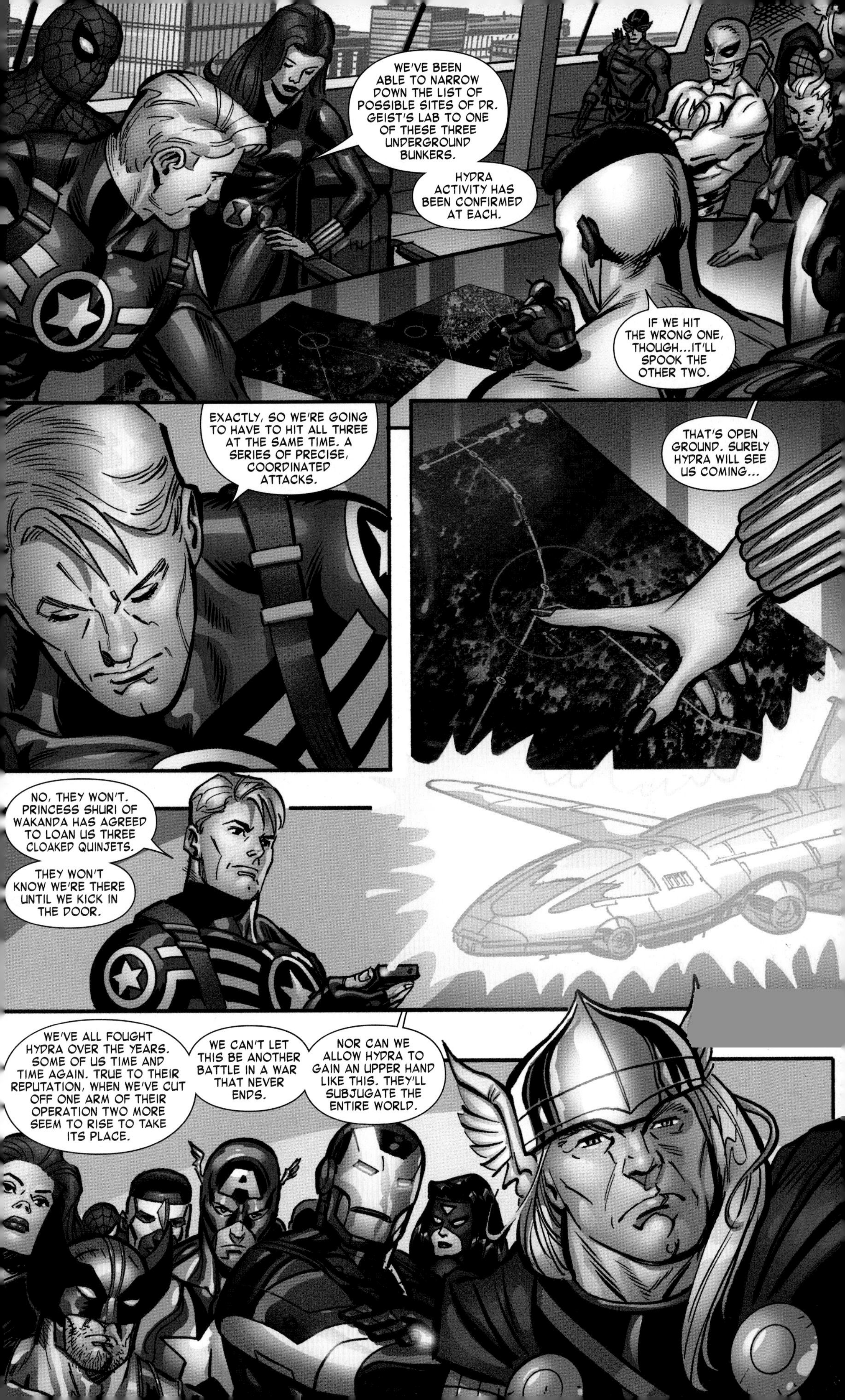
WE'VE BEEN ABLE TO NARROW DOWN THE LIST OF POSSIBLE SITES OF DR. GEIST'S LAB TO ONE OF THESE THREE UNDERGROUND BUNKERS.
HYDRA ACTIVITY HAS BEEN CONFIRMED AT EACH.
IF WE HIT THE WRONG ONE, THOUGH...IT'LL SPOOK THE OTHER TWO.
EXACTLY, SO WE'RE GOING TO HAVE TO HIT ALL THREE AT THE SAME TIME. A SERIES OF PRECISE, COORDINATED ATTACKS.
THAT'S OPEN GROUND. SURELY HYDRA WILL SEE US COMING...
NO, THEY WON'T. PRINCESS SHURI OF WAKANDA HAS AGREED TO LOAN US THREE CLOAKED QUINJETS.
THEY WON'T KNOW WE'RE THERE UNTIL WE KICK IN THE DOOR.
WE'VE ALL FOUGHT HYDRA OVER THE YEARS. SOME OF US TIME AND TIME AGAIN. TRUE TO THEIR REPUTATION, WHEN WE'VE CUT OFF ONE ARM OF THEIR OPERATION TWO MORE SEEM TO RISE TO TAKE ITS PLACE.
WE CAN'T LET THIS BE ANOTHER BATTLE IN A WAR THAT NEVER ENDS.
NOR CAN WE ALLOW HYDRA TO GAIN AN UPPER HAND LIKE THIS. THEY'LL SUBJUGATE THE ENTIRE WORLD.

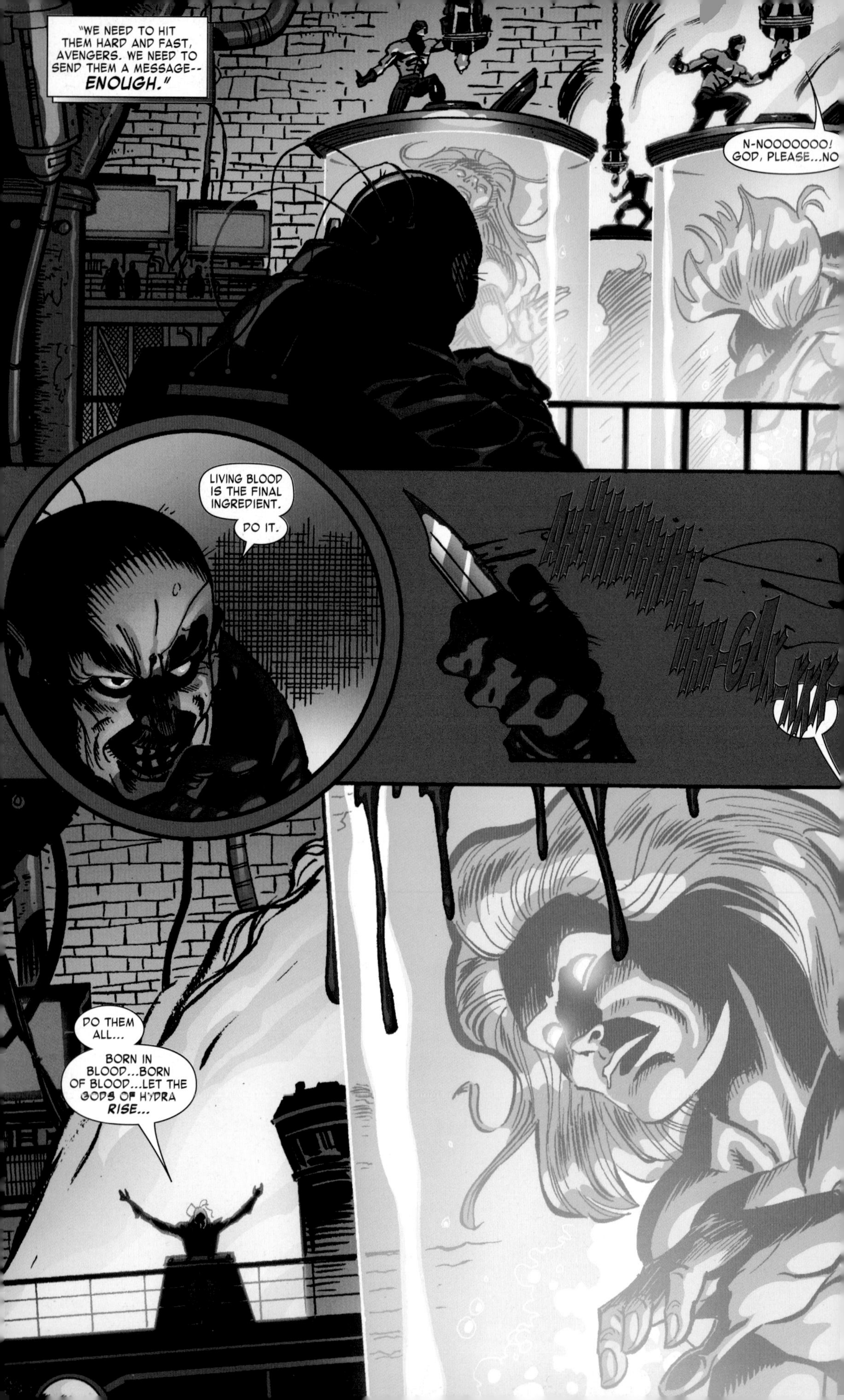
"WE NEED TO HIT THEM HARD AND FAST, AVENGERS. WE NEED TO SEND THEM A MESSAGE-- ENOUGH."
N-NOOOOOOO! GOD, PLEASE...NO
LIVING BLOOD IS THE FINAL INGREDIENT.
DO IT.
DO THEM ALL...
BORN IN BLOOD...BORN OF BLOOD...LET THE GODS OF HYDRA RISE...

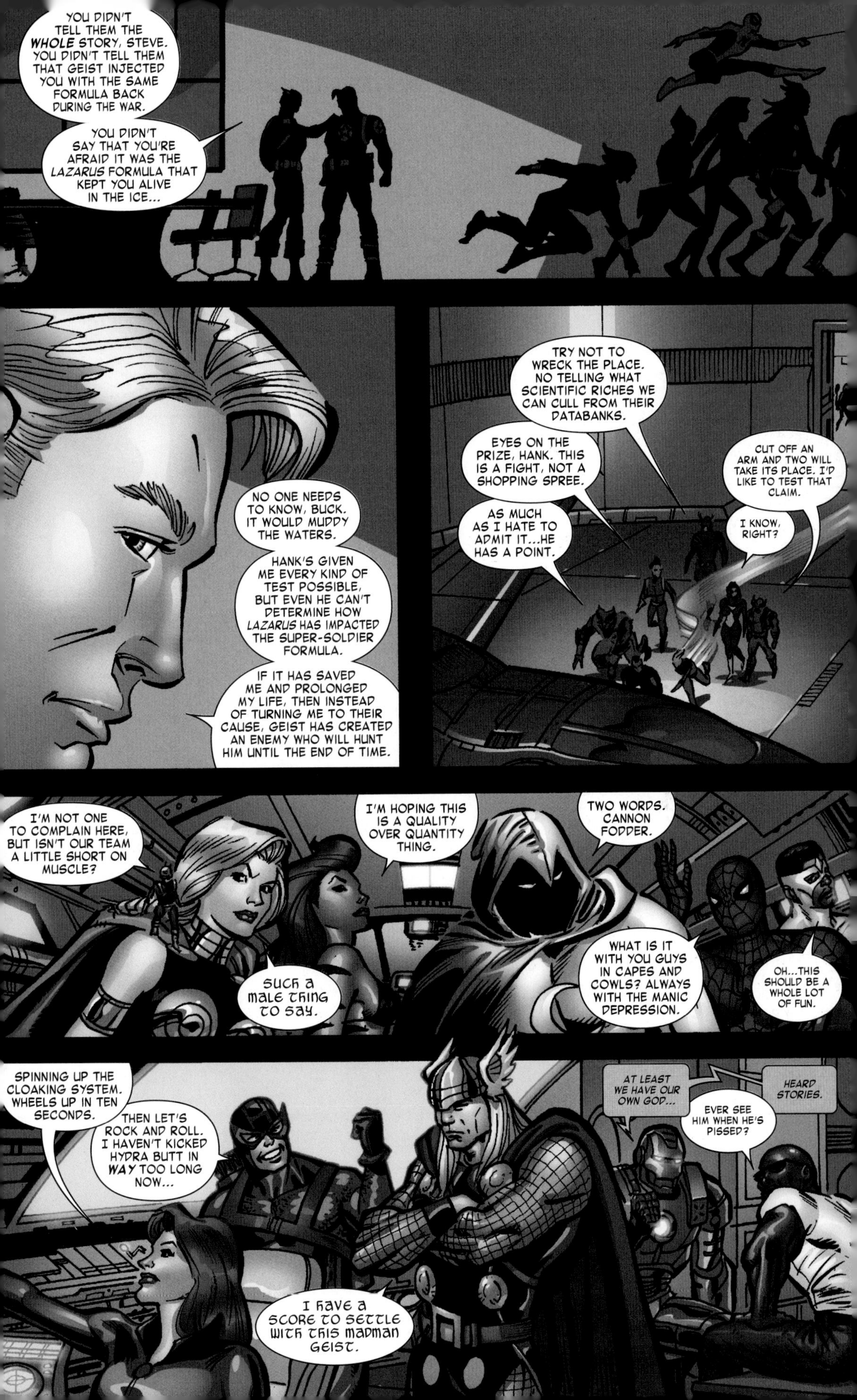
YOU DIDN'T TELL THEM THE WHOLE STORY, STEVE. YOU DIDN'T TELL THEM THAT GEIST INJECTED YOU WITH THE SAME FORMULA BACK DURING THE WAR.
YOU DIDN'T SAY THAT YOU'RE AFRAID IT WAS THE LAZARUS FORMULA THAT KEPT YOU ALIVE IN THE ICE...
NO ONE NEEDS TO KNOW, BUCK. IT WOULD MUDDY THE WATERS.
HANK'S GIVEN ME EVERY KIND OF TEST POSSIBLE, BUT EVEN HE CAN'T DETERMINE HOW LAZARUS HAS IMPACTED THE SUPER-SOLDIER FORMULA.
IF IT HAS SAVED ME AND PROLONGED MY LIFE, THEN INSTEAD OF TURNING ME TO THEIR CAUSE, GEIST HAS CREATED AN ENEMY WHO WILL HUNT HIM UNTIL THE END OF TIME.
TRY NOT TO WRECK THE PLACE. NO TELLING WHAT SCIENTIFIC RICHES WE CAN CULL FROM THEIR DATABANKS.
EYES ON THE PRIZE, HANK. THIS IS A FIGHT, NOT A SHOPPING SPREE.
AS MUCH AS I HATE TO ADMIT IT...HE HAS A POINT.
CUT OFF AN ARM AND TWO WILL TAKE ITS PLACE. I'D LIKE TO TEST THAT CLAIM.
I KNOW, RIGHT?
I'M NOT ONE TO COMPLAIN HERE, BUT ISN'T OUR TEAM A LITTLE SHORT ON MUSCLE?
SUCH A MALE THING TO SAY.
I'M HOPING THIS IS A QUALITY OVER QUANTITY THING.
TWO WORDS. CANNON FODDER.
WHAT IS IT WITH YOU GUYS IN CAPES AND COWLS? ALWAYS WITH THE MANIC DEPRESSION.
OH...THIS SHOULD BE A WHOLE LOT OF FUN.
SPINNING UP THE CLOAKING SYSTEM. WHEELS UP IN TEN SECONDS.
THEN LET'S ROCK AND ROLL. I HAVEN'T KICKED HYDRA BUTT IN WAY TOO LONG NOW...
I HAVE A SCORE TO SETTLE WITH THIS MADMAN GEIST.
AT LEAST WE HAVE OUR OWN GOD...
HEARD STORIES.
EVER SEE HIM WHEN HE'S PISSED?

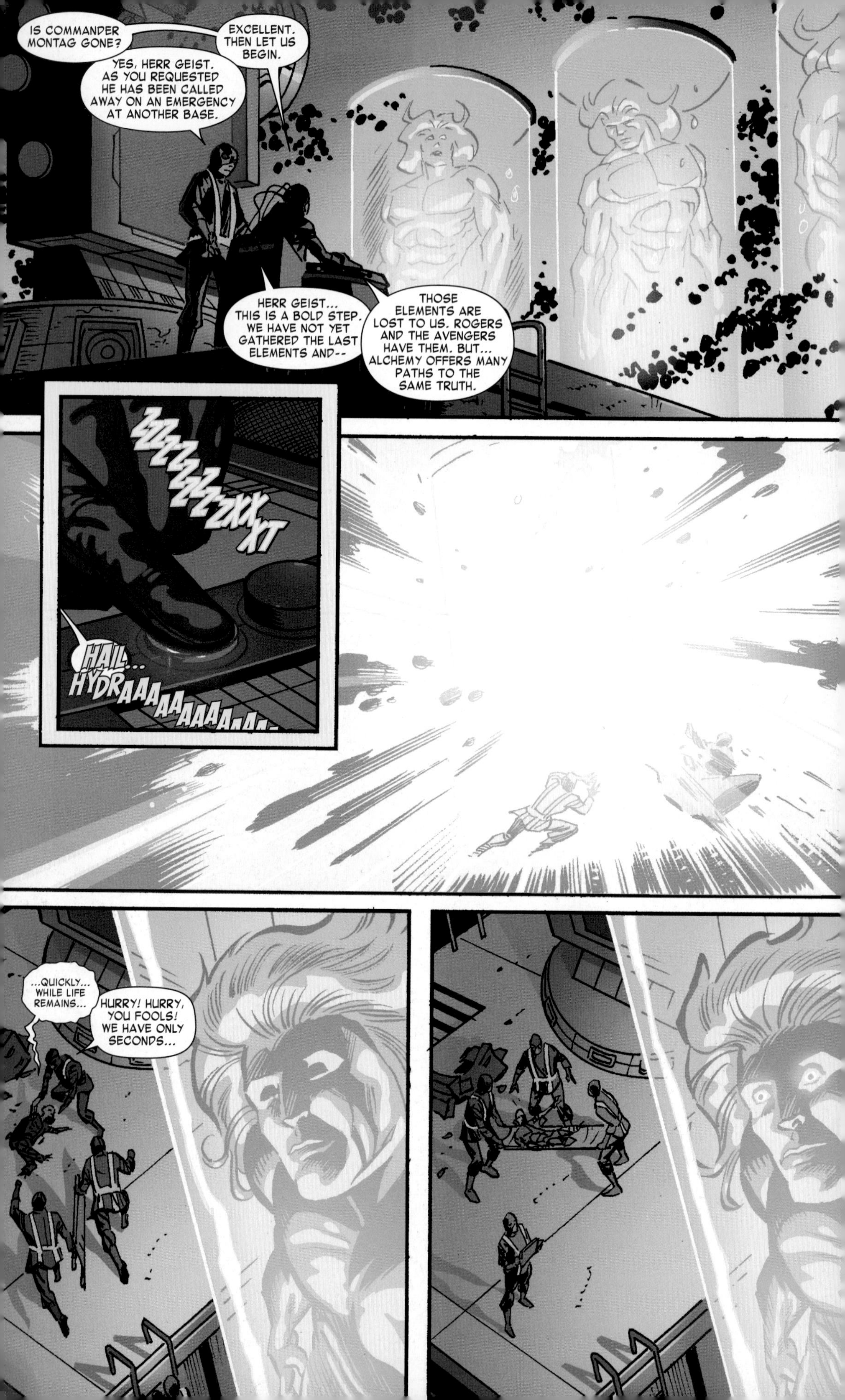
IS COMMANDER MONTAG GONE?
YES, HERR GEIST. AS YOU REQUESTED HE HAS BEEN CALLED AWAY ON AN EMERGENCY AT ANOTHER BASE.
EXCELLENT. THEN LET US BEGIN.
HERR GEIST... THIS IS A BOLD STEP. WE HAVE NOT YET GATHERED THE LAST ELEMENTS AND--
THOSE ELEMENTS ARE LOST TO US. ROGERS AND THE AVENGERS HAVE THEM. BUT... ALCHEMY OFFERS MANY PATHS TO THE SAME TRUTH.
ZZZZZZZZZXKXT
HAIL... HYDRAAAAAAAAAAAA-
...QUICKLY... WHILE LIFE REMAINS...
HURRY! HURRY, YOU FOOLS! WE HAVE ONLY SECONDS...

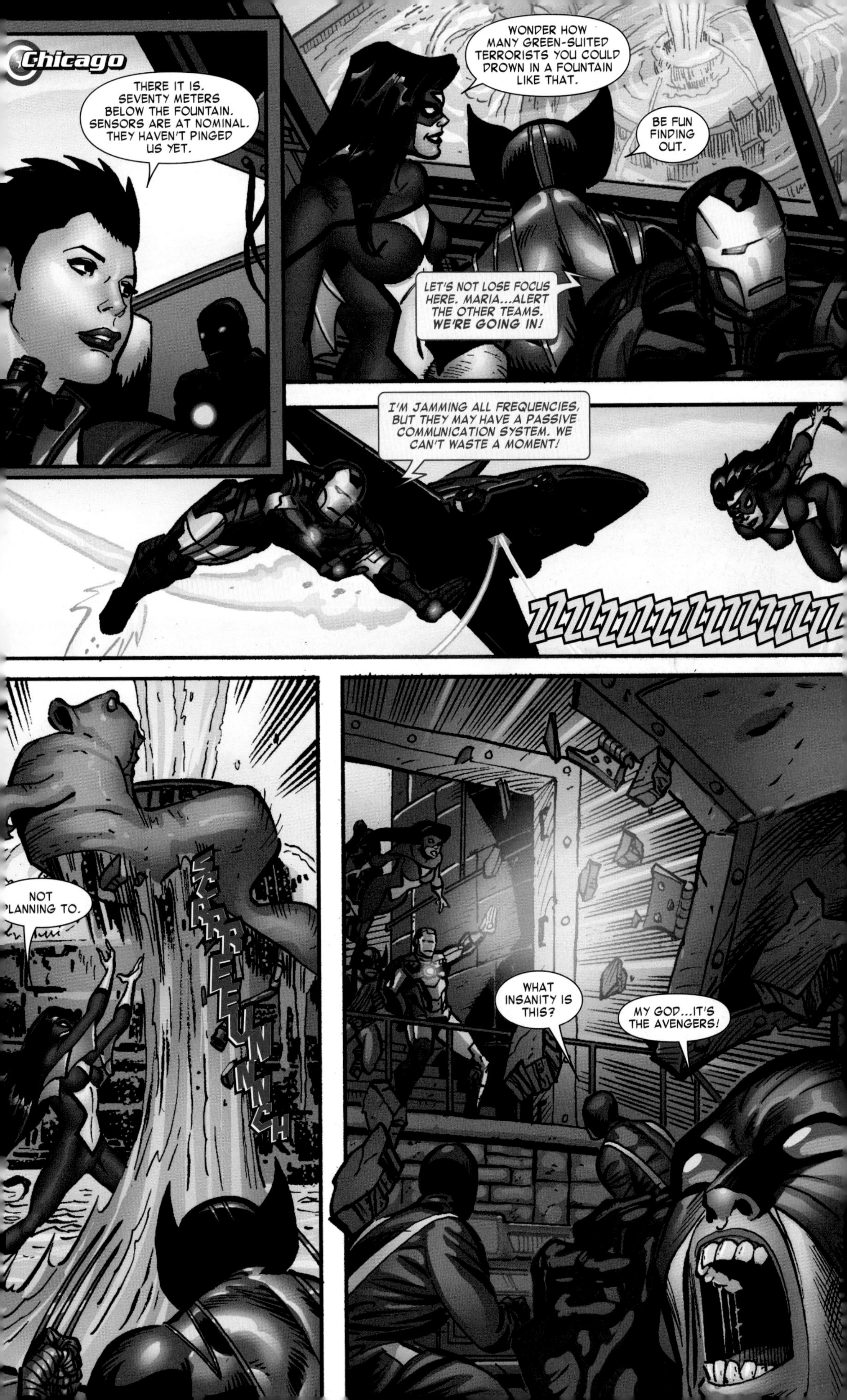
Chicago
THERE IT IS. SEVENTY METERS BELOW THE FOUNTAIN. SENSORS ARE AT NOMINAL. THEY HAVEN'T PINGED US YET.
WONDER HOW MANY GREEN-SUITED TERRORISTS YOU COULD DROWN IN A FOUNTAIN LIKE THAT.
BE FUN FINDING OUT.
LET'S NOT LOSE FOCUS HERE. MARIA...ALERT THE OTHER TEAMS. WE'RE GOING IN!
I'M JAMMING ALL FREQUENCIES, BUT THEY MAY HAVE A PASSIVE COMMUNICATION SYSTEM. WE CAN'T WASTE A MOMENT!
ZZZZZZZZZZZZZZZZZZZZZZ
NOT PLANNING TO.
SKRRREEUNNNCH
WHAT INSANITY IS THIS?
MY GOD...IT'S THE AVENGERS!

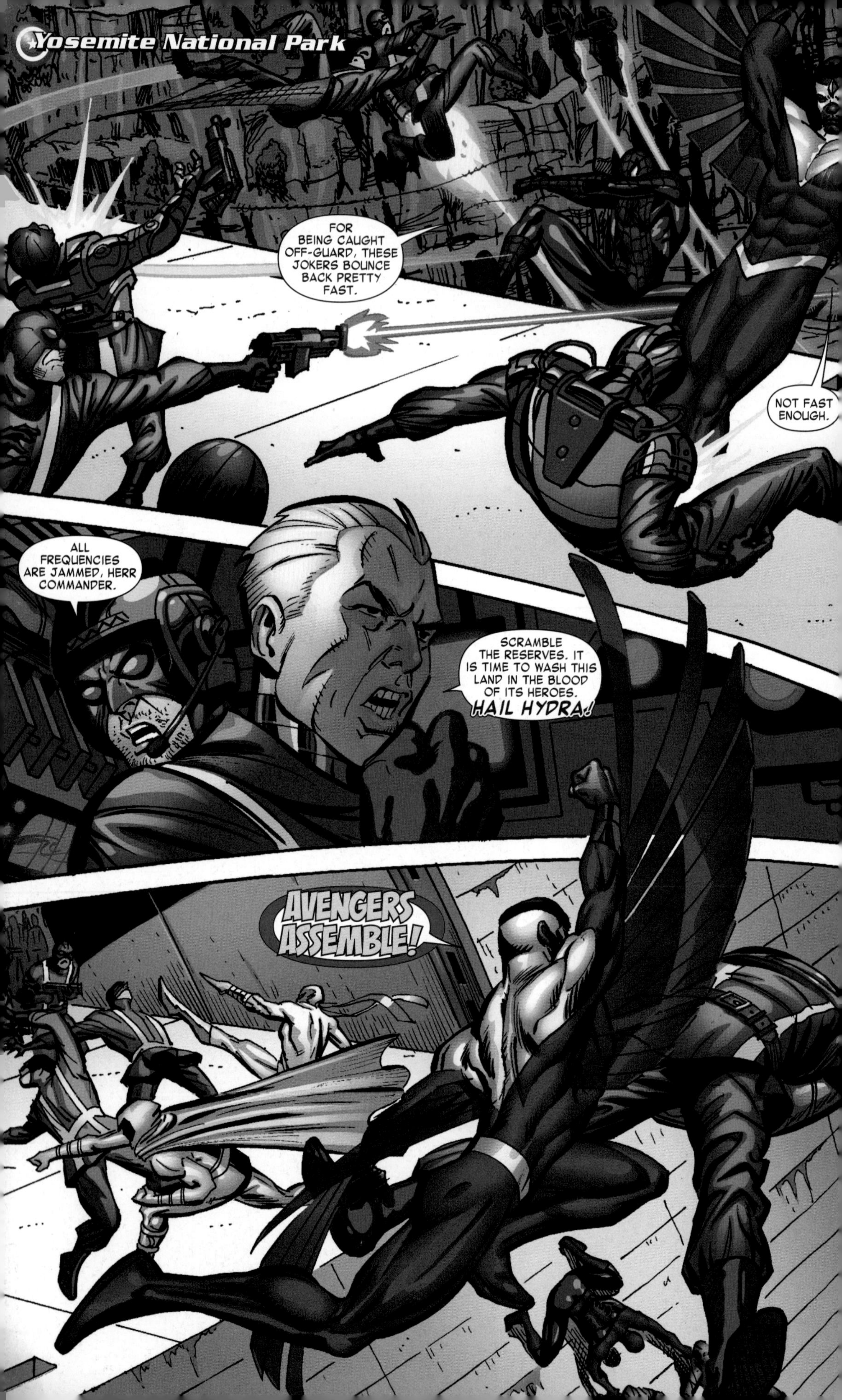
Yosemite National Park
FOR BEING CAUGHT OFF-GUARD, THESE JOKERS BOUNCE BACK PRETTY FAST.
NOT FAST ENOUGH.
ALL FREQUENCIES ARE JAMMED, HERR COMMANDER.
SCRAMBLE THE RESERVES. IT IS TIME TO WASH THIS LAND IN THE BLOOD OF ITS HEROES. HAIL HYDRA!
AVENGERS ASSEMBLE!

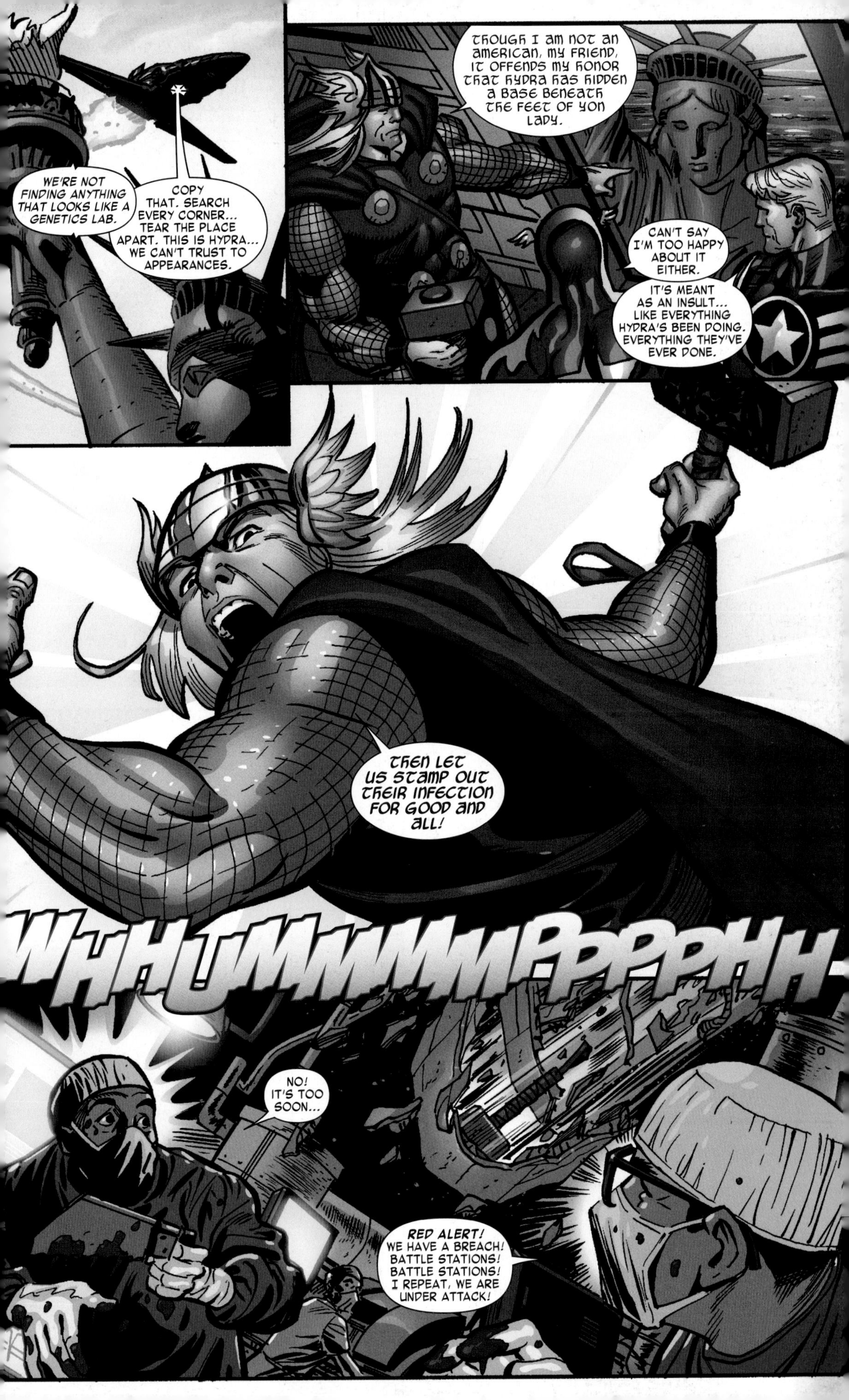
WE'RE NOT FINDING ANYTHING THAT LOOKS LIKE A GENETICS LAB.
COPY THAT. SEARCH EVERY CORNER... TEAR THE PLACE APART. THIS IS HYDRA... WE CAN'T TRUST TO APPEARANCES.
THOUGH I AM NOT AN AMERICAN, MY FRIEND, IT OFFENDS MY HONOR THAT HYDRA HAS HIDDEN A BASE BENEATH THE FEET OF YON LADY.
CAN'T SAY I'M TOO HAPPY ABOUT IT EITHER.
IT'S MEANT AS AN INSULT... LIKE EVERYTHING HYDRA'S BEEN DOING. EVERYTHING THEY'VE EVER DONE.
THEN LET US STAMP OUT THEIR INFECTION FOR GOOD AND ALL!
WHHUMMMMMPPPPHH-
NO! IT'S TOO SOON...
RED ALERT! WE HAVE A BREACH! BATTLE STATIONS! BATTLE STATIONS! I REPEAT, WE ARE UNDER ATTACK!

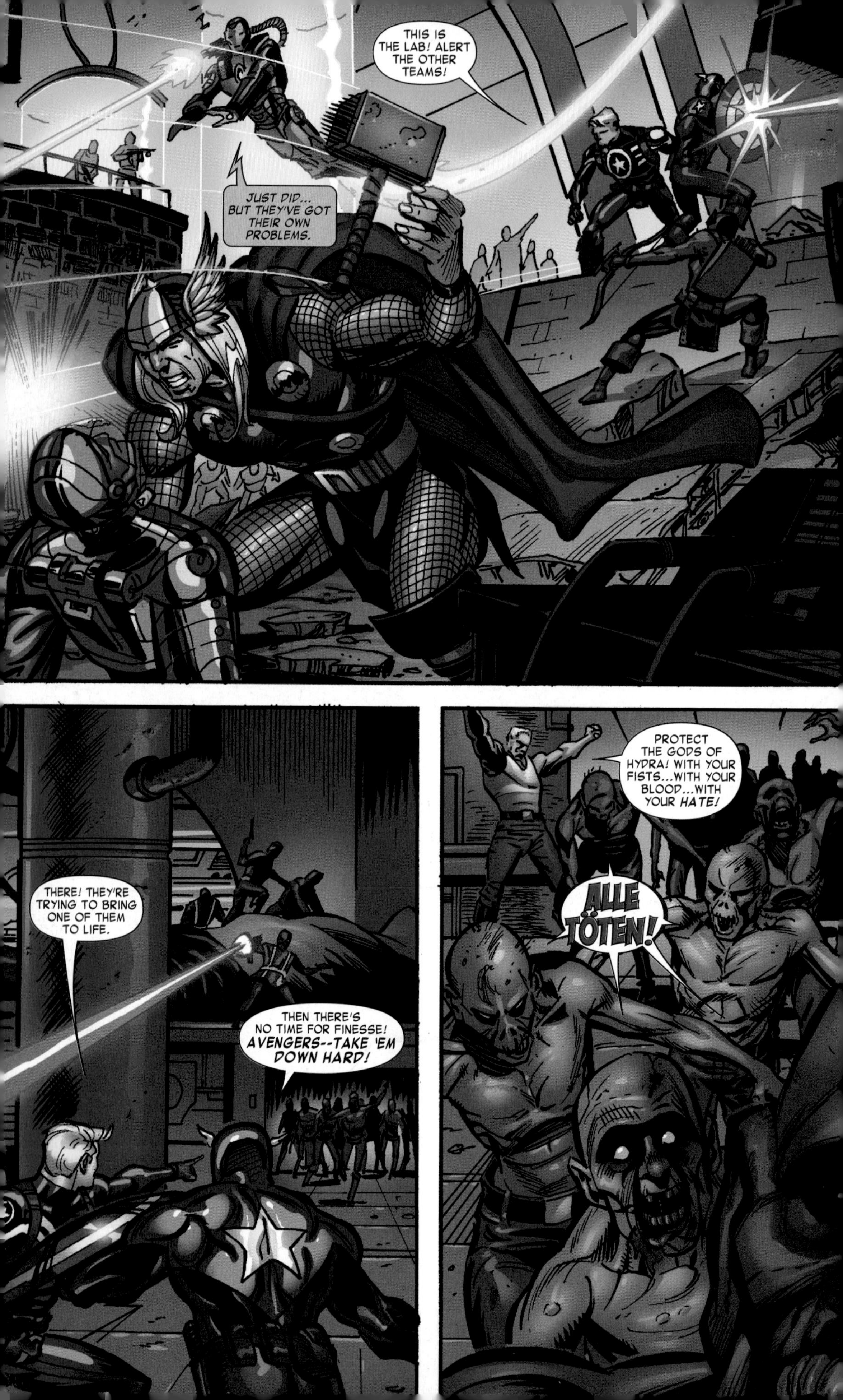
THIS IS THE LAB! ALERT THE OTHER TEAMS!
JUST DID... BUT THEY'VE GOT THEIR OWN PROBLEMS.
THERE! THEY'RE TRYING TO BRING ONE OF THEM TO LIFE.
THEN THERE'S NO TIME FOR FINESSE! AVENGERS--TAKE 'EM DOWN HARD!
PROTECT THE GODS OF HYDRA! WITH YOUR FISTS...WITH YOUR BLOOD...WITH YOUR HATE!
ALLE TÖTEN!

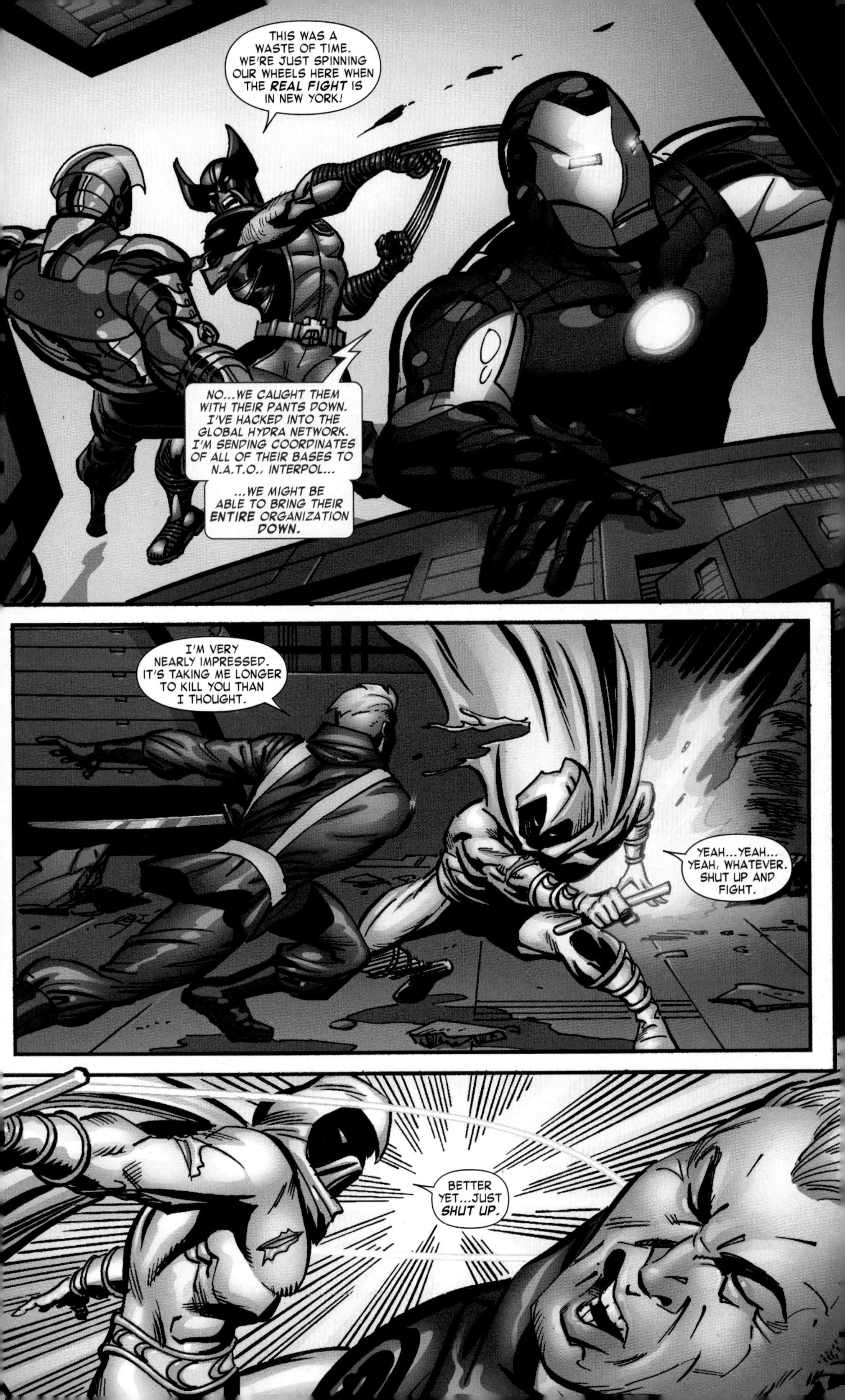
THIS WAS A WASTE OF TIME. WE'RE JUST SPINNING OUR WHEELS HERE WHEN THE REAL FIGHT IS IN NEW YORK!
NO...WE CAUGHT THEM WITH THEIR PANTS DOWN. I'VE HACKED INTO THE GLOBAL HYDRA NETWORK. I'M SENDING COORDINATES OF ALL OF THEIR BASES TO N.A.T.O., INTERPOL...
...WE MIGHT BE ABLE TO BRING THEIR ENTIRE ORGANIZATION DOWN.
I'M VERY NEARLY IMPRESSED. IT'S TAKING ME LONGER TO KILL YOU THAN I THOUGHT.
YEAH...YEAH... YEAH, WHATEVER. SHUT UP AND FIGHT.
BETTER YET...JUST SHUT UP.

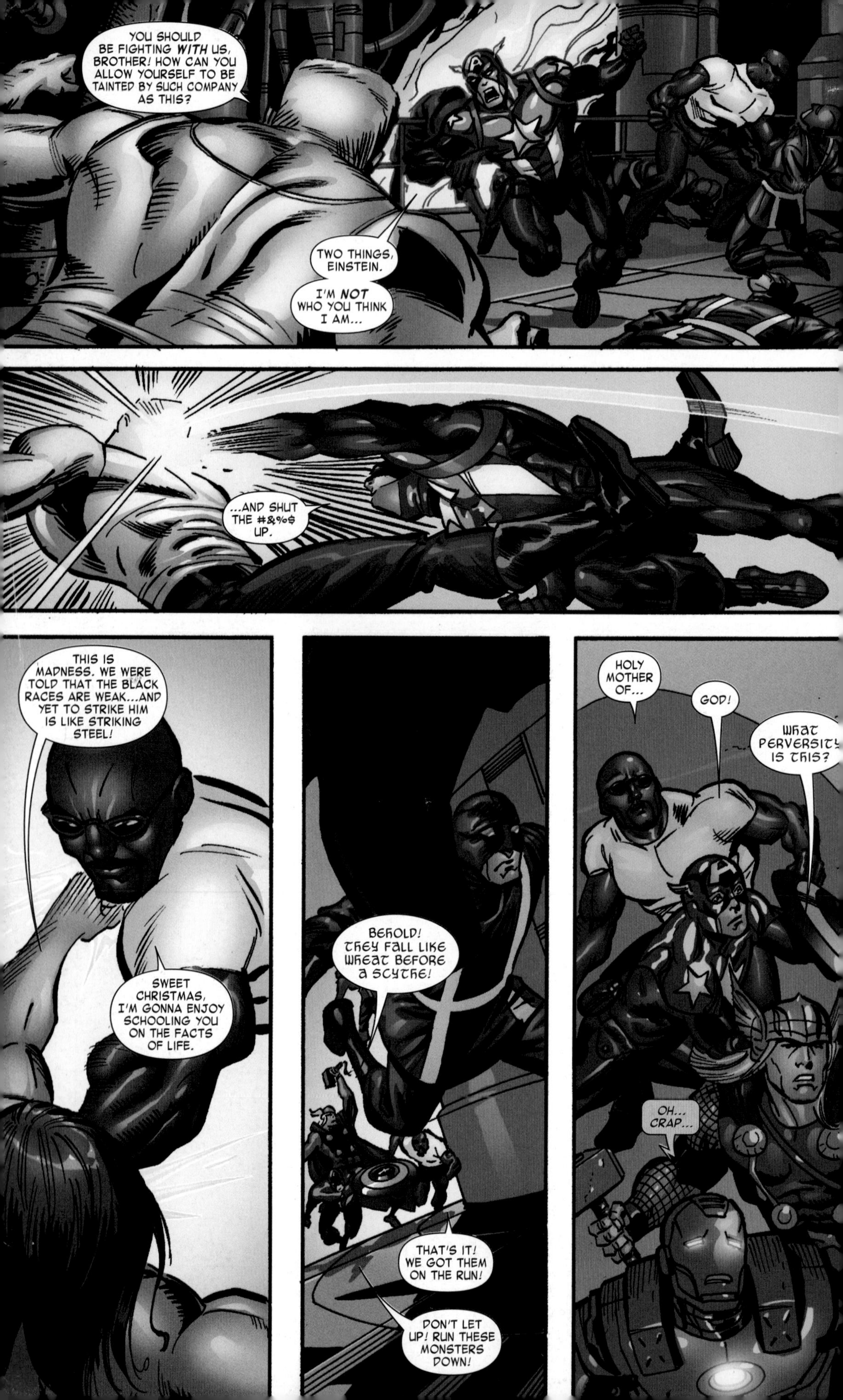
YOU SHOULD BE FIGHTING WITH US, BROTHER! HOW CAN YOU ALLOW YOURSELF TO BE TAINTED BY SUCH COMPANY AS THIS?
TWO THINGS, EINSTEIN.
I'M NOT WHO YOU THINK I AM...
...AND SHUT THE #&%$ UP.
THIS IS MADNESS. WE WERE TOLD THAT THE BLACK RACES ARE WEAK...AND YET TO STRIKE HIM IS LIKE STRIKING STEEL!
SWEET CHRISTMAS, I'M GONNA ENJOY SCHOOLING YOU ON THE FACTS OF LIFE.
BEHOLD! THEY FALL LIKE WHEAT BEFORE A SCYTHE!
THAT'S IT! WE GOT THEM ON THE RUN!
DON'T LET UP! RUN THESE MONSTERS DOWN!
HOLY MOTHER OF...
GOD!
WHAT PERVERSITY IS THIS?
OH... CRAP...

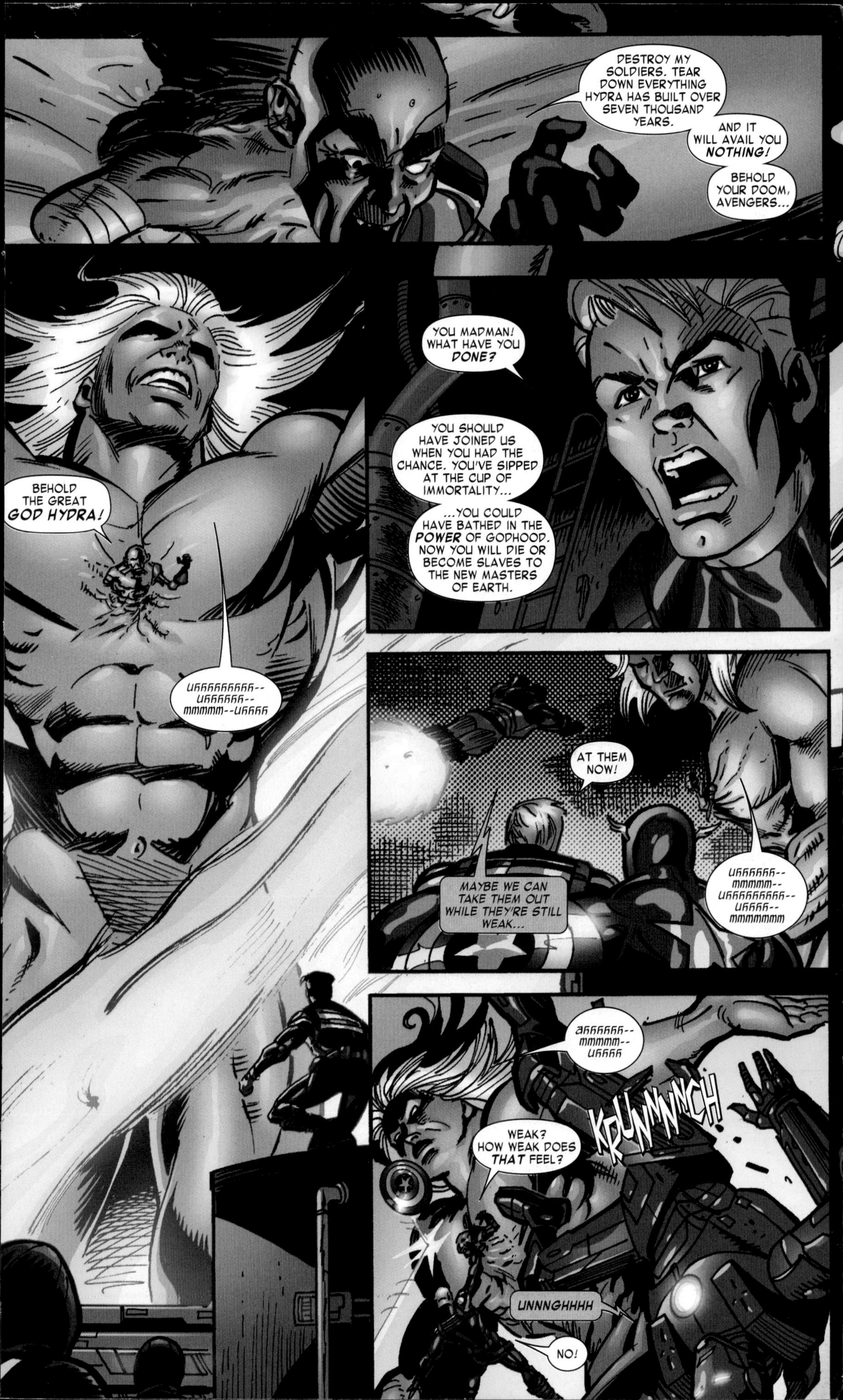
DESTROY MY SOLDIERS. TEAR DOWN EVERYTHING HYDRA HAS BUILT OVER SEVEN THOUSAND YEARS.
AND IT WILL AVAIL YOU *NOTHING!*
BEHOLD YOUR DOOM, AVENGERS...
BEHOLD THE GREAT *GOD HYDRA!*
UHHHHHHHH-- UHHHHHH-- MMMMM--UHHHH
YOU MADMAN! WHAT HAVE YOU *DONE?*
YOU SHOULD HAVE JOINED US WHEN YOU HAD THE CHANCE. YOU'VE SIPPED AT THE CUP OF IMMORTALITY...
...YOU COULD HAVE BATHED IN THE *POWER* OF GODHOOD. NOW YOU WILL DIE OR BECOME SLAVES TO THE NEW MASTERS OF EARTH.
AT THEM NOW!
MAYBE WE CAN TAKE THEM OUT WHILE THEY'RE STILL WEAK...
UHHHHHH-- MMMMM-- UHHHHHHHHH-- UHHHH-- MMMMMMM
AHHHHHH-- MMMMM-- UHHHH
KRUNNNNCH
WEAK? HOW WEAK DOES *THAT* FEEL?
UNNNGHHHH
NO!

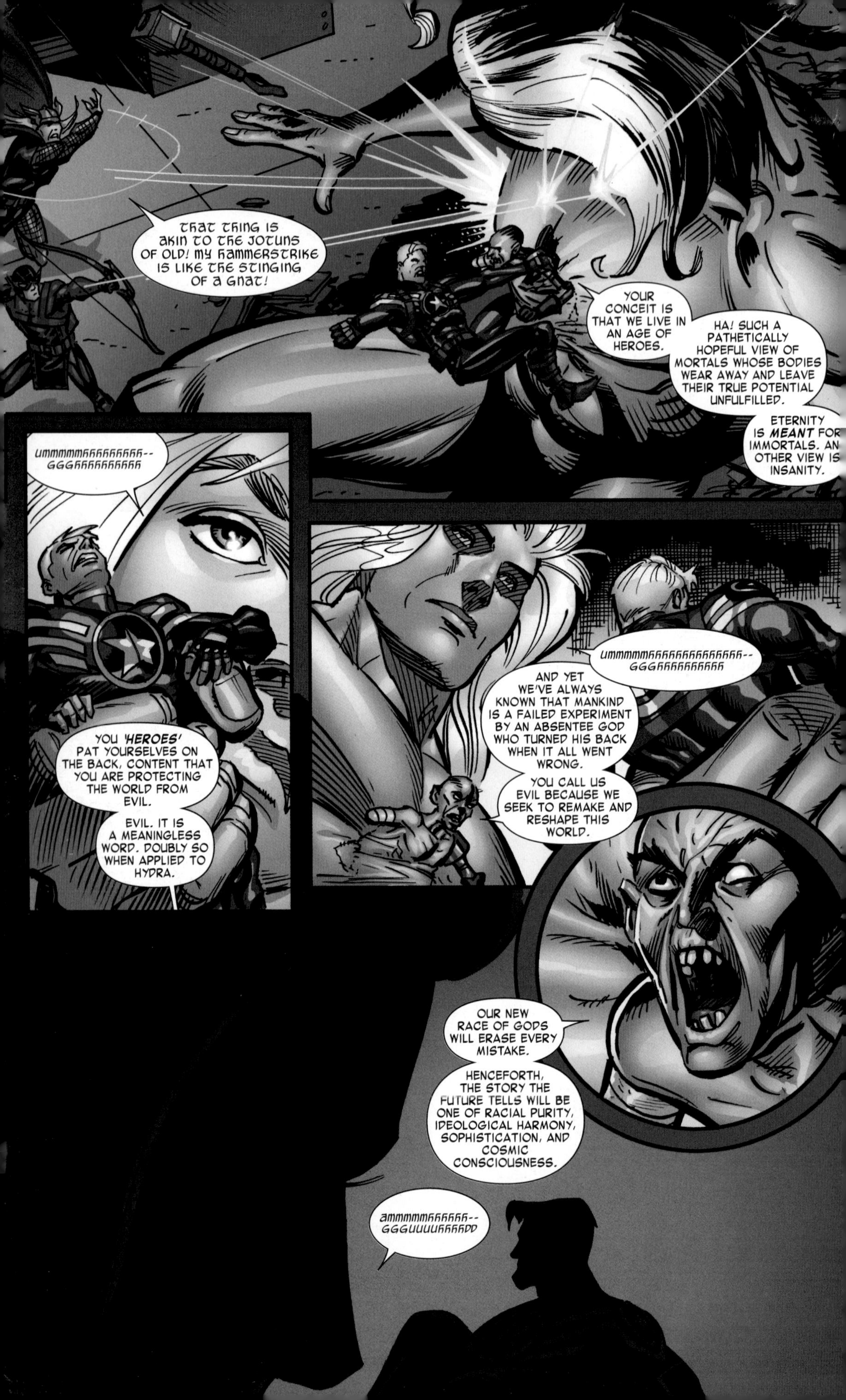
THAT THING IS AKIN TO THE JOTUNS OF OLD! MY HAMMERSTRIKE IS LIKE THE STINGING OF A GNAT!
YOUR CONCEIT IS THAT WE LIVE IN AN AGE OF HEROES.
HA! SUCH A PATHETICALLY HOPEFUL VIEW OF MORTALS WHOSE BODIES WEAR AWAY AND LEAVE THEIR TRUE POTENTIAL UNFULFILLED.
ETERNITY IS **MEANT** FOR IMMORTALS. AN OTHER VIEW IS INSANITY.
UMMMMMHHHHHHHHH--GGGHHHHHHHHHH
YOU '**HEROES**' PAT YOURSELVES ON THE BACK, CONTENT THAT YOU ARE PROTECTING THE WORLD FROM EVIL.
EVIL. IT IS A MEANINGLESS WORD. DOUBLY SO WHEN APPLIED TO HYDRA.
UMMMMMMHHHHHHHHHHHHHH--GGGHHHHHHHHH
AND YET WE'VE ALWAYS KNOWN THAT MANKIND IS A FAILED EXPERIMENT BY AN ABSENTEE GOD WHO TURNED HIS BACK WHEN IT ALL WENT WRONG.
YOU CALL US EVIL BECAUSE WE SEEK TO REMAKE AND RESHAPE THIS WORLD.
OUR NEW RACE OF GODS WILL ERASE EVERY MISTAKE.
HENCEFORTH, THE STORY THE FUTURE TELLS WILL BE ONE OF RACIAL PURITY, IDEOLOGICAL HARMONY, SOPHISTICATION, AND COSMIC CONSCIOUSNESS.
AMMMMMHHHHHH--GGGUUUUHHHHDD

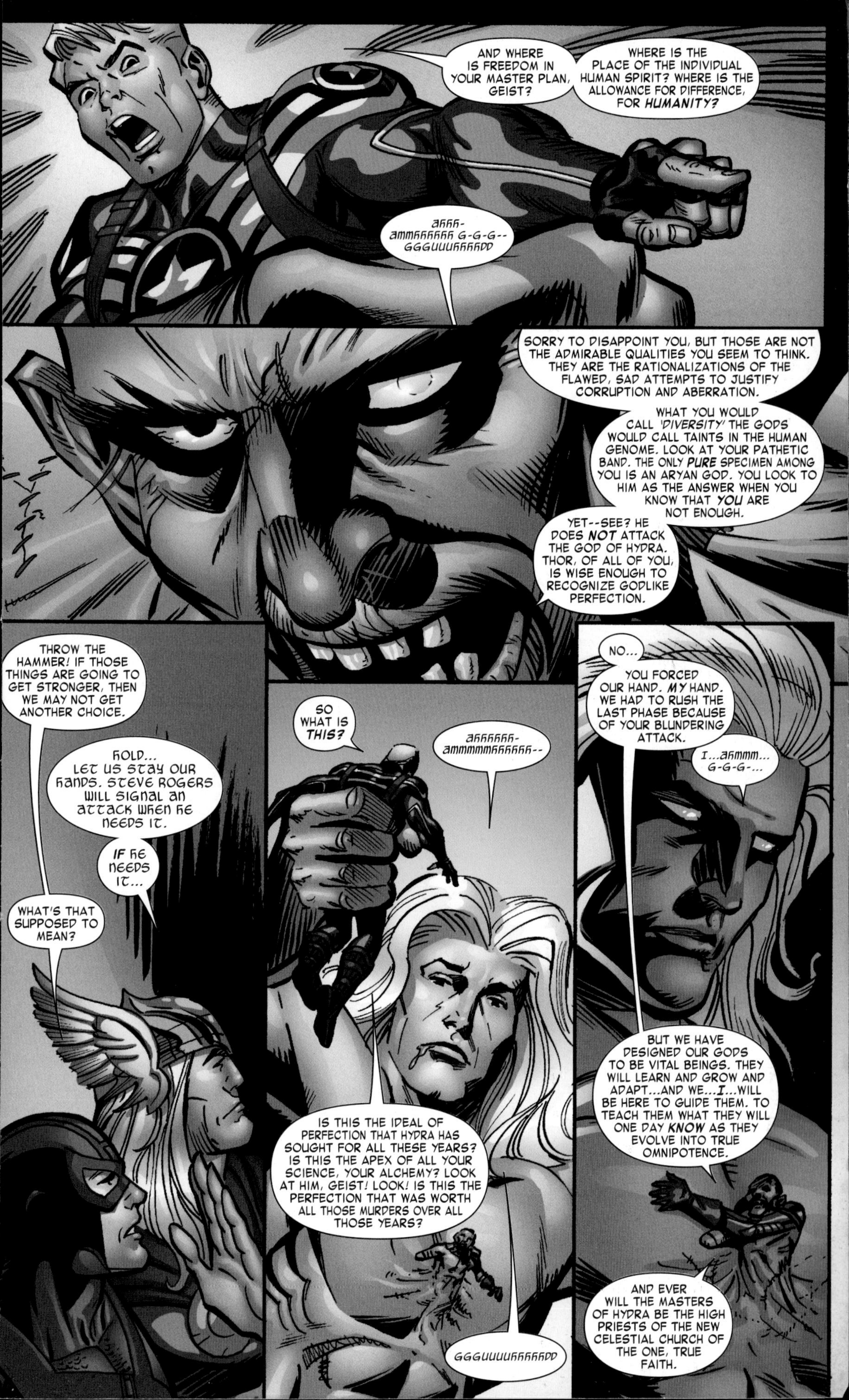
AND WHERE IS FREEDOM IN YOUR MASTER PLAN, GEIST?
WHERE IS THE PLACE OF THE INDIVIDUAL HUMAN SPIRIT? WHERE IS THE ALLOWANCE FOR DIFFERENCE, FOR HUMANITY?
AHHH-AMMHHHHH G-G-G--GGGUUURRRRDD
SORRY TO DISAPPOINT YOU, BUT THOSE ARE NOT THE ADMIRABLE QUALITIES YOU SEEM TO THINK. THEY ARE THE RATIONALIZATIONS OF THE FLAWED, SAD ATTEMPTS TO JUSTIFY CORRUPTION AND ABERRATION.
WHAT YOU WOULD CALL 'DIVERSITY' THE GODS WOULD CALL TAINTS IN THE HUMAN GENOME. LOOK AT YOUR PATHETIC BAND. THE ONLY PURE SPECIMEN AMONG YOU IS AN ARYAN GOD. YOU LOOK TO HIM AS THE ANSWER WHEN YOU KNOW THAT YOU ARE NOT ENOUGH.
YET--SEE? HE DOES NOT ATTACK THE GOD OF HYDRA. THOR, OF ALL OF YOU, IS WISE ENOUGH TO RECOGNIZE GODLIKE PERFECTION.
THROW THE HAMMER! IF THOSE THINGS ARE GOING TO GET STRONGER, THEN WE MAY NOT GET ANOTHER CHOICE.
HOLD... LET US STAY OUR HANDS. STEVE ROGERS WILL SIGNAL AN ATTACK WHEN HE NEEDS IT.
IF HE NEEDS IT...
WHAT'S THAT SUPPOSED TO MEAN?
SO WHAT IS THIS?
AHHHHHH-AMMMMMHHHHHH--
IS THIS THE IDEAL OF PERFECTION THAT HYDRA HAS SOUGHT FOR ALL THESE YEARS? IS THIS THE APEX OF ALL YOUR SCIENCE, YOUR ALCHEMY? LOOK AT HIM, GEIST! LOOK! IS THIS THE PERFECTION THAT WAS WORTH ALL THOSE MURDERS OVER ALL THOSE YEARS?
GGGUUUUHHHHHDD
NO...
YOU FORCED OUR HAND. MY HAND. WE HAD TO RUSH THE LAST PHASE BECAUSE OF YOUR BLUNDERING ATTACK.
I...AHMMM... G-G-G-...
BUT WE HAVE DESIGNED OUR GODS TO BE VITAL BEINGS. THEY WILL LEARN AND GROW AND ADAPT...AND WE...I...WILL BE HERE TO GUIDE THEM. TO TEACH THEM WHAT THEY WILL ONE DAY KNOW AS THEY EVOLVE INTO TRUE OMNIPOTENCE.
AND EVER WILL THE MASTERS OF HYDRA BE THE HIGH PRIESTS OF THE NEW CELESTIAL CHURCH OF THE ONE, TRUE FAITH.

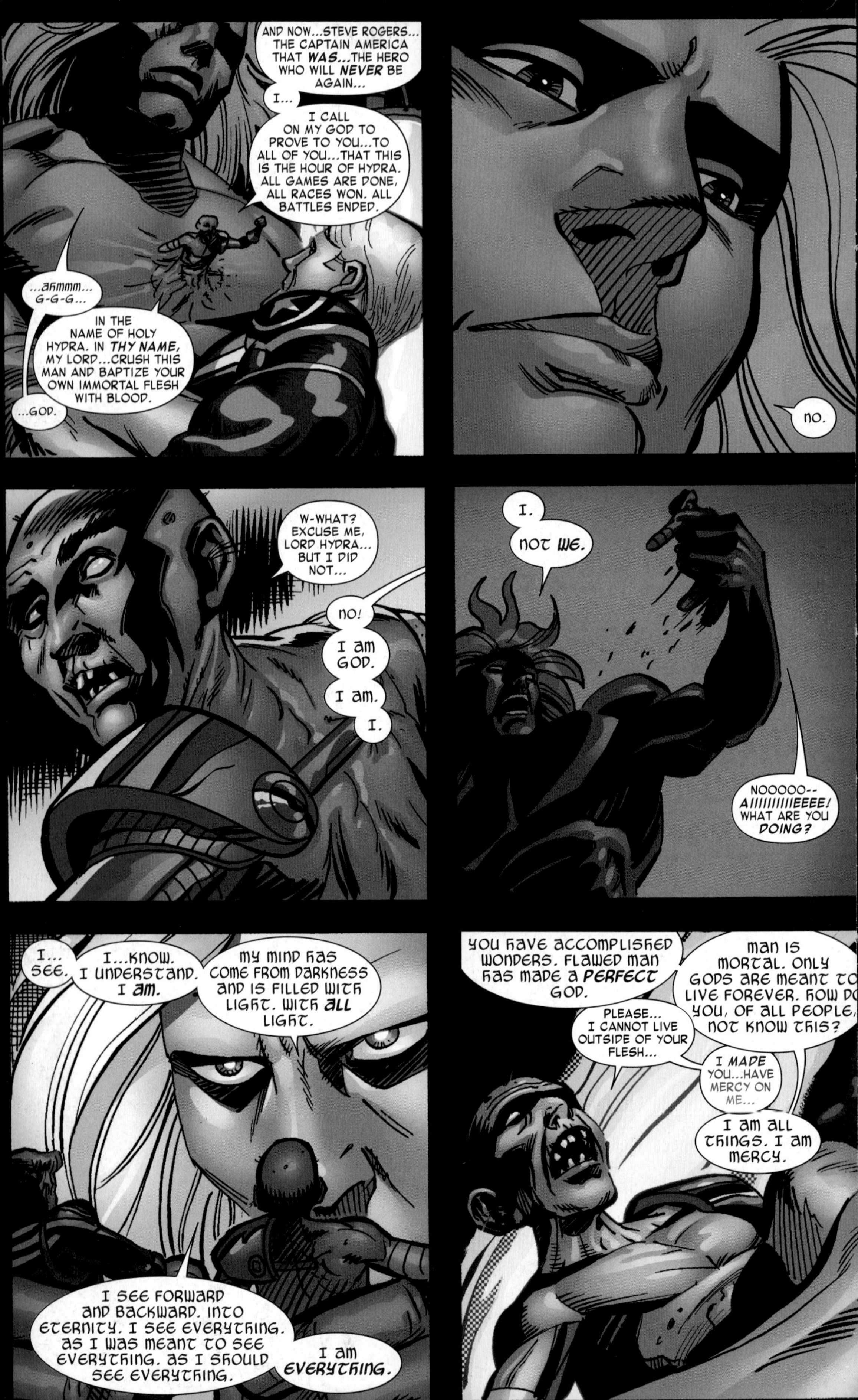
AND NOW...STEVE ROGERS... THE CAPTAIN AMERICA THAT WAS...THE HERO WHO WILL NEVER BE AGAIN...
I...
I CALL ON MY GOD TO PROVE TO YOU...TO ALL OF YOU...THAT THIS IS THE HOUR OF HYDRA. ALL GAMES ARE DONE, ALL RACES WON. ALL BATTLES ENDED.
...AHMMM... G-G-G...
IN THE NAME OF HOLY HYDRA. IN THY NAME, MY LORD...CRUSH THIS MAN AND BAPTIZE YOUR OWN IMMORTAL FLESH WITH BLOOD.
...GOD.
NO.
W-WHAT? EXCUSE ME, LORD HYDRA... BUT I DID NOT...
NO!
I AM GOD.
I AM.
I.
I.
NOT WE.
NOOOOO-- AIIIIIIIIIEEEE! WHAT ARE YOU DOING?
I... SEE.
I...KNOW. I UNDERSTAND. I AM.
MY MIND HAS COME FROM DARKNESS AND IS FILLED WITH LIGHT. WITH ALL LIGHT.
I SEE FORWARD AND BACKWARD. INTO ETERNITY. I SEE EVERYTHING. AS I WAS MEANT TO SEE EVERYTHING. AS I SHOULD SEE EVERYTHING.
I AM EVERYTHING.
YOU HAVE ACCOMPLISHED WONDERS. FLAWED MAN HAS MADE A PERFECT GOD.
MAN IS MORTAL. ONLY GODS ARE MEANT TO LIVE FOREVER. HOW DO YOU, OF ALL PEOPLE, NOT KNOW THIS?
PLEASE... I CANNOT LIVE OUTSIDE OF YOUR FLESH...
I MADE YOU...HAVE MERCY ON ME...
I AM ALL THINGS. I AM MERCY.

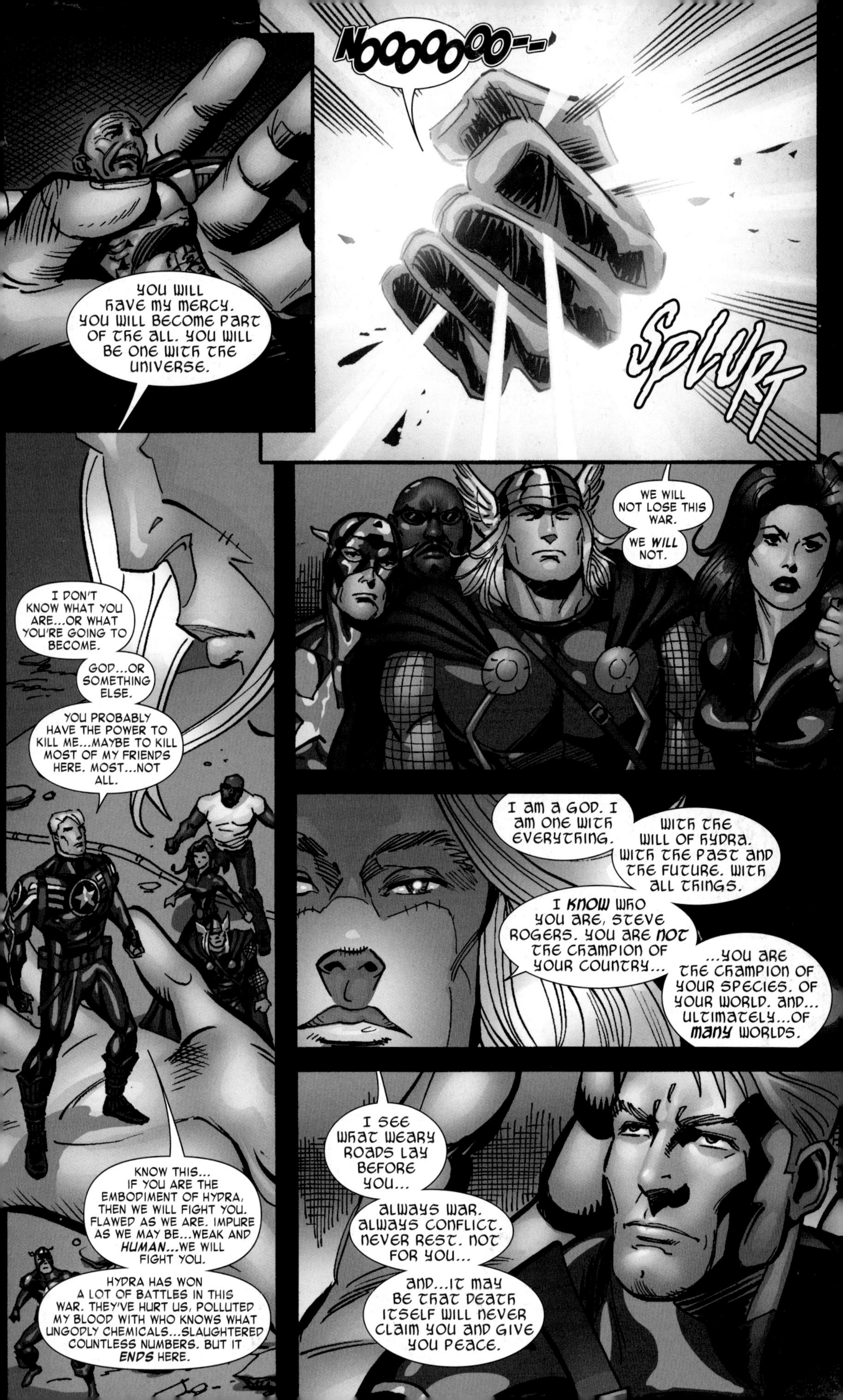
YOU WILL HAVE MY MERCY. YOU WILL BECOME PART OF THE ALL. YOU WILL BE ONE WITH THE UNIVERSE.
NOOOOOOO--
SPLURT
I DON'T KNOW WHAT YOU ARE...OR WHAT YOU'RE GOING TO BECOME.
GOD...OR SOMETHING ELSE.
YOU PROBABLY HAVE THE POWER TO KILL ME...MAYBE TO KILL MOST OF MY FRIENDS HERE. MOST...NOT ALL.
KNOW THIS... IF YOU ARE THE EMBODIMENT OF HYDRA, THEN WE WILL FIGHT YOU. FLAWED AS WE ARE. IMPURE AS WE MAY BE...WEAK AND HUMAN...WE WILL FIGHT YOU.
HYDRA HAS WON A LOT OF BATTLES IN THIS WAR. THEY'VE HURT US, POLLUTED MY BLOOD WITH WHO KNOWS WHAT UNGODLY CHEMICALS...SLAUGHTERED COUNTLESS NUMBERS. BUT IT ENDS HERE.
WE WILL NOT LOSE THIS WAR.
WE WILL NOT.
I AM A GOD. I AM ONE WITH EVERYTHING.
WITH THE WILL OF HYDRA. WITH THE PAST AND THE FUTURE. WITH ALL THINGS.
I KNOW WHO YOU ARE, STEVE ROGERS. YOU ARE NOT THE CHAMPION OF YOUR COUNTRY...
...YOU ARE THE CHAMPION OF YOUR SPECIES. OF YOUR WORLD. AND... ULTIMATELY...OF MANY WORLDS.
I SEE WHAT WEARY ROADS LAY BEFORE YOU...
ALWAYS WAR. ALWAYS CONFLICT. NEVER REST. NOT FOR YOU...
AND...IT MAY BE THAT DEATH ITSELF WILL NEVER CLAIM YOU AND GIVE YOU PEACE.

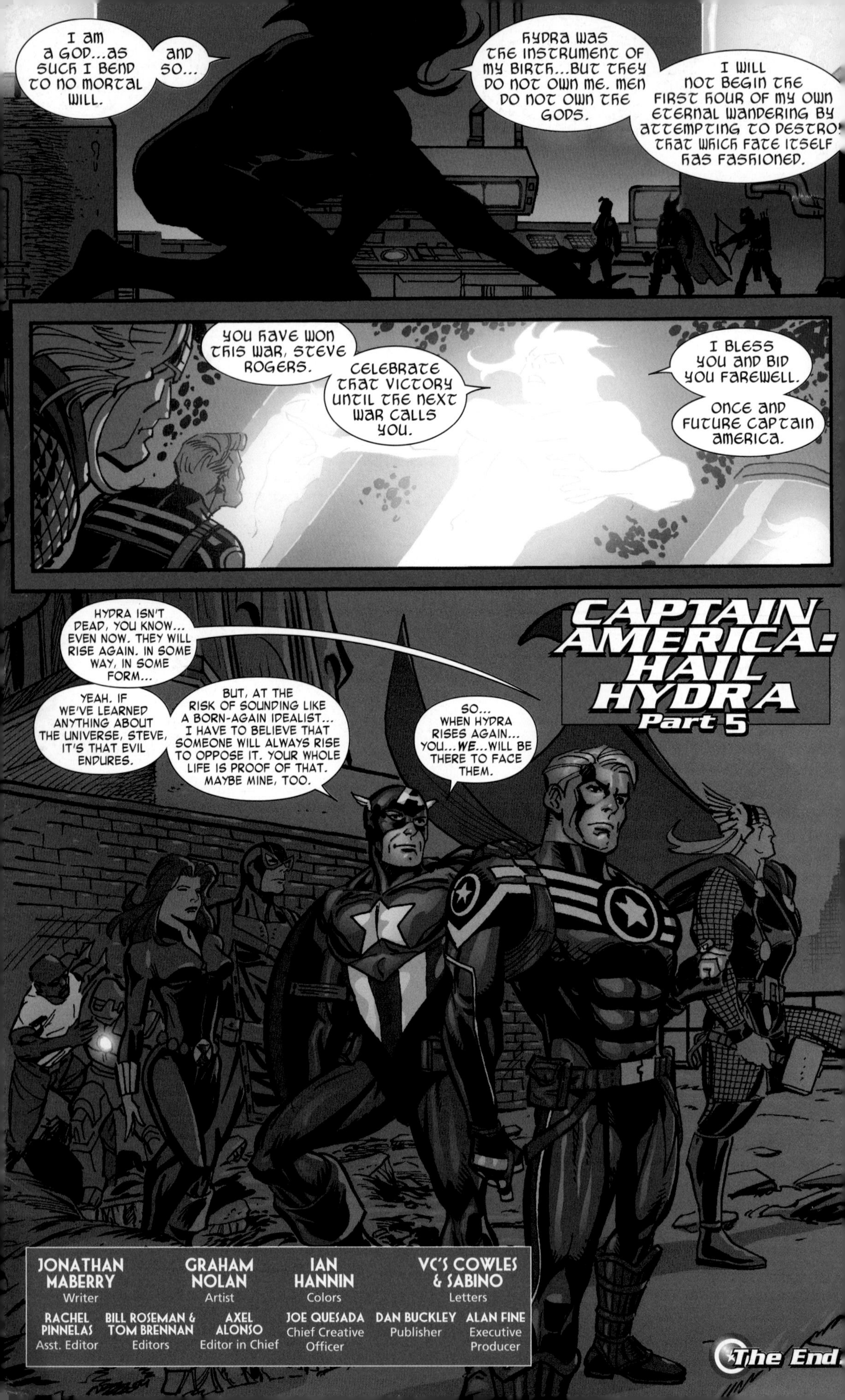
I AM A GOD...AS SUCH I BEND TO NO MORTAL WILL.
AND SO...
HYDRA WAS THE INSTRUMENT OF MY BIRTH...BUT THEY DO NOT OWN ME. MEN DO NOT OWN THE GODS.
I WILL NOT BEGIN THE FIRST HOUR OF MY OWN ETERNAL WANDERING BY ATTEMPTING TO DESTRO THAT WHICH FATE ITSELF HAS FASHIONED.
YOU HAVE WON THIS WAR, STEVE ROGERS.
CELEBRATE THAT VICTORY UNTIL THE NEXT WAR CALLS YOU.
I BLESS YOU AND BID YOU FAREWELL.
ONCE AND FUTURE CAPTAIN AMERICA.
CAPTAIN AMERICA: HAIL HYDRA Part 5
HYDRA ISN'T DEAD, YOU KNOW... EVEN NOW. THEY WILL RISE AGAIN. IN SOME WAY, IN SOME FORM...
YEAH. IF WE'VE LEARNED ANYTHING ABOUT THE UNIVERSE, STEVE, IT'S THAT EVIL ENDURES.
BUT, AT THE RISK OF SOUNDING LIKE A BORN-AGAIN IDEALIST... I HAVE TO BELIEVE THAT SOMEONE WILL ALWAYS RISE TO OPPOSE IT. YOUR WHOLE LIFE IS PROOF OF THAT. MAYBE MINE, TOO.
SO... WHEN HYDRA RISES AGAIN... YOU...WE...WILL BE THERE TO FACE THEM.
JONATHAN MABERRY Writer
GRAHAM NOLAN Artist
IAN HANNIN Colors
VC'S COWLES & SABINO Letters
RACHEL PINNELAS Asst. Editor
BILL ROSEMAN & TOM BRENNAN Editors
AXEL ALONSO Editor in Chief
JOE QUESADA Chief Creative Officer
DAN BUCKLEY Publisher
ALAN FINE Executive Producer
The End.

PENCILS FROM ISSUE 1, PAGES 1-4

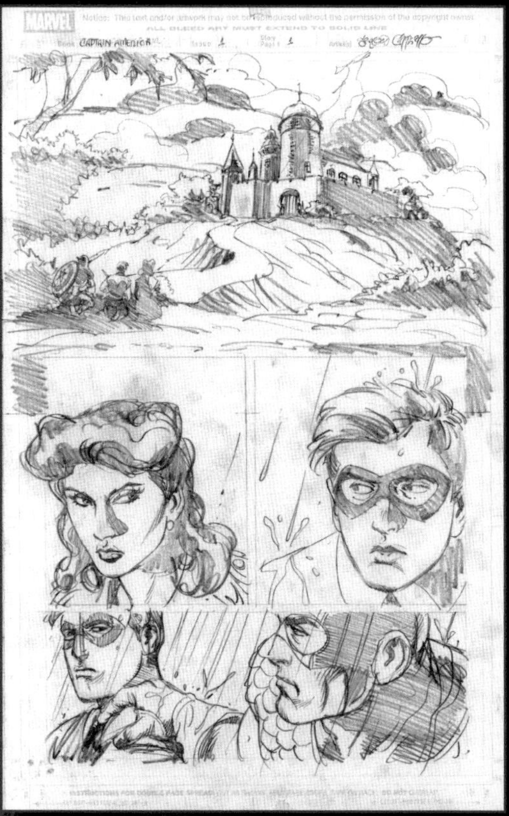

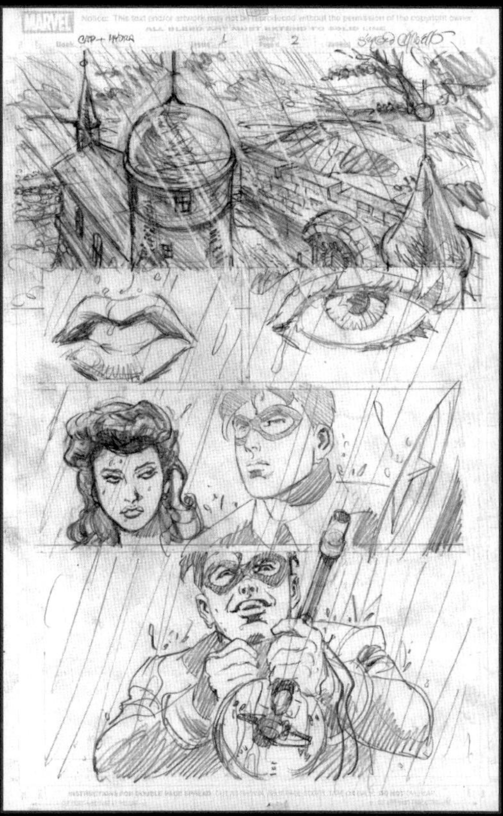

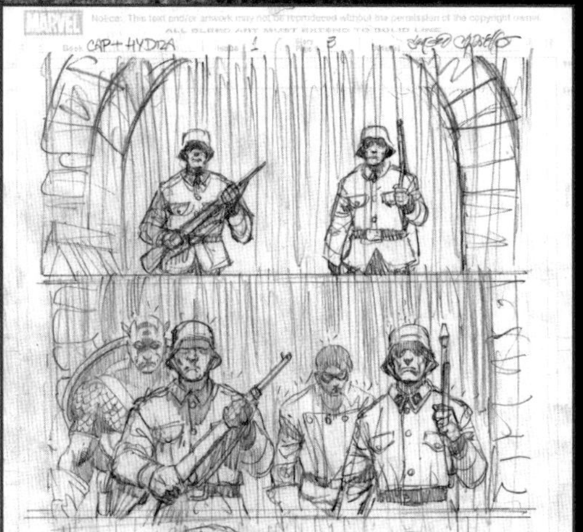

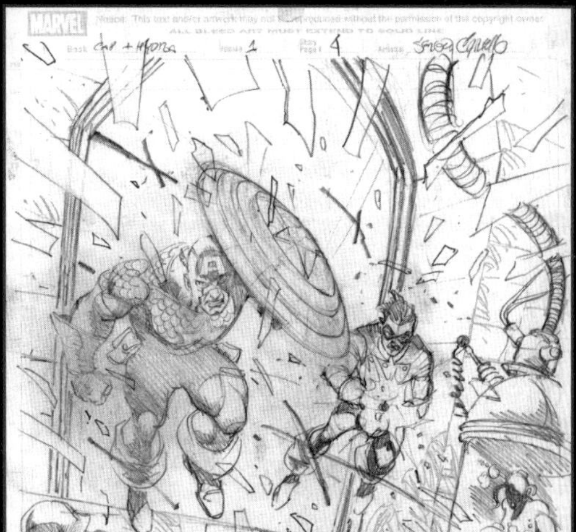

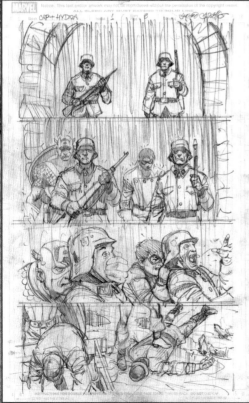

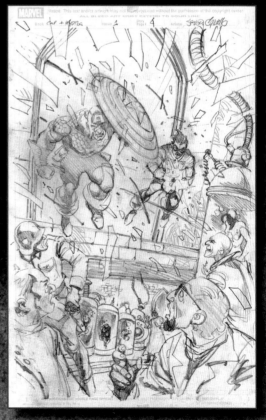

COVER SKETCHES BY ADI GRANOV

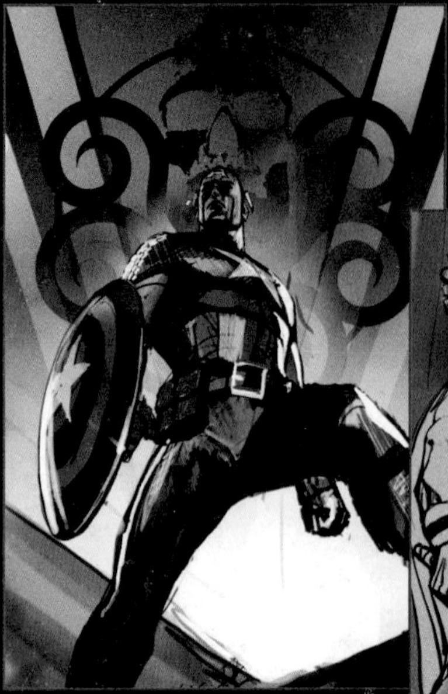

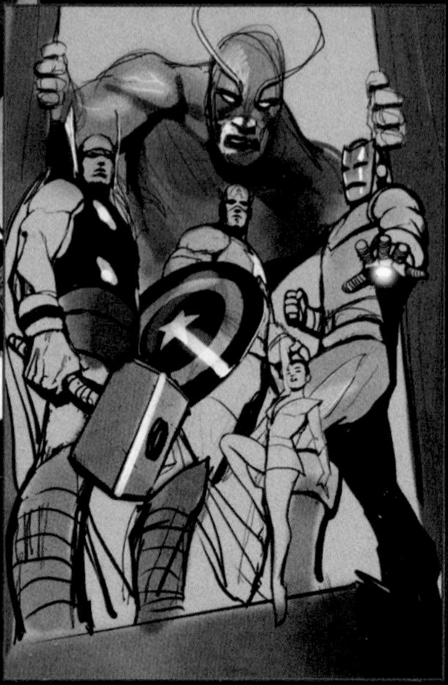

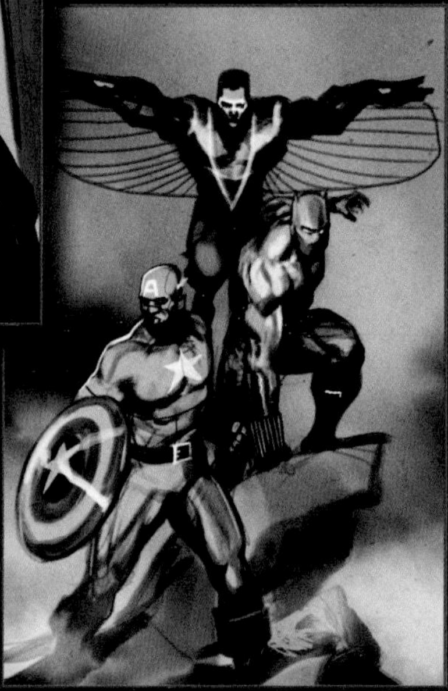

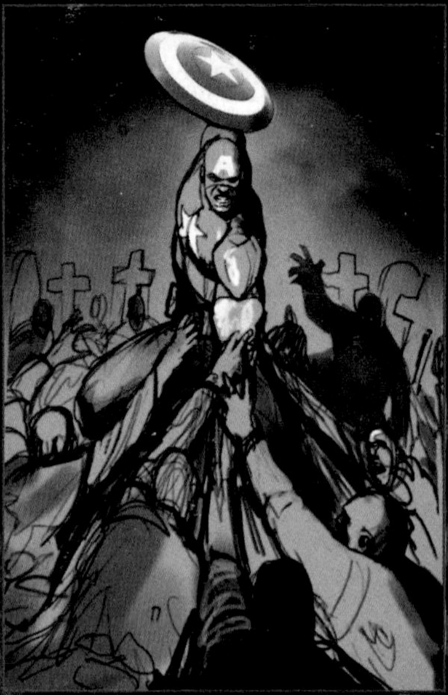

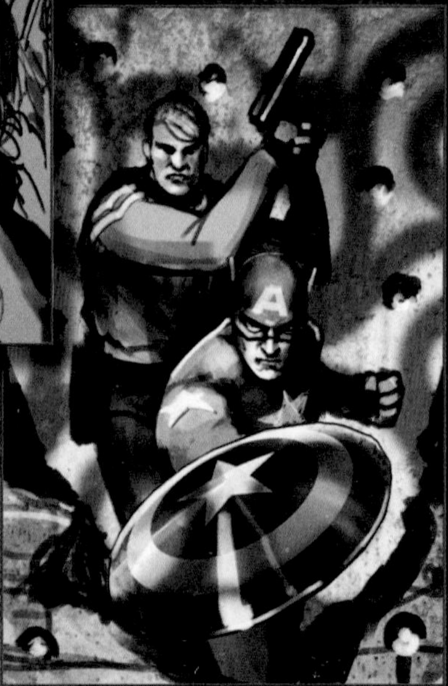